Portraits

⟶ of ⟵

American
Architecture

PORTRAITS
OF
AMERICAN ARCHITECTURE

A GALLERY OF VICTORIAN HOMES

PAINTINGS AND TEXT BY HARRY DEVLIN

GRAMERCY BOOKS

New York • Avenel

To my friend Gilbert G. Roessner

This 1996 edition is published by Gramercy Books,
a division of Random House Value Publishing, Inc.,
40 Engelhard Avenue, Avenel, New Jersey 07001.
http://www.randomhouse.com

Gramercy Books and colophon are trademarks of
Random House Value Publishing, Inc.

Random House
New York • Toronto • London • Sydney • Auckland

Printed and bound in Hong Kong

Library of Congress Cataloging-in-Publication Data
Devlin, Harry.
    Portraits of American architecture: a gallery of Victorian homes / by Harry Devlin.
        p.   cm.
    ISBN 0-517-15015-8
    1. Devlin, Harry—Themes, motives. 2. Houses in art. 3. Architecture, Domestic—
United States—Pictorial works. 4. Architecture, Victorian—United States—Pictorial works.
I. Title
ND237.D43A4 1996
759.13—dc20   96-12648
                                                                                              CIP

8 7 6 5 4 3 2 1

Black-and-white illustrations courtesy of the Library of Congress
Frontispiece: *Stockerton Mourning House*

Contents

Introduction

A MEASURE OF ROMANTICISM marks those who love old houses. There is a yearning to know more about an old house—to see beyond the bricks, wood, and mortar into a dwelling that may have sheltered generations of a family or, perhaps, nurtured the tangled plot of a Gothic tale. In writing and painting PORTRAITS OF AMERICAN ARCHITECTURE I wish to encourage that very Romanticism by celebrating the Victorian era in America, an epoch that produced vital, exuberant, and *miraculous* architectural expressions—miraculous because the extraordinary circumstances and climate of the period will never occur again.

History, sociology, and aesthetics all come alive when viewed through the windows of a nineteenth-century house. But old houses are jealous of their secrets, and Romanticists must pass unrequited unless they understand something of the history of the era and the fascinating *mood* in which its buildings were conceived.

The houses I have portrayed were chosen because they are accepted versions of the array of architectural styles that appeared in the last century. Many are, or were, in New Jersey. Influences from the South came to New Jersey by way of Philadelphia, while New England's architectural contributions arrived there via New York City. By the time styles reached New Jersey, building methods and stylistic characteristics had evolved to forms that would remain essentially constant as they moved westward across the continent.

Woven into the narrative and into the words accompanying the paintings are references to arts other than architecture, as no single art fares well in isolation. The Gothic mood, for example, affected literature, architecture, drama, music, and painting. Therefore, names of otherwise disparate individuals figure in the seventy-year span this book encompasses. Madame de Staël, Thomas Jefferson, Frances Trollope, Sir Walter Scott, Aaron Copland, Mary Shelley, and Dolly Madison all find some commonality in the pages that follow. Almost forgotten names are resurrected: Batty Langley, Capability Brown, and Orson Squire Fowler, in their time, exerted great influence on our landscape, our architecture, and our very way of thinking.

The portraits of the structures are factual, but liberties were taken with backgrounds and foregrounds for clarity and composition. I have cut down forests of trees, utility poles, and other offending objects to present clearly the nature of the subjects. I have also made more subtle selections. Just as human portrait subjects have their best sides, so do houses. Houses convey varying moods at different seasons and times of day and, needless to say, many visits were required to catch the subjects at their best.

The development of my personal interest in architecture—specifically nineteenth-century houses—can be traced back to my college years. The journeys between my home in Elizabeth, New Jersey, and Syracuse University were frequent and the routes I took were varied. Those were late Depression years and the roads through Pennsylvania and New York were memorable for their noble houses in sad decay.

At that time, I had no architectural understanding—I simply found ancient houses entirely fascinating. Information about these old places was hard to come by and it was an era when anything Victorian was held in contempt. But in time I learned to identify Greek Revival, Gothic, and Mansard. Italianates, Queen Annes, and the Stick Style were mysterious terms to be introduced in years to come.

On leaving Elizabeth for the journey north, the first structure to fire my youthful imagination was a hotel, the Cochran House of Newton, New Jersey, which has since been destroyed. It was a masterpiece of carpenter's lace and lathesman's art. Across the Delaware in Milford, a number of Romantic houses, unlike anything I had ever known, gradually gave way to farms and forests and then to architecturally barren areas near Pennsylvania coal mines. On Route 11, in Great Bend, I saw my first Greek Revivals. A little further on, at the approach to Binghamton, there rose a great deserted Victorian that might have been home to the Magnificent Ambersons. A year later, it was gone, fallen to flame or the wrecker's ball. The loss I felt for the Binghamton house foretold the future of an artist determined to recapture the mood and ambience of an architectural epoch so thoroughly maligned.

My post-college years found me in my first studio in Greenwich Village, which was a few steps away from the Jefferson Market building, a whimsical mélange of vari-colored stone and sand castle forms that I found immensely pleasing. Many years later, restored and freed of the visual distraction of the 6th Avenue El, that structure was seen in a very different way. The years between had added to an understanding of the history of architecture and now the old market building became Ruskinian Gothic and the rich allusions associated with that form added aesthetic and intellectual pleasure to visual enjoyment.

Later during World War II, as an artist in the Identification and Characteristics Section of Navy Intelligence, I worked with architects—some recently graduated from the Cranbrook Academy School of Architecture and very much under the general influence of the Bauhaus and the particular influence of the great Eliel Saarinen. The password was "form follows function" and questions about nineteenth-century architecture commonly went unanswered. It was deemed that styles of that era were best forgotten and there was a brave new world to be faced once the war was won.

T.H. Robsjohn-Gibbins' devastating put-down of traditional design values in his "Goodbye, Mr. Chippendale" (1944) seemed to say it all. An exception to that implied consensus was Lieutenant George E. Kidder-Smith whose superb architectural photographs paid homage to diverse forms of building in Europe and the Americas.

Houses became the focus of many illustrations I produced in the heyday of magazine illustration. By 1955, magazines supporting illustration all but disappeared, the victim of a voracious medium—television. In the ensuing years, my artistic output was varied and included a number of childrens' books written by my wife, Wende. The books became a congenial outlet for my predeliction for old houses. The Jug and Muffin Tearoom in *Old Black Witch* and Maggie and Grandmother's home on the bogs in *Cranberry Thanksgiving* are mild caricatures of early American houses.

In 1965, I proposed a book for young readers—a kind of primer of American domestic architecture to be illustrated with detailed paintings. It was fortunate that Wende's distinguished children's book editor, Alvin Tresselt, was also an old house enthusiast who cheerfully endorsed the project. In 1964, *To Grandfather's House We Go* was published.

In most artists' lives, there is some major happening—some heartening breakthrough that confirms whatever inner convictions the artists may have. City Federal Savings Bank's accession of the forty-four paintings from the two architectural books was the event that persuaded me to create a body of paintings re-introducing Americans to their nineteenth-century architectural heritage.[1]

Further incentive came from the Morris Museum of Arts and Sciences. In December 1979, the museum gave me a one-man show of architectural paintings. Some wonderful friends organized the reception and

---

1. The 1976 accession was a noteworthy event. CityFed, a pioneering financial institution, joined me in a *droit de suite* (right of follow-up) contract, an enlightened agreement that allows the creator a share in any accrued value should the works, in time, be sold.

produced a catalogue and our son, Jeffrey, designed a poster. The showing was favorably reviewed and Jeffrey's poster won the 1980 Art Director's gold medal. Exhibitions followed at World Headquarters of General Electric, The Union League Club (its gallery was designed by a Hudson River School painter) at Schering-Plough Corporation and others. Historical recognition came with an exhibition at the New Jersey Historical Society and an award from the New Jersey Historical Commission.

In 1977, the film director, Louis Presti, asked me to write and host a series of films on domestic architecture for New Jersey Public Broadcasting (now New Jersey Network). Our collaboration produced three documentaries: "The Pattern Ended Houses of Salem County," "The Dutch Houses of the Hackensack Valley," and "The Federal Houses of Princeton," all under the general title of "Fare You Well, Old House." These films were followed by "To Grandfather's House We Go," which encompassed the major architectural styles of nineteenth-century New Jersey.

In the background of this activity was a major project begun in 1968. Readers of *To Grandfather's House* and its companion piece suggested that I write an in-depth version of those books for adult audiences. Most interest centered on nineteenth-century Victorian structures and this came as no surprise as I was aware of the enthusiasm kindled by John Maass' 1957 *The Gingerbread Age*. Maass, born in Vienna, came to America in 1941 to view the Victorian architecture of this nation with a fresh eye and to tell his adopted country that "Victorians actually enjoyed more comfort, light and air, and certainly more originality than we have realized." My own determination was to make evident the forces which shaped the dynamic forms of Victorian or American Romantic architecture. The book would span the years between 1830 and 1900, years when the reigning mood was Romanticism.

Painting seemed an ideal way to present the essence of the structures of that period. Obstructive trees, tele-

phone poles, or other intrusive elements could be eliminated while areas in deep shadow would be intensified or lightened to explain important details. In time, seventy paintings were completed. While painting, words and ideas woven into the paintings grew into brief essays to accompany each architectural example. The research and the overview text involved many summers. In 1984, transparencies and the completed texts were submitted to the publisher, David R. Godine of Boston.

Inevitably, over the years my painting style underwent changes. The straightforward exposition of earlier paintings have evolved to a more pliant handling of subject. Larger canvasses seem to enhance painterly possibilities. While the camera[2] remains an ally, there is less and less dependence on the foregrounds and backgrounds the instrument provides. Now paintings are recomposed and elements substituted or placed at altered depths and angles to achieve a mood befitting the dictum that Victorian houses are "monuments to a Romantic mood." Completion of the paintings for *Portraits of American Architecture* brings a new challenge. Limitations imposed by demands of the book are now part of a disciplined past. Architectural themes will always provide content for my paintings, but freedom from literary restrictions permits a sweep of possibilities that I hope will lead to new expressions "worthy of esthetic consideration."

Harry Devlin

---

2. The camera obscura was the ally of artists so distant as Jan Vermeer (1632–1675). The executor of Vermeer's will was Anton van Leeuwenhoek (1632–1723) of microscope fame. Canaletto used the instrument extensively and Impressionist painters found black and white photography invaluable.

I. The Romantic Mood

AN OLD ARTISTS' TENET states that style and content are the two great essentials in understanding any art. A third element, however, adds dimension to that understanding. The third element pertains to the two moods, called Classical and Romantic, in which art is produced. The moods are antithetical and successively dominate whole periods of history. They condition circumstances of everyday life and are the catalysts in a wide range of social, corporate, and aesthetic decisions. To quarrel with a prevailing mood is not a fruitful undertaking even for the most daring revolutionists, corporate heads, or artists.

During most of the nineteenth century the Romantic mood ruled Europe. Preceded by the Classical period of the eighteenth century, it was followed by a second Classical era that began about 1900. The twentieth-century Classical era died in the 1960's in a tempestuous social and moral revolution which gave unexpected birth to yet another Romantic era. It has always been thus: the Classical is followed by the Romantic. Sometimes either of the moods has endured for many generations. The ancient Egyptians, under the pharaohs and the priesthood, lived for centuries in a tyranny of Classicism. Only briefly would a Romantic interlude break through the restrictions of the Classical into a radiance of change and freedom. During the Eighteenth Dynasty, Amenhotep IV proclaimed one god, changed his own name to Akhenaton, closed down the temples, and allowed artists and other groups to create forms other than the familiar profiled shoulders and lock-step conventions. Akhenaton ruled for only fourteen years, but a remarkable Romantic art flourished in that brief time and somehow survived the vengeance of the returning priesthood. Most familiar to us of the works of the period is the graceful bust of Akhenaton's queen, Nefertiti.

Of the many scholarly descriptions of the Romantic and the Classical, I borrow one of the best, from Louise Dudley and Austin Faricy's, *The Humanities* (McGraw Hill Book Co., 1960).

The qualities that characterize classicism are clarity, simplicity, restraint, objectivity and balance. The qualities that characterize romanticism are love of the remote and indefinite, escape from reality, lack of restraint in form and emotions, preference for picturesqueness or grandeur or passion. Classicism and Romanticism are fundamentally in opposition; what is Classic is not Romantic, and what is Romantic is not Classic. The Classic is finished, perfect; it has great beauty of form; the Romantic is unfinished, imperfect and often careless of form. The Classic is simple, the Romantic complex; the Classic is objective, the Romantic is subjective; the Classic is finite, concerned only with projects that can be realized and accomplished; the Romantic is infinite, concerned with plans that can never be realized, affecting 'thoughts co-equal with the clouds'.

At this writing we are living in a Romantic interval. Nevertheless, under the conditions of a Romantic mood something like a cult has arisen seeking to characterize individuals as Romantics or Classicists. There are people who are essentially Classicists—whose decisions and outlooks, in the view of Romanticists, are reserved, rationally conceived, and grimly colorless. There are personalities who are undoubtedly Romantic. Their decisions and outlooks, in the eyes of the Classicists, are utterly optimistic and insanely impractical. Jean Shepard might refer to Classicists as "official people." The official people will refer to Romanticists as dreamers at best and dangerous at worst. Shepard named Romanticists "night people."

Other qualities also distinguish the Romantic: love

of the orient or orientalism, a delight in the morbid or melancholy, paradoxical views of constancy and inconstancy, fascination with diabolism and the occult, and a predilection for works on the abodes of the dead and on the far reaches of space.

How did the dual vision of the Romantic and Classic come about? Considering time elements and the indistinct boundaries of the moods, it took keen perception to formulate the theory. Credit for the perception goes to August Wilhelm von Schlegel (1767–1845) and his brother Friedrich (1772–1829), whose essays captivated the dashing Madame de Staël (1766–1817). Her lectures on the von Schlegels' Classical–Romantic hypothesis influenced thinking in the intellectual salons of Europe. Madame de Staël's own life, immersed in revolution,

Madame de Staël

was a model of Romanticism. The lady's lovers included Talleyrand, and she was allied intellectually with the leaders of the Romantic movement. Like Beethoven, she first admired and later despised Napoleon. (Beethoven had the pleasure of literally scratching Napoleon's name from the dedication of his *Eroica* Symphony.) Madame

de Staël was exiled by the Royalists, by the Reign of Terror, and by Napoleon—a distinction that gave her considerable satisfaction.

Although the von Schlegels and Madame de Staël were the first to describe the Classical–Romantic dichotomy, Jean Jacques Rousseau (1712–1778) was the first major force in Romanticism. Rousseau reintroduced the noble savage,[3] that sentimentalized primitive so much admired by Romantics (at a safe distance) and immortalized in France by Chateaubriand and in America by James Fenimore Cooper. Rousseau further subscribed to the glorification of feelings over ideas, love of nature, distrust of any established order, and a reverence for imagination and introspection—all Romantic ideas eerily akin to those expressed by the youth of the 1960's.

In Germany a generation of young writers late in the eighteenth century established *Sturm und Drang* ("storm and stress"), the literary movement that kindled an intellectual awakening to Romanticism. Of the literary works that grew out of the awakening, one work is noteworthy, Goethe's *The Sorrows of Young Werther* (1774, 1787). Although today's readers may consider *Werther* a milestone of sentimental, romantic nonsense, this lugubrious tale of a poet's unselfish, impossible, and unfulfilled love was a sensation in its time. Its influence induced a rash of suicides, and its popularity lasted over many generations.

---

3. The first use of the term "noble savage" is ascribed to Dryden in his play *The Conquest of Granada* (1670), but early Greek authors lavished praise on "uncontaminated" primitives to underline excesses in their own times. Educated Europeans of the late eighteenth century were intrigued by the flora and fauna of the New World. Of the fauna, Europeans found the "savage"—uncivilized man living in the state of nature—to be most fascinating and eagerly welcomed any report on newly found aboriginal groups. Some reports were pure fiction, slanted to suit the fancy of individuals dissatisfied with their own societies. The religious life of savage tribes was extolled for its simplicity and lack of competing dogmas, while the natives' closeness to nature was hailed as an incomparable virtue. Of all the books touching on the New World's wealth of flora and fauna, none was greeted by European audiences with greater enthusiasm than William Bartram's *Travels Through North and South Carolina, Georgia, East and West Florida* (1791). Bartram was a botanist, an artist, and a keen observer who described Indians accurately and without sentimentality. Despite many negative aspects of his descriptions, his book was thought to ennoble the original Americans and was a boon to those who sought to further the myth of the noble savage.

With Goethe and *Werther* here we encounter a trait that was to become commonplace throughout the Romantic experience: to the Romantics it seemed perfectly plausible that Goethe could write Romantic works on one hand and respectably maintain a career as a Classical scientist on the other. Not since the Renaissance had such duality been so favored. Classicists admire specialists.

Samuel Taylor Coleridge (1772–1834) made the first Classical–Romantic distinction in England, but only after the movement was well under way. Also in England Alexander Pope (1688–1744), whose acid pen earned him the agnomen "The Wicked Wasp of Twickenham," was a model Classicist, but in his late years he fell under the spell of Romanticism and built a sham grotto and an Italianate villa. Pope then totally abandoned his classical literary style and wrote "Elegy to an Unfortunate Lady," all about gloomy caverns, ruins, and a sword-pierced ghost. Pope's "Elegy" in fact had all the trappings of the Gothic novel yet to be invented.

Romantic tho[...]t ranged just below the level of consciousness [...] found their way into the imagination[...]ntsia, and other elements of th[...]ptance in minds sensitiv[...]49, five years after P[...]7–1797), a rich youn[...]uilding a modest ho[...]d the house into an e[...]

Th[...]eate a Gothic buildir[...]ds of the people at th[...]e term. Things Goth[...]eserted, haunted, for[...]ords that were to de[...]s of Gothic novels. T[...]es. After all, Goths [...]ravaged Rome. Their [...]struction, decline, and [...]nore benign vision of the

Gothic. In his travels in Europe he had recognized the magnificence of the great cathedrals, many of which were approaching ruin. There was a melancholy ambience to these structures that stimulated in Walpole a melancholy mood he would later embody in his novel *The Castle of Otranto* (1764).

Beyond the titillations of melancholy the eighteenth-century Romantic sensed an alliance with the generations that built the great ecclesiastical structures. Certainly the dreamers who realized the monumental, aspirant, towering cathedrals "had thoughts co-equal to the clouds." It was pleasurable for the Romantic to disagree with the consensus opinion that anything Gothic was awful. Ever since the Renaissance some three hundred years earlier, when the term "Gothic" had first come into use, Europeans had chosen to view their Gothic heritage as barbarous. The Romantics correctly pointed out that the cathedrals—open skeletons of stone held in form by thrusts and counterthrusts of interdependent elements—were wonders of construction produced by an inspired people. To Walpole, in the relative security of late-eighteenth-century Twickenham, the labors and achievements of the thirteenth- and fourteenth-century builders must have seemed incredible. Despite incessant warfare, famine, marauding bands of plunderers, peasant uprisings, and most calamitous of all, the Black Death, those dedicated laborers had created the most awe-inspiring monuments in Europe.

The whole idea of the Gothic was appealing to Walpole's kind, therefore, and in the neo-Gothic architecture that was to come, the dominant theme was the recreation of the cathedrals' reaching, aspirant mode.

From its beginnings, the Gothic Revival style of building heralded an important change in the way people regarded architecture. Classicists considered buildings beautiful by virtue of their line, proportion, and form. Romanticists felt that beauty in architecture could be judged through buildings' associations with literary and historical images. Thus "picturesque" and "evocative" became key terms to the Romantic builders.

Gothic literature, however, took another route. Its theme stressed decay, mystery, and those twilight elements related to the sinister.

It is remarkable that the first Gothic Revival structure and the first Gothic novel were created by the same person. Horace Walpole took years to complete "Strawberry Hill," his neo-Gothic castle. It wasn't until 1764 that he had the dream that would launch the Gothic novel. Walpole, exhausted after preparing a pamphlet to defend a friend in trouble with the law, dreamed he was in a mouldering castle. High above an enormous stairway appeared a colossal hand in armor. Fresh from this fragment of a dream, and in feverish excitement, Walpole wrote his *Castle of Otranto* over the next two months. It became the model of countless Gothic novels that swept Europe and America. For seventy-five years the Gothic novel reigned as Europe's most original literary form, to be superseded only by Dickens's humor in *Pickwick Papers* and his realism in *Oliver Twist*. In Germany the Gothic story stayed on in one form or another until 1900. In the 1960's, the Gothic novel once again made its appearance, featuring innocent but determined maidens, despotic and very rich uncles, and Gothic manor houses. The form suited the escapist needs of the new Romantics perfectly.

Literature obviously led the way in creating the Romantic mood of the eighteenth and nineteenth centuries, and while it was influencing the thoughts of Europeans in general, the mood was also affecting other arts. Mozart, who was superbly equipped to sense new directions, nevertheless died too young (1791) for his music to be significantly touched by the growing Romantic mood. His music remained essentially Classical. Beethoven, born fourteen years later than Mozart, began his musical life as a Classical composer, moving, at the height of his creativity, toward musical Romanticism. Beethoven's Romantic Ninth Symphony, the great choral symphony embodying Schiller's "Ode to Joy," was completed in 1823, but he had given serious consideration to its setting as early as 1793.

It cannot be said that everyone was affected by the growing Romantic mood. There were those who wanted no part of the Romantic revolution. Older values or a desire to place content over fashion led many to renounce Romanticism. Jane Austen, for one, regarded the trappings of the mood with contempt. In 1815, while in London, she was invited to meet Madame de Staël, then the most famous woman writer in Europe. Miss Austen declined, feeling she had little in common with that conspicuous supporter of the Romantic theme.

In America as in Europe, most people had few contacts with the elements that produce a cultural mood. Many groups espoused spiritual or intellectual pursuits that ran contrary to the prevailing Romanticism. During the Romantic era, the Shaker Sect not only produced pure, Classical form-follows-function architecture and furniture, they also created hymns that joyfully set forth their beliefs. Later, Aaron Copland celebrated the Shaker hymn " 'Tis a Gift to be Simple" as a major theme in his *Appalachian Spring* suite. To be simple is not a Romantic trait.

In American building, Thomas Jefferson, a Classical Revival architect, Benjamin Henry Latrobe, William Strickland, Asher Benjamin, Minard Lafever, and Thomas Ustick Walter, leading Greek Revival architects all, thought of themselves as Classicists. They would have been bemused, puzzled, or possibly outraged to have been remembered as architects of the Romantics. Nevertheless their enterprise was Romantic: reviving the past, and reaching back into antiquity to create a kinship between a new republic and the ideals of ancient Greece and Rome, is a Romantic action.

Romanticism in architecture has been in eclipse for most of our own century, but it shows signs of revival. On March 5, 1988, Prince Charles, heir to the Throne of England, spoke to a joint conference of the American Institute of Architects and the Royal Institute of British Architects, held in Pittsburgh. In his plea for a return to traditional architectural styles, he said, "If we encourage a renaissance of craftsmanship and the art of embellishing buildings for man's pleasure and for the sheer joy in beauty itself, as opposed to mere functionalism, then we shall have made our cities centers of civilization once again." (*New York Times*, March 6, 1988.)

The Prince of Wales' remarks were met with a standing ovation. Yet many of his listeners represented an architectural establishment whose credos have embraced the "form-follows-function" strictures of Classical architecture. Prince Charles had touched a responsive chord in those architects who now perceive the swing to the elements of Romanticism.

Arts in the Romantic Mood

Of all the arts literature was best suited to have expressed the Romantic mood. Rousseau, Goethe, Balzac, Hugo, Keats, Byron, Shelley—Percy and Mary—Scott, Hawthorne, and Poe come directly to mind as influential literary figures caught up in the Romantic movement. No other force or art had such direct influence on architecture as literature. The works of the eighteenth- and nineteenth-century writers and poets expressed the Romantic mood long before other arts felt the tides of change. As always there are some exceptions—landscape architecture seems to have found Romantic expression very early on. But *writing* was the prime conveyer of the elements that made the mood to which architects and architecture responded.

It can also be argued that architecture influenced literature. Gothic architecture, especially vine-strangled, mossy, and crumbling specimens, gave writers a focus for that part of the Romantic movement that embraces the mysterious, the morbid, and the murky. While literature's effect on architecture was unplanned and indirect, some popular writing in nineteenth-century America was aimed directly at architecture to influence its course. Essays and tracts advised, cautioned, and encouraged prospective builders. No editorial writer was

thought worthy of his post who failed to make occasional comment on the state of American architecture.

Next to writing, music was best able to voice the illusory qualities of Romanticism, yet it was some fifty years after the onset of literary Romanticism that a Romantic composer challenged Classical music. To underline the great Romantic revolution and the time factors that so affected nineteenth-century music, it has been said that Mozart was entirely a Classical composer; Beethoven, a Classical and a Romantic composer; and Brahms, entirely Romantic.

It was Beethoven (1770–1827) who introduced the elements of revolt that led music to break away from the molds of formalism and artificiality that had too often typified the Classical period. His later works sang out the emancipation of human emotions just as he personally proclaimed his freedom from the demeaning strictures of patronage. At the sight of Goethe kneeling before royalty, Beethoven felt constrained to remark angrily, "It is they who must make way for us, not we for them."

The earliest years of Beethoven's career showed the Classical influences of Haydn and Mozart, but as he matured his music began to flame with such power and individuality that he was universally marked as a new force in the musical realm. The years 1810–1817 were comparatively unproductive in Beethoven's life. Termed his *Sturm und Drang* years, they occurred almost thirty year after von Klinger's drama, *Sturm und Drang*, which had given the literary movement its name. After 1817 the majority of Beethoven's works were written in the minor keys with an especial predilection for C minor. With his *Missa Solemnis* and his later string quartets and trios, Beethoven not only became a Romantic, but a seer and a mystic as well. Of the F-minor sonata *Appassionata*, Ernst von Elterlein was moved to write, "Dismal spectral shadows rise, as it were, out of the lowest depths; soft wailings issue from the heart, and fate is heard knocking at the door. Suddenly a mighty storm bursts forth. . . ." How better to describe the

Gothic aspects of the great composer's work?

Ludwig van Beethoven died March 26, 1827, during a violent thunderstorm. Shortly before his death he had written his Opus 131 in C sharp minor. Wagner pronounced the first movement as "the most melancholy sentiment ever expressed in music." It was the Romantic way to go.

Tragically, Beethoven's great predecessor, Mozart, lived only thirty-five years. He died in 1791, just before the first stirrings of the *musical* Romantic period. What that incomparable genius might have done with the freedoms in which Beethoven flourished we can only conjecture. In his biography of Mozart in *The International Cyclopedia of Music and Musicians*, Pitts Sanborn wrote, "The only element lacking in his cosmos is an appreciation of the out-of-doors, of Nature—which was to mean so much to Beethoven." The appreciation of the out-of-doors and of Nature are elements of Romanticism that, had Mozart lived, he would surely have mastered magnificently.

The first performance of Victor Hugo's play *Hernani* occurred in 1830 and constituted an open revolt against Classicism and the academicians of Paris. In the same year Hector Berlioz (1803–1869) conducted the first performance of his *Symphonie fantastique*, a pi-

Hector Berlioz

oneer work in realism and programmatic music. Early in his career, on reading Goethe's *Faust*, Berlioz wrote to a friend: "I could not lay it down, but read and read and read—at tables, in streets and the theater." Berlioz provides us with a direct example of the influence of literature on music. In time the composer wrote ten songs from *Faust* and a major work, *The Damnation of Faust*.

Jacques Offenbach around 1880 composed *The Tales of Hoffmann*, a musical pageant saturated with sinister Gothic allusions based on E. T. A. Hoffmann's stories published sixty years before. Saint-Saëns' *Danse Macabre* (1874) was considered so provocative that a near-riot occurred at its first performance. Paul Dukas's symphonic poem *L'Apprenti sorcier* musically paraphrased Goethe's eerie tale of a disorderly broom and a sorcerer's apprentice. Moussorgski's *Night on Bald Mountain*, Paganini's *Dance of the Green Devil*, and Dvorak's *Noon Day Witch* all evoked Gothic subjects. With the *Symphonie fantastique* of Berlioz, these programmatic pieces make appropriate fare for present-day Halloween performances or for horror-film sound tracks.

Themes of national pride were introduced to music as patronage shifted from the courts of the nobility to the state. The revolutions of 1848 further democratized Europe and inspired Polish, Bohemian, Hungarian, and Czech composers to a frenzy of nationalism. Schubert's thematic music and Schumann's subjective themes moved the musical art into another aesthetic sphere within the Romantic movement. Carl Maria von Weber helped introduce the Romantic opera which Richard Wagner would bring to a tumultuous crescendo.

The symphonic poems of Liszt, the introspective and often melancholy works of Tschaikowsky—*None but the Lonely Heart, Symphonie pathétique*—the tone poems of Richard Strauss, and Rachmaninoff's passionate concertos carried the Romantic movement through the nineteenth century and into the first quarter of the twentieth. The American composer Howard Hansen unabashedly titled his moving second symphony *The*

Romantic. It survived the indifference of the twentieth-century Classicists to become a standard in the repertoires of major symphonic organizations throughout the world.

Not only were compositions of the early Romantic writers and composers Romantic, their lives seemed to echo the most Romantic ideals. Berlioz's poverty-ridden life was plagued by a seemingly hopeless love affair with an untamed, debt-stricken Irish actress, Henrietta Smithson. After countless dismissals she eventually married him, only to face neglect and a lonely and alcoholic end.

Berlioz's brain was filled with unrealizable dreams. He once wrote a dramatic work, the *Judex crederis*, for 465 instruments including thirty pianos and as many harps. It was never performed. In the best Romantic tradition Berlioz failed to achieve critical acceptance in his lifetime in his native France, but ironically his death brought immediate recognition and acclaim to his music. With his music he also left behind letters and memoirs that are models of Romantic prose.

Victor Hugo's long life (1802–1885) could have been written by himself in one of his most imaginative moods. He lived most of his life in political exile, but, unlike Berlioz, Hugo was not poor. His *Hernani*, introduced to Paris with the aid of a large claque of long-haired youth, was the hit of the 1830 season. At age twenty-eight he was on his way to great fame and considerable fortune. While Hugo was a model husband, his wife, Adèle, found pleasure in secret meetings with Hugo's closest friend. Their trysts were held in deserted churches—no doubt for the Gothic effect. Adèle and Victor remained married, but as a token of penance, Adèle gave her husband permission to take a mistress. For fifty years the actress Juliette Drouet accepted that role, and Madame Hugo condoned the arrangement. The great author spent his exiled years at St. Peter Port in the Channel Isle of Guernsey near the picturesque ruins of a Gothic church.

Victor Hugo

Madame Victor Hugo

The interaction of the arts on each other and on their audiences brought the Romantic era to its zenith in the mid-nineteenth century. The cultural time lapse between Europe and America was ever shortening, so that for the first time it is possible to refer to Europe and America without time compensations to explain lags in development. By the 1860's, costume had reached its romantic peak aided and abetted by the other arts. Hooped skirts sixteen feet in circumference ballooned from tightly corseted, sixteen-inch waists and décolleté bodices. Military uniforms were at their Graustarkian best, and facial adornments—whiskers, side chops, and baroque moustaches—were the subjects of enthusiastic cultivation.

Landscape architecture is an art often slighted as a mere handmaiden to architecture, but it was itself an important influence on the architecture of the Romantic era. Especially under the leadership of Batty Langley (1696–1751), landscape architecture became an art unto itself as early as the 1750's. Langley was able to combine Gothic and Picturesque motifs into "wildernesses," groves, labyrinths, and other landscape themes that would challenge the established formality of gardens everywhere in Europe. A. J. Downing found Langley's books an indispensable resource. Many Downing tenets originated a century before his time from Langley and his associates. As Langley died in 1751, his perceptions of the Gothic feeling make him one of the earliest adventurers in the Romantic movement.

Prior to the 1960's, in the twentieth-century Classical era, humanists taught that painting was not an art that could cope with the elements of Romanticism. Romanticism was in such ill favor that to name a master as a Romantic painter was to denigrate his reputation. It was proclaimed that Romanticism was never a part of the mainstream of the development of the visual arts. Historical figures who gave evidence to the contrary, such as William Blake and his friend Henry Fuseli, were, it was held, able to express elements of Romanticism in their art, but only in concordance with literary themes. Another name put forth as a Romanticist was Delacroix, whose reputation was so powerful that art historians hedged, conceding that he was able to convey Romantic themes without surrendering aesthetic ideals.

The twentieth-century Classical assessment of Romantic painting went on to say that the shudderingly delicious horror, the unrequited or platonic love, the impossible dream, the exiled soul, and what Ruskin called the pathetic fallacy (conscienceless cruelty assigned to nature, for example) found better expression in literature, music, and the theater than in painting.

The reawakening of interest in the works of William Blake may have been a factor in the re-evaluation of Romantic painting in recent years. Gradually Romanticism lost its negative connotation in art criticism. Painters of great stature were reclassified, and many were correctly reassigned. The late Lord Kenneth Clark's authoritative *The Romantic Rebellion: Romantic versus Classic Art* (Harper & Row, 1973), listed Turner, Goya, and Géricault, among others, as Romantic painters. To present-day viewers, it seems inconceivable that those masters could have been considered otherwise.

Today's views of Romanticism have been altered. Association with literary themes is no longer required. Kenneth Clark's 1973 book never mentioned the Pre-Raphaelite Brotherhood, since that group's reputation was then at its nadir, but in the years since *The Romantic Rebellion*, a great interest in the lives and works of Dante Gabriel Rossetti, John Everett Millais, William Holman Hunt, and others of the Brotherhood has arisen. There's an irony here, as the Brotherhood was pretentiously Classical, yet history has placed it in the Romantic arena.

Nineteenth-century Romantic thought embraced dicta that were to become the targets of twentieth-century Classical criticism: "Through works of art, men become conscious of moral responsibility," "The aim of art should be noble simplicity and calm grandeur," "Art should excite the emotions," and, in the Gothic vein, "Fear is the source of the sublime." Hardly any phase of life—the arts, commerce, politics, or the military, was untouched by the first conscious Romantic movement. The elements of the revived movement that began in the 1960's have not yet developed in enough detail or given enough perspective to indicate how pervasive their effect will have been on the fabric of our society. Mood watchers have long waits.

Plate 1   *Hand-hewn Beams*

Hand-hewn Beams

*At Millfield, not far from Ohio University, in Athens,
log cabins and post-and-beam houses survive in the Appalachian quiet. I painted the stacked remains of a post-and-
beam house to mark the end of an era.* Portraits of American Architecture *begins with the simultaneous acceptance
of the steam-driven saw, the mill-cut nail, and balloon-
frame construction, inventions that revolutionized America's concepts of building in the nineteenth century.*

*The log cabin has long been an important symbol to
Americans. It was a place to rise from to become President; it denoted independence, industry, individuality, ruggedness, honesty, and the pioneering spirit. It was a
straightforward, form-follows-function, Classical construction built from available materials with available tools. Its
only decoration might have been antlers or a horseshoe
over the doorway. In New York's Adirondacks, in Tennes-*

*see, and in Kentucky, log cabins are built to this day. In
New England post-and-beam construction has made a recent comeback in good numbers. In 1820 the post-and-
beam house was the norm for new house construction, and
the reigning style for the well-to-do was the Adamesque–
Federal, a Classical form with finite and delicate Classical
decoration. In the ensuing sixty years America's muse had
utterly transformed the American psyche.*

*The use of extremes will best illustrate the transition
in tastes and values that took place in those tumultuous
years: imagine a log cabin or a rugged post-and-beam
farmhouse placed next to a Cape May cottage. Aesthetically, technologically, and philosophically, the structures
are worlds apart—almost totally unrelated. Before the Industrial Revolution, rudimentary technology limited construction details to the output of skilled craftsmen. Before*

the Civil War the American temperament held building to a reasonably sober line, with Greek Revival, Gothic, and Italianate decorations excused by their association with history and noble sentiments. After the Civil War, with technology flourishing and the Age of Innocence behind us, the way was clear for experimentation, invention, and excesses. Association with history or religion became vague, and decorative elements overpowered or obliterated the functional outlines of the building itself.

If the tenets of the Romantic–Classic theory are to be observed, the construction today of classical log cabins must be regarded as a Romantic exercise, because nostalgia—a looking backward—is the motivating force.

Olana

"Olana," a Moorish fantasy, is a breathtaking reflection of the Romantic vision. Built by Hudson River School painter Frederick Edwin Church (1826–1900) following travels in the Holy Lands, Olana faces that great river at Hudson, New York. Although it is over a hundred years old, the house still looks transplanted and alien in the verdure of the Hudson River Valley.

At his death Frederick Edwin Church was utterly unknown to the rising generation. Forty years earlier he had been perhaps the best known and admired artist in America.

Some years ago one of Church's paintings, of the ghostly remnants of a sailing vessel in a brooding arctic landscape, made headlines in the nation's newspapers. The Icebergs, *painted in 1861, sold at a 1979 auction to a private collector for $2.5 million.[1] In his productive years Church made a fortune charging admission (usually 25 cents) to view his canvasses of Niagara Falls, the Andes, the ruins of the Rose Red City of Petra, etc. In the 1930's and '40's, however, his works could be bought at very low prices. Buyers were not interested in Church. The 1970 edition of* The Oxford Companion to Art *failed to list Church, although* The London Art Journal *once named him the successor to Turner. Before the sale of* The Icebergs, *most biographies mentioned only that he had studied with Thomas Cole and classified him as a Hudson River School traditionalist. In fact there was far more interest in the successful efforts of preservationists to save Olana for the public than there was in Olana's builder.*

David C. Huntington's The Landscapes of Frederick Edwin Church *(1966, George Braziller & Co.) helped to revive interest in Church, and the mood of the succeeding years helped enormously.*

Olana, translated, *means "our place on high." Church*

---

1. The painting had been lost for a hundred years. It was discovered at a home for delinquent boys in Manchester, England. The cover illustration of Icebergs *in David Huntington's book on Church was reproduced from an 1860's chromolithograph of the painting.*

described the architecture as "Persian, adapted to the occident." The artist's home, before Olana, was a modest cottage inspired by Andrew Jackson Downing, author of The Architecture of Country Houses. The principal architect of Olana was Calvert Vaux, author of Villas and Cottages.

David Huntington provides an excellent description of the elements of Olana's architecture: "In the pointed arches, the block-like massing, the steep-pitched roof of the tower, and the 'constructional' polychromy of the original house, one can make out the connections with Gothic Revival, Italian Villa, French Mansard and Ruskinian Venetian stylistic idioms. The studio wing in its delicacy and lightness brings to mind the later Shingle Style."

Shortly after Church's death, Mrs. M. E. W. Sherwood wrote in the New York Times, "If only we hold on to our idols, they will come back."

Plate 2   *Olana*

Plainfield Term

In architecture the word "term" (also "terminus") derives from "terminal figure." It is one of a group of architectural devices used in place of, or to adorn, brackets, columns, pilasters, and pillars. The most familiar such figure is the caryatid, *a freestanding female figure supporting overhead structures. Male counterparts are* atlantes. *A three-quarter figure serving as a bracket is a* telamon, *and* terms *are carved into tapering pedestals merging at the top into human, animal, and mythological figures. A* Persian *is a telamon portrayed in male Persian dress. A* bifrons *has two heads, and a* quadrifrons *is a column topped with four heads looking north, east, south, and west, while a* gaine *is a decorative anthropomorphic pedestal tapering downward and rectangular in cross section, like the* herm, *which is a rectangular post surmounted by a human head. Finally,* canephorae *are caryatids with baskets on their heads.*

The term in the painting decorates a small nineteenth-century office building in Plainfield, New Jersey. It is one of a pair flanking an arched doorway, and it is important only because it illustrates the pride of the Victorian builder, who felt that his building was an extension of himself and, to some degree, an extension of his beliefs. The absentee landlord existed in the last century, of course, but most owners lived in the community in which their businesses and their buildings were located. In a business district it was common practice to name a building for its builder, and that builder wanted his name to be honored by the structure. Even a small business office in a small town was a powerful status symbol if the building met with general approval—and disapprobation could bring ridicule to the builder and his business.

Victorians were only beginning to accept the accelerated change going on about them. Values were under attack, and the post-Civil War climate suggested that permanency was a thing of the past. Yet many Victorians clung to the ideal that a building, whether a residence or a

Plate 3   *Plainfield Term*

business structure, should last, to be handed down with pride from generation to generation.

It is fortunate for us that the ideal of permanency persisted. In our cities the passerby has inherited much to be wondered at and to be enjoyed in Victorian/Romantic expressions if the viewer can relate what is seen to the history and philosophy inherent in the urban landscape.

In 1988, the arms of the Plainfield terms were broken off by vandals.

II. The Victorian Impact

IT IS UNFORTUNATE THAT the contemporary image of the period known as Victorian is so associated with prudery, complacency, smugness, and hypocrisy. The immediate followers of the Victorians (and the Edwardians), were the Classicists of the 1900's, who in their zeal to discredit all that had immediately gone before them chose to air the most negative aspects of their predecessors to give luster to their own brave new world.

It is true that American Victorians were an unlikely mixture of Romantics and Puritans, and to some extent it is true that the Victorian nature was conformist. But we forget that Victorian houses were far more individualistic than our mass-produced shelters of recent decades. The denigration of conformity and elevation of individuality that have so entertained our past few generations have provided ironic results. Individuality was placed at a premium, but the result has been a mass individuality that has become its opposite: rigid conformity in codes of speech, dress, ideals, and behavior was the norm for the students and flower children of the sixties. The Victorians seem unique, even remarkable, by comparison.

Perhaps the most confusing aspect of the Victorians were the contradictions and the dualities of their society. It was an age that pointed in pride to freedom but somehow could, to a point, tolerate slavery. Victorian America prided itself on equality, but it delighted in covert aristocracies symbolized by New York's Four Hundred, Boston's Brahmins, and Philadelphia's Main Line. Victorians doted on the image of innocent childhood as characterized in Longfellow's "Children's Hour," but ignored the evils of the sweatshop and child labor. Victorian taboos regarding sex are legend, yet Victorian dress emphasized the salient sexual features of the wearers, male or female. All the while moral earnestness was the overt ideal. As Longfellow wrote:

> Life is real! Life is earnest!
> And the grave is not its goal;
> Dust thou art, to dust returnest,
> Was not spoken of the soul.

Apparently formal resolutions and agreements reached by duly constituted bodies were acceptable so long as these statements didn't actually impinge on the practices of the community. The vastly successful Seneca Falls Convention of 1848, which laid the foundations for all the women's-liberation movements that were to come, was largely applauded by the community—so long as no change really came of it. More to the community's liking was the verse excerpted from Tennyson's "In Memoriam":

> For him she plays, to him she sings
> Of early faith and plighted vows;
> She knows but matters of the house,
> And he, he knows a thousand things.

"In Memoriam" was written two years after the Seneca Falls Convention.

Victorians believed that they could control the destiny of mankind and shape the future for mankind's benefit. Part of that belief was expressed in their earnest moral efforts to subdue passion. It was clearly understood that if one could only overcome passion, the way would be clear to a future where evil was aberrant.

On both sides of the Atlantic Queen Victoria symbolized the dual themes of home and domesticity. The home was where the Victorian heart dwelled. The era was receptive to the outlooks and values of a confident and optimistic middle class. The home of the Victorian served purposes beyond shelter. It was the setting where Mother transmitted the higher ideals of religion, spiritual love, and general uplift. For Father the home was the symbol of his success, a statement to his neighbors of his status.

The United States, as the Victorian period continued, realized its "Manifest Destiny," pushing westward beyond the Mississippi. This was also a period of growing sectionalism—of splitting into two regions, North and South, each with its own social and economic system. We tend to forget how the War Between the States threatened to tear the nation apart. Even in comparison with recent conflicts, its casualties were appalling. One out of every four Civil War soldiers died in battle, of wounds, or from disease. The South, fielding one of the greatest armies in history—superb, natural fighting men led by brilliant generals—stood no chance against the overwhelming manpower and industrial might of the North.

The War ended an age of innocence. It hardened America and introduced a conscious cynicism into the late-Victorian ethic. Beyond Walt Whitman's sorrowful evaluation of the war as a "strange, sad war of Americans fighting Americans, often brother fighting brother," was the public—the political—knowledge that some Americans who made no sacrifices, did make enormous fortunes from the war in previously unacceptable ways. The same entrepreneurs, after the war, increasingly controlled railroads, banks, and trusts. Through manipulations frequently aided by political connivance, the newly rich and powerful became an entrenched elite, able to further enrich themselves and their allies.

The conspicuous wealth displayed by the robber barons did not bother or anger the post-war American Victorians as it would have enraged the citizenry of only twenty years before. Europe had been the scene of mid-century revolutions, but here there was relatively little social rebellion after the Civil War. The rich were envied, but there was always the hope that with a little luck and considerable sweat, one could rise to a similar position. Or if not oneself, then certainly one's children.

The Victorian ethic and the Romantic mood continued to dominate the latter decades of the nineteenth century, leading to an erosion of its spirit. The Mauve Decade, 1890–1900 was cynical, overblown, and ready for intellectual and social cleansing. Excesses could no longer entertain, excuse, or direct the senses away from the staleness and the ennui that prevailed. The scales were tipping, the colors softening, the hyperbole cooling, and a new mood was being felt throughout the land.

The Victorian era did not die with Queen Victoria in 1901. Most historians concede that the end of the era (and the mood), came eleven years later with the sinking of the *Titanic*. A survivor is quoted as saying, "I'll never believe in anything again." When the great ship went down on her maiden voyage the Victorian spirit drowned with her. World War I brought whatever remained of the structure of Victorian confidence and optimism crashing in ruins.

Now, in the closing decades of our own century, we can look back to the Victorian spirit—its eccentricities, its grandiose dreams, its wild romanticism—and find ourselves admiring Victorian achievements. The Victorians have left us a legacy, their courageous Romantic outlook and their moral vigor. We can benefit by contemplating it.

The living legacy of the Victorians is their architecture. It began in America with the Greek Revival.

Antiques Bazaar

In its years the Victorian store played host to an almost endless list of enterprises. High ceilings and generous display windows made the space attractive to merchants of every description. While the buildings housing the store areas were built to accommodate businesses, additional living space was gained by the addition of apartments overhead. The building in the painting could house four to six income-producing apartments.

Enterprises that originally occupied the store were very stable during the prime years of the Victorian-era neighborhood. Several generations of grocers, haberdashers, butchers, bakers, etc. rented the premises from generations of owners. But as neighborhoods changed, succession ended as the heirs of prosperous small businesses turned to the professions in the upwardly mobile manner of the times. Older neighborhoods declined or were replaced by the buildings of corporate ventures. In declining areas the nature of the businesses changed at an ever-increasing pace. In such a neighborhood saloons, laundries, carpentry, roofing, and plumbing establishments succeeded the greengrocers, clothiers, and ice cream parlors as the area became increasingly commercial.

Neighborhoods that maintained a residential character also saw change as family grocers gave way to chain stores. A&Ps, Acmes, Nationals, Eagles, Butlers, Piggly Wigglys, Handy Andys, and Grand Unions held forth as corner-store entities for a few more generations. Sometimes the faint imprints of Salada, Tetley, or Lipton remain in the windows where once the handsome raised gold letters advertised the teas featured in the stores. As supermarkets replaced the corner groceries, the space might become a paint and hardware store, handling a variety of wares appealing to the homeowners of a generation deprived of the services of the once indispensable nineteenth-century handyman. Sporting goods were added to the wide-ranging hardware line. Union Hardware was the standard name in roller skates for sixty years.

Victorian furniture stores of the western states served (behind the scenes) as undertaking establishments. Coffins were considered a form of furniture. In many parts of the west, particularly in Nebraska and the Dakotas, the custom still prevails.

The Island Heights, New Jersey, emporium of the painting is playing out another role—this time as a bazaar for period pieces, baskets, Japanese fish kites, and novelties for a summer trade. The faded, billowing sheets of flags almost cover the identifying brackets of the Mansard structure. The painting was my last for this book. I intended it to be exuberant and immensely cheerful, but, somehow, it's a little saddening.

Lenoir's

At the southern end of the New Jersey Turnpike, the soaring Memorial Bridge arcs over the Delaware River into Delaware itself. Immediately a modest highway sign points to New Castle, an early capital of Delaware. Peter Stuyvesant and William Penn figured in its early history, and among its treasures is an early-eighteenth-century Wrenish courthouse, one of the oldest public buildings in the United States.

The wonderful thing about New Castle is that it has always been so well preserved that restoration has played only a minor role in its survival. A colonial arsenal in the center of the old town is now the pleasantest of restaurants, and there are eight or so blocks of eighteenth- and nineteenth-century town houses lined around an old Village Green. One group of town houses is the subject of my detailed painting. I painted it to show how well certain Victorian touches agree with Classical structures.

The shuttered doorway at the right has the Adamesque fanlight typical of the Federal era, dating the building to around 1800. The brickwork is of interest, as it shows partial replacement, a sign of continuing maintenance if not exactly preservation. The building to the left of Lenoir's is in such mint condition that the brick façade may have been restored in the past fifty years. The little console over the doorway is Victorian, but the transom light over the doorway indicates that the doorway itself may have originated during the Greek Revival tenure. The storefront faces the village green and was proportioned by a carpenter who had a fine instinct for suitability. It is remarkably simple, yet it conveys a sense of style—understated Victorian style.

The old brick sidewalks are swept with sand by the New Castle residents. The abrasive action scours the brick so that the salmon-colored surface is always fresh and appealing. That pink goes nicely with the blue-gray of the cobblestones in the streets. Ground-floor shutters are robustly paneled, and their hooks and hinges have the generous measurements of hand-crafted hardware.

Plate 5   *Lenoir's*

Don't knock on the door at Number 11. Lenoir's hasn't been a store for a long time. In discussing with neighbors their plans to return Lenoir's to its town-house status, the new owners sensed that, in New Castle, change was anathema. Even the removal of the faded Dry Goods and Notions sign, which "had always been there," seemed wrong on reconsideration. So Lenoir's remains unchanged. The room behind the storefront is lined with books. The shelves that once held notions now hold ideas.

In early spring New Castle has a Flag Day celebration. The arsenal, once manned by Redcoats, flies British flags alongside The Stars and Stripes, and almost every house in the old town is represented with banners or bunting. It's an exciting day in a beautiful old town.

Stockerton Mourning House

Stockerton, Pennsylvania, is about eight miles north of Easton. Alongside the Forks Church, the Forks Cemetery basks in the peaceful surroundings of a farming community. Names on the gravestones indicate predominantly German ancestry. Outstanding are two lovingly made mourning houses. Both are octagons, built to provide shelter for mourners attending services during inhospitable weather. It is remarkable that the cheerful nature of the structures never offended bereaved Victorians, who made mourning such an elaborate ritual.

In an age when the external evidences of mourning have almost disappeared, the mourning customs of the

Plate 6   *Stockerton Mourning House*

middle and upper classes in the Romantic era are pertinent to the understanding of Victorians' attachment to symbolism.

Some notes: directly after the death of a family member, the dressmaker was notified. She bought yards and yards of black bombazine for mourning dresses. Black gloves, black-bordered handkerchiefs, and black-bordered calling cards and stationery were also ordered. The closeness of the deceased relative determined the width of the borders. Diamonds were reset in black. Men wore black crepe around their top hats. (The blue-nosed cartoon character representing Prohibition wore that same kind of funereal hat.) If the cemetery where burials occurred was an adjunct to the church, the sexton tolled the bell, one strike for each year of the deceased's life.

The Victorians practically made a sacrament of mourning. Among collectors of Victoriana are some who treasure lachrymatories, solemnly decorated phials for collecting and preserving tears. The Victorian widow was the center of a great deal of interest. For three months after the death of her husband, the widow was "immured," a word we now regard as a synonym for imprisoned. After three months the widow could attend art galleries or concerts, but not the theater. Custom also demanded her piano be closed!

The widow's veil was a gauge which measured the duration of her bereavement. In the deep mourning period, the veil covered her face. After two years the veil was turned back to form a trailing element. From time to time the crepe was shortened until propriety considered it no longer essential. Then white cuffs and collars were introduced, followed by a succession of purple, violet, lilac, and soft gray to herald a return to post-mourning normalcy.

Wealth and social status were expressed in the symbols of the Victorian funerals. The hearse might be drawn by six horses, preferably black and decked out with black-dyed plumes. Elegant horse-drawn carriages followed with masses of flowers prominently displayed. It was all part of the conspicuous consumption that so enraged Thorstein Veblen and was so much a part of the Romantic age.

The architecture of the mourning house in the painting expresses no specific style. The structure is, of course, an octagon, and it has Italianate brackets, pierce work, etc., but this form of gazebo can only be called Victorian.

The Pink House

Architectural historian Dr. Alan Gowans referred to the sort of ornamentation that graces this house as "a kind of costume to be put on or taken off." Cape May documents list the place as the Eldridge Johnson house, circa 1880. In the 1960's it was moved a few blocks to its present location from its original site near the venerable Congress Hotel in Cape May, New Jersey. With all the carpenter's lace removed, it is a simple gable-ended house with an interior of surprising finish. A parlor fireplace is of marbelized slate, and rich moldings curve around the corners of window and door frames. The house is known as "The Pink House" and is thought to have been planned by Charles Shaw. It is one of the most photographed houses in America.

The Pink House is described as a side-hall pitched-roof cottage. The first floor consists of two moderate-sized rooms in tandem flanked by a side stair toward the rear. This room arrangement allowed cross ventilation and ample light. The kitchen and pantry were in a small addition at the rear. The layout suggests that the houses of this type were especially built as summer residences.

A tall turned finial and pendant adorn the gable, and the windows of the third floor are arcuated. Cusped decorations at the bottom of the porch arches look somewhat Saracenic, but other elements seem more inspired by Carpenter Gothic examples.

The careers of older architects in the post-Civil War era were jeopardized by constant change. The movement away from older, conservative ideas of style toward the new and the daring was swift and constant in large urban communities but more cautious in outlying areas. This fact

Plate 7   *The Pink House*

was a blessing for architects who were willing to forsake big city offices, as commissions dwindled, for smaller, more conservative towns. The smaller towns wanted no part of the new ideas sweeping through the cities and were content with styles already becoming vernacular. Cape May's cottages are an example: in scale and in essential form they are quite conservative, and despite their frothy predilections, they are expressive of the earlier ideas and Republican ideals expressed in pre-Civil War writings such as Downing's Country Houses. For a long while Cape

May stayed stylistically frozen in time—to the great advantage of the architects who had turned away from the arena of change.

I have been asked if it isn't difficult to part with paintings. The answer is, yes. The painting of The Pink House was one of my favorites, as it allowed me to use the colors that the wonderfully bright atmosphere of seashore communities bestow. I parted with this painting with great reluctance.

III. The Greek Revival

IT WAS WHILE AT COLLEGE that I saw my first Greek Revival buildings. Syracuse and the majestic surrounding countryside had many Greek survivors. I had seen a few in my home state of New Jersey but had no reason to consider them, beyond noticing their obvious crisp beauty. Only after learning their reason for being was I able to look at them with anything approaching the enthusiasm with which I now view these structures. As pieces of the story of the upstate Greek Revivals joined, the historical, artistic, and humanistic elements that contributed to the style all fell into place. Understanding the history of any architectural style provides dimension and color to an appreciation of buildings in that style.

The earliest information available to me on the Greek Revival in upstate New York was a patchwork of fact and folklore. As the houses had been around in abundance since the 1830's, a considerable body of myth about them had developed. Facts and myths were beguiling to one who was to find this growing interest a lifelong pleasure.

In those late-depression years at Syracuse, my travels included many of the roads that were key to the development of New York in the days of the Erie Canal. In the 1930's, a discouraging number of deserted nineteenth-century houses were in a state of final decay in the region. The abandoned buildings dated from the 1860's onward. The Greek Revivals, though older, seemed much less affected by neglect than their Victorian neighbors. The higher cost of maintenance was the overriding factor in the demise of so many Victorians, but there was another reason.

Since 1900, entire generations of Americans have been indoctrinated in the belief that anything Victorian was garish, excessive, ugly, foolish, and in bad taste.

Things Victorian were cheerfully destroyed by the enlightened iconoclasts whose "individual" thoughts had been so carefully shaped by contemporary pundits of fashion. Greek Revival houses (and items associated with them) found better treatment than other Victorian artifacts. Somehow they were honored by the Classical-minded generations of the 1930's. No doubt the Classical directness and the simplicity of most of the Temple Style houses earned them the respect of neo-Classicists.

The surprising anomaly here is that the Greek Revival style was very much a Romantic style. A yearning for a mythical past and the reverence for ancient civilizations, implied in the Greek Revival, are both marks of Romanticism. Despite their Classical forms and their apparent simplicity, the Greek Revival house is America's first Romantic configuration. The Adamesque–Federal houses immediately preceding these Greek Revivals used Classical forms, but only as restrained and delicate relief. The Adamesque–Federal style was part of a long and sensible evolution that provided shelter with a touch of style. The Greek Revivals were monuments to a mood.

That mood was pervasive in its time. The names Syracuse, Ithaca, Attica, Troy, Macedon, Marathon, Mycenae, Ionia, Apulia, and Pharsalia designate New York cities, towns, and villages. Greek or Greek related, they were chosen as place names by early-nineteenth-century surveyors who, in their education as engineers, were taught a modicum of Greek because knowledge of and admiration for anything Greek were considered fashionable. Prior to the use of Greek place names, America's earliest settlers chose nostalgic English-based names for their new homes: New London, New York, New Jersey, New Bedford, and New Brunswick fall into this category. An alternative for the colonists were names that indicated an allegiance to one's monarchs. Elizabeth, Charlottesville, Williamsburg, Charleston, and Georgetown were named for royal figures. After the American Revolution, founders of towns turned to the Bible and came up with Zions, Jerichos, Bethels, etc. From 1820, however, the Spartas and the Athenses cropped up in every state, north and south, because America visualized itself a re-creation of a Periclean ideal.

J. L. David's painting of Mme. de Récamier (1777–1849). Both her gown and the Récamier on which she sits were taken from classical Greek styles.

In France, interest in the history, myth, furniture, dress, and architecture of the ancient Greeks had begun in the 1770's. By Napoleon's time the interest had grown to a national passion much encouraged by the emperor. Napoleon's empress (and President Madison's Dolly), dressed in the Greek Revival style usually referred to as Empire style except in England, where the term "Regency" is favored. The painter Jacques-Louis David (1748–1825), posed his female subjects in short-waisted, décolleté gowns with long pleated skirts resembling the fluted columns of Greek temples. He and Ingres painted them in traditional reclining positions on Empire chaise longues. Reclining itself thus became fashionable, and the haut monde of Paris entertained in the reclining position.

The French went beyond venerating all things Greek by adding to the Hellenic mystique an uncritical admiration of ancient Rome. David's paintings of subjects that typified civic virtues, stoicism, and self-sacrifice also illustrated the sentiments of revolutionary ardor. His *Oath of the Horatii* (1787), helped establish a trend to Classical revivalism. David thought himself a Classicist, but perspective places him firmly in the camp of Romanticism.

The turbulent history of France from its revolution to the final exile of Napoleon had little effect on French talent for style and fashion. While the guillotine, the Reign of Terror, and Napoleonic adventures wrought havoc, French fashions in clothing, furniture, and architecture continued on their evolutionary and influential course. In Russia the second language of educated classes was French. French fashions were adopted by the Russian elite prior to and even after Napoleon's invasion of Russia. Russian architecture was thoroughly influenced by the French, and Temple Style buildings found their way to the Russian landscape. So many Greek Revival houses were built that a number of Russian towns could have served as the film settings for *Birth of a Nation, Gone with the Wind,* or *Mourning Becomes Electra.*

Between the French and Americans there has always been a love-hate relationship. In war we have been allies, but in many elements of our cultural and political life we have been at odds. The beginning of the Greek Revival era in America saw America in a pro-French stance. At the mere mention of the Marquis de Lafayette, trumpets sounded in the minds of our countrymen. An unparalleled hero's welcome marked his triumphant return to America in 1824–1825. Rugged Virginia farmers were reduced to tears when Mr. Jefferson and the marquis embraced on the lawns of Monticello (Classical Revival architecture).

Contributing to Americans' affection for France was their seething anger against France's ancient rival, England. In a way our war for independence was an act akin to a rebellious son's breaking with his father. Family ties and a common institutional heritage continued to bind us to England, however. Only two years after Corn-

Monticello

wallis's surrender, the two nations were negotiating trade pacts in a move to normalize relations. But the War of 1812 put an end to rapprochement. Injury to pride and property brought rage to a nation so openly jealous of its sovereignty; the sack of Washington severely alienated Americans.

A page from Mrs. Frances Trollope's book describing her travels in America, *Domestic Manners of the Americans* (1832), tells it all:

> We received, as I have mentioned, much personal kindness; but this by no means interfered with the national feeling of, I believe, unconquerable dislike, which evidently lives at the bottom of every truly American heart against the English.

By the advent of the Greek Revival from France, the stage was set for Americans to exercise further independence from England by enthusiastically adopting the fashions and goods of France. For years wallpapers, fabrics, and furniture, if imported, were brought over from France. An enthusiasm for ancient Greece was one of these imports.

In view of these circumstances it is perplexing to learn that the first Greek Revival architecture was introduced to America by the English-born, English-trained architect Benjamin Henry Latrobe (1764–1820). In 1798 he designed and supervised the building of the Bank of Pennsylvania in Philadelphia. That Ionic-order building was the first of a long line of public and domestic buildings whose style would come close to as-

suming the proportions of a national style, although not until thirty years later, or some fifteen years after the War of 1812. At that point, feeling themselves to be inheritors of the Periclean ideal, Americans could adopt the Greek Revival style as eminently suitable for a democratic people. The nobility of the Temple Style and the American sense of destiny seemed a fitting partnership.

The countryside surrounding Syracuse, New York, has a rich heritage of Greek Revivals because of the Erie Canal. George Washington, foreseeing the importance of communication between the country west of the Alleghenies and the seaboard, had advocated the canal in the 1780's. The canal was begun, in parts, as early as 1792, but major construction was not resumed following the War of 1812 until 1817. The colossal task of joining the Great Lakes to the Hudson River, from Buffalo to Albany, attracted immigrant labor and opened western New York to commerce. The first journey from Buffalo via canal and lakes to Albany and thence downriver to New York City was accomplished in 1825. The commerce created along the canal attracted investors, entrepreneurs, and builders. A building boom followed the Erie Canal, in which schools, churches, banks, and homes were mostly built in the Greek Revival style.

Bank of Pennsylvania, Philadelphia

As building progressed westward, there was considerable departure from the prototypical Greek forms, with aspects of folk art and local idiosyncracies appearing in the interpretations. There were adaptations for every pocketbook, and for the leaner purses the Greek application was little more than tacking pilasters onto a simple house and the suggestion of entablature and pediment at the eave-end. The more important houses had columns, often squared, which stood away from the house and created a form that was new in America. With few exceptions, houses had been placed with their long sides facing the road. With the Greek Revivals, the eave ends faced the road so that everyone could admire those gleaming white pillars.

A Greek style farm house

Purists felt that the columns of a Greek Revival house should be massive and squat. According to Asher Benjamin's *American Builder's Companion* (sixth edition, 1827), "The thickness of the columns at the base exceed the breadth of the door and windows." In his *Companion* Benjamin foresaw objections to Greek Revival church architecture that would be raised by the Gothic Revivalists who were to come. He wrote, "In sacred places all obscene, grotesque and heathenish representations ought to be avoided; for indecent fables, extravagant conceits, or instruments and symbols of pa-

gan worship are very improper ornaments in structures consecrated to Christian devotion." His advice was scrupulously heeded. The Greek Revival churches I have seen are chaste and simple.

The roofs of Greek Revivals presented a special problem to their builders. To fit the form of their Greek models, they must be flat or low pitched. But considerable bracing was required to withstand the weight of the heavy northern snowfalls. The roof of a handsome Greek building on the campus of Drew University in Madison, New Jersey, has ingenious mechanical bracing which allows it to settle under pressure of heavy snow. While some roofs were covered with tiles or slate (adding to the weight problem), the most popular covering was standing-seam metal, which gave the owners their only choice in coloring, as the houses themselves were invariably painted white. Typically, roofs were painted red or green. Shutters were rarely hung on Greek Revivals until the waning days of the style. Fanlights, which were common in the preceding Adamesque–Federal style, were replaced by oblong transom lights to retain the *trabeated* (that is, without arches) feeling of the Greek style. Windows too were trabeated. Decoration was varied and usually limited to Greek fret and anthemia, but there were, of course, elaborate exceptions.

As the style progressed farther westward and to the south, unorthodox builders produced naively singular variations. Original interpretations of the Greek Revival, created by housewrights far removed from the sophistication of Asher Benjamin's ideas, abound in Ohio, Indiana, and Michigan. Some of the best of American instinctive architecture comes from the less formal expressions. My painting of the pristine Greek Revival at Milford, Pennsylvania (plate 8), shows a shed addition on the left. Someone with an eye for form understood that a slanting roof spoiled the solemn and noble temple effect and appended a false front to the offending addition. From the street, at least, the illusion succeeds. In other folk-inspired Greek Revivals, craftsmen nailed strips of wood to pilasters to create the fluted effect of

Grecian originals. In one Ohio house the effect of reeding was achieved by gluing actual reeds to surfaces and overpainting them. In the transmutation of marble to wood the 1830's craftsmen often found themselves unable to cope with the demands of the Grecian forms and were forced to resort to ingenious building methods.

Not everyone delighted in America's preoccupation with classical architecture. Mrs. Trollope, who in her time was the most hated author in America, had some acid observations on the Greek Revival style. In Cincinnati she wrote to the effect that no sooner had Americans cleared the woods of their native inhabitants than they built wooden temples in the wilderness. Mrs. Trollope was particularly scornful of homes and public buildings made of wood. She had this to say about Buffalo:

> Of all the thousand and one towns I saw in America, I think Buffalo is the queerest looking; it is not quite so wild as Lockport, but all the buildings have the appearance of having been run up in a hurry, though everything has an air of great pretension; there are porticos, columns, domes, and colonnades, but all in wood.

Later in her life, when Frances Trollope had gained great fame, she softened her views of America. In her novel *The Old World and the New*, her English-born family finds America to its liking and, becoming very successful in their various enterprises, build, on a bluff overlooking the Ohio River, a square edifice of three stories, sixty feet to a side, with "a colonnade of well-proportioned Doric pillars round the entire building." Mrs. Trollope endowed her fictional English family with a southern plantation prototype.

In Virginia and to the south, the transition from British-inspired architecture to the Greek Revival style was smoothly paved by the earlier interposition of Jeffersonian Classicism, which incorporated Adamesque elements such as semicircular fanlights over principal doorways. The Jeffersonian structures also employed

University of Virginia Pavilion.
An example of Jeffersonian Classicism.

domes and arches, which are not Greek, but Roman. While the pediment, frieze, columns, and balustrades were painted white, the body of the building was red brick. Mr. Jefferson's taste and designs were essentially Roman rather than Greek and were to some extent inspired by his exposure to ancient Roman buildings in southern France during his ambassadorship to that country (1785–1789). Monticello and buildings at the University of Virginia are living examples of Jeffersonian Classicism.

The Greek Revival style thus moved from the seaboard to the Ohio and then west to the Mississippi and southward to become the foremost antebellum style of the southern states. "Tara," in *Gone with the Wind*, a fictional mansion built by an Irish planter in a sadly divided nation, remains the most enduring vision of the southern plantation. It is described as a Greek Revival house. One of the tragedies of the Civil War was that the war itself and then the economics of the post-war period saw the destruction and decay of so many noble Temple Style structures.

New Jersey has only a small number of Greek survivors. One of my favorites is the Boisaubin Mansion, (plate 9), in Chatham Township near Convent Station and Morristown. It was built in 1793 and was once the home of a French emigré and his retinue. Although not Greek in its original construction, it soon grew identical pediments and Doric columns fore and aft. The mansion was a stop on the underground railway, and the columns to the left in the picture concealed ladders that led to a refuge in the pediment. In the lawn that swings down to the road, underground caverns stored ammunition as insurance against the possibility of Confederate incursions, which were feared as far north as New Jersey. Later on, the house was the home of the American cartoonist, illustrator, and painter A. B. Frost, who called it "Moneysunk."

Other countries besides the United States built energetically in imitation of the Greeks but confined that building almost exclusively to public structures. There are residences in the Greek Revival mode in France, England, and Russia, but it was only in America that the style was so widely embraced for domestic building. Nevertheless, the Romantic mood was slow to penetrate the American psyche. In the eighteenth century the nation was too preoccupied in battling the wilderness, the Indians, and the British to sense the subtle tugs of a cultural and intellectual mood. By the 1830's, however, enough of the mood had comingled with patriotic pride, with the economic expansion, and with the desire for independent expression to create the startling proliferation of the American Greek Revival.

The Egyptian Revival: A Compatriot Style to the Greek Revival

Even in his dominant period, not every campaign Napoleon waged was a success. His Egyptian campaign (1798), launched to frustrate the ambitions of the British empire builders, was spectacular, but it was thwarted by tangential defeats, military and political. The campaign is important to architectural history because a group of Napoleon's officers were fascinated by the relics and ruins of ancient Egypt and returned home with drawings which became a source of fascination for the West. The West was already indulging in the exotica of orientalism. Mozart's *Abduction from the Seraglio*, and Beethoven's Turkish fantasies were a few examples from a long list of works intended to please a public endlessly enamored of the mysteries of the East. In 1802 Napoleon's archaeologist, Baron de Denon, published a work that lent authority to existing sketchy notions of the tombs, temples, and obelisks of Egypt. Most of the subsequent adaptations of Egyptian Revival architecture derive from that work.

The Egyptian Revival architectural style never had great impact on building in Europe, but in America there was a certain enthusiasm for it. The architects and builders who built in the style were chiefly Greek Revivalists and went over to the Egyptianate only as an alternative form. The year 1830 was the high-water mark for the style. Minard Lafever, Thomas U. Walter, Thomas Stewart, and William Strickland, the staunch Greek Revivalists, were the noteworthy architects who contributed to the Egyptian Revival.

A favorite expression of Egyptian architecture is Minard Lafever's Whalers' Church at Sag Harbor, Long Island, New York. My painting of the church (plate 10) has confused some viewers into thinking that the vertical perspective was forced. Actually the walls, like their ancient Egyptian antecedents, are *battered*, or inward slanting, to imply a sense of massiveness. This sense of monumentality led other builders to use the Egyptian style in prisons, in bank buildings, and in other solemn edifices. The old Tombs in New York City are an outstanding example of that massive (and gloomy) application. Because of the solemnity and mystery of the style, it was favored for the entrance ways to cemeteries, which were beginning to enter the stage of their evolution in which they resembled formal parks. Halls of justice, the Medical College of Virginia at Richmond, and a few churches were also part of the original revival. Much later, in the 1920's, a re-revival brought forth Egyp-

The old Tombs in New York City in the Egyptianate style

Grove Street Cemetery, New Haven, Connecticut

tianate movie theaters, banks, and even a gas station or two.

The Sag Harbor Whalers' Church (Presbyterian) was said to have been built by shipwrights. It once had a spire that reminded people of a mariner's telescope, although it was decorated with a potpourri of Classical ornaments. The steeple, which was twice the height of the body of the church itself, parted company with the church during the disastrous hurricane of 1938—ninety-five years after it was built. The decorations along the eaves are representations of whalers' flensing spades, and the pews are graced with heavy ropes carved of wood in a nautical motif. Surrounding the church are the wind-carved gravestones of young sailors lost at sea in the perilous pursuit of the whale. The total cost of the church, in 1843, was $17,000, including Mr. Lafever's fee.

The Egyptian Revival is the easiest to identify of all the revival styles. It takes a good eye to tell certain Adamesque–Federals from Georgians, and Greek Revivals can be confused with Classical or Jeffersonian structures. But the Egyptianate style *looks* Egyptian. Tall windows narrow at the top to accommodate the battered wall effect. Sun disk (*Aten*) and vulture emblems, symbols of protection, decorate massive lintels, and the columns are so distinctive as to be associated exclusively with Egyptian temples and colonnades.

The period 1825 to 1840 was a period of dynamic change, particularly in the north. New England built mills and factories in compliance with the demands of the Industrial Revolution. Farm hands became mill hands, forced to move from widely separated farmsteads to the confinement of factory towns and tenements. The wrenching adjustment led to a far-reaching revolution of mores, aspirations, and attitudes. City life meant rapid exchange of ideas and an examination of existing moral tenets. The Romantic movement in America was gathering momentum.

Back to Mrs. Trollope, who was, oddly, a patron—of sorts—of the Egyptian Revival, having come to America from England to invest what was left of a family fortune in the founding of a department store in Cincinnati, which she called her "Bazaar." Frances Trollope's husband was an invalid, she had two tubercular children, and her golden dream was to create a source of ready income to support the family. The Bazaar was a disaster, her fortune was exhausted, and her future looked bleak when she returned to England in defeat in 1827. The publication of *Domestic Manners of the Americans*, five years after her visit to America, brought her from poverty and humiliation to reasonable prosperity. Her husband died, however, and so did her two ailing children.

Perhaps the loss of her Bazaar could have been averted had Mrs. Trollope not built so lavishly and in a style so contrary to the "Classical" styles that Ohioans found to be suitable. In 1829 the *Cincinnati Chronicle* commented on the newly finished building. It spoke of four Egyptian columns on one side and of "three arabesque windows with arches, supported by four Moorish stone pilasters with capitals." Above that was a wall decorated with "gothic battlements, each of which supports a stone sphere." Surmounting this architectural medley was a huge Turkish crescent. The amazing assemblage was forthwith dubbed "Trollope's Folly."

The building, of course, was a complete failure. The Whalers' Church had cost $17,000, but Mrs. Trollope's rash architectural adventure cost $24,000, not including the land. Mrs. Trollope lived to be eighty or so, writing endless novels and watching her book on America go through at least five editions, but she died without learning that her son, Anthony, would become one of the great literary figures of the nineteenth century.

Walter Swain, the third generation art specialist in Plainfield, New Jersey, called my attention to the yellowed under-backing of a framed print of the 1860's. It was a folded and stitched page of *The Albany Morning Express*, dated December 22, 1863, the year of Frances Trollope's death. An item in bold print read: "The late Mrs. Trollope did not commence her literary career until she was fifty years of age. She failed as a milliner." The terse comment all too clearly exhibited the prevailing animosity toward Mrs. Trollope who had written fifty novels and books on travel, "Domestic Manners of the Americans" (1832) in her fifty-second year, and her minor masterpiece, "The Vicar of Wrexhill" (1837), in her fifty-seventh year.

In the end it took Mark Twain to set Mrs. Trollope in perspective. He wrote:

> It was for this sort of photography that poor candid Mrs. Trollope was so handsomely cursed and reviled by this nation. Yet she was merely telling the truth, and this indignant nation knew it. She was painting a state of things which did not disappear at once. It lasted to well along in my youth, and I remember it. . . .

There is irony in Mrs. Trollope's detestation of America's wooden temples. For, what our doughty Mrs. Trollope didn't know was that the *original* temples of ancient Greece were also made of wood and garishly painted.

By the late 1850's, the Greek Revival was no longer a contending style. It continued to live only in the Great Lakes region. Anthropologists note that Greek Revival houses built after the mid-nineteenth century can be classified as folk architecture.

Plate 8 *Greek Revival (Milford, Pa.)*

Greek Revival

In 1835 James Wallace, of Milford, Pennsylvania, built a house for one of his twin daughters. It had three rooms and was one-and-a-half stories high. By 1850 it had grown to fourteen rooms with three staircases. At the near end of the house a shed roof is knowingly disguised with a false front to maintain formality and dignity. Of all the Greek Revivals I encountered, I chose this one to paint, because of that shed and the taste it evinces.

Houses of the Milford type were not planned by architects as we know them today. They were built by carpenters whose abilities to translate information from builders' manuals into sturdy and fashionable dwellings eventually brought them the status of contractors. Minard Lafever moved from carpenter to architect through his books, which were inspiration to other carpenters.

The carpenter's skills in the 1830's were admirable. A good carpenter ranked very high among artisans. One of the requisites of a good carpenter was a "good eye"—an eye that understood the three dimensions of proportion and an eye that knew when something looked right.[2] To the Milford carpenter, who finished off the little shed at the side of the house, the slant of the shed roof looked wrong with the more formal structure, so the false front was added to satisfy an inborn sense of fitness.

If the carpenter grew in experience, and if he were endowed with leadership and business sense, he drew around him a group of workers who became specialists. One such 1830's specialist was a well-digger, who was often not available when plowing or seeding or other farm chores took priority. A typical contract between builder and well-digger might read like the following actual contract drawn in October 1834:

> James S. Fletcher agrees to dig and wall a good well, with durable and permanent water—the well hole after walling to be three ft. diam.—the wall to be good and substantial and the owner to pay when the job is finished, one fourth in money and ¾ in store goods, a sum which shall be calculated by the following rates—50¢ per ft. for the first 25 ft.—75¢ per ft. for the next 5 and $1 per ft. for the remaining part of said well—but if in digging said Fletcher comes into rock digging sooner than 25 ft., then the 75¢ per foot to commence from that point.[3]

How water was assured is a mystery. Rhabdomancy (divination by forked branches, often called "dowsing") was used with remarkable success, but it should be remembered that the water table throughout the east and midwest was much higher in the nineteenth century.

What about the other twin daughter? Mr. Wallace built her a house right next door.

Greek Revival Mansion

A. B. Frost (1851–1928), the painter, illustrator, and cartoonist, lived here. He called his nineteenth-century home "Moneysunk." The historic marker at the roadside names it the Boisaubin House. The house, placed on one of General Washington's campsites, was built without the columns, pediment, and entablature by the retinue of a French émigré. The Classical elements were probably appended in the early 1830's, although local historians can find no substantiating documents. The back of the house duplicates the Greek Revival elements of the front, an unusual feature, as most Temple Style builders adorned their houses with columns only on the end facing the road. The Boisaubin mansion has another distinction. Inside one of

---

2. A "good eye" is also important in the arts. A canon in cartooning is: if it looks right, it is right. If it looks wrong, fix it!

3. From Early Homes of Ohio, I.T. Tracy, Garret & Massie, Inc., Richmond, Virginia, 1936.

Plate 9   *Greek Revival Mansion (Boisaubin House)*

the squared Doric columns at the front, stairs lead to a hiding place in the pediment. The Boisaubin mansion was a stop on the Underground Railroad, which flourished in this area in the 1830's. Later the sweeping lawn in front of the mansion held a sodded-over cavern in which a cache of arms and ammunition was hidden to supply Union troops if ever hostilities should reach as far north as Chatham Township, New Jersey.

The bricks of the Boisaubin House were made in a furnace on the property, but mules had to carry marble sills for windows and fireplaces from a hundred miles away.

Frost's paintings and illustrations were often inspired by the woods and rolling fields that surrounded his Moneysunk. The highly prized sporting prints, reproduced from his paintings of hunting, fishing, and golf, have assured Frost of a place of importance in that genre, but he is equally remembered for his Uncle Remus illustrations and for some very pungent cartoons.

A few miles away from Moneysunk, in Madison, New Jersey, another outstanding Greek Revival building dominates the campus of Drew University. To conform to Greek architectural ideals, a building's roof must be very low pitched, but the great area of the Drew University roof presented a problem in bearing the weight of a heavy snow. The architects who built the roof braced it in such a manner that the huge braced supporting timbers can settle outward under stress. The 1830's produced remarkable engineers whose ingenious work in wooden construction has been brushed over too lightly.

Plate 10
Whaler's Egyptianate Church

Whalers' Egyptianate Church

Sag Harbor, Long Island, should be a goal for anyone with a desire to see unaltered Greek Revivals, salt-weathered, shingled vernaculars, and an astounding Presbyterian church in the Egyptianate Style. Of all the treasures in this unhurried old whaling town, the Whalers' Church is the rarest. Even without its immense spy-glass steeple (Corinthian details), lost in the hurricane of 1938, it has a striking presence. For generations the church was a landmark for homing mariners.

The architect of the Whalers' Church was Minard Lafever, of Greek Revival fame. In the tradition of Horatio Alger heroes, Lafever had walked from the family farm in Watkins Glen to Geneva, New York, to buy his first book on architecture. At age eighteen he had built his first house, and at thirty-one, published his first book, The Young Builder's General Instructor. By 1830 Lafever felt able to adopt the title of architect. Three years later he wrote the influential Modern Builder's Guide, which became the principal handbook for builders throughout the Ohio Valley and westward. His reputation was further increased by the publication of The Beauties of Modern Architecture in 1835.

Lafever's present-day fame comes from his association with the Greek Revival, but his greatest commissions involved the Gothic form. I can find no other example of Lafever's use of the Egyptianate mode, but by the time he planned the Sag Harbor church, it was an accepted style suited to prisons, cemeteries, medical schools, and synagogues. As early as 1808 Benjamin Henry Latrobe (1764–1820) had proposed the Egyptianate for the Library of Congress in Washington.

The Whalers' Church, like Greek Revival houses and the Carpenter Gothic, imitates stone forms with shingles and wooden elements. The walls are battered: from the base they slant inward, making any photograph of the building look distorted.

The shingles are cedar, rough cut and generously proportioned to create a handsome display of light, shade, and texture. In my painting of the Whalers' Church, I used a terra rosa ground—a brick-red color to cover the entire white canvas. Throughout the painting I let the color come through as shadow to create the effect of cedar exposed by the weathering of white paint.

Basking Ridge Greek Revival

Early-nineteenth-century settlers in the Morris County area of New Jersey watched deer and other wild animals come up from the lowlands of the Great Swamp to bask in the sun and named the rise "Basking Ridge." In 1776, at nearby White's Tavern, General Charles Lee, second to Washington in command of the Continental Army, was taken prisoner by British troops.

Much earlier, in 1717, Scotch Presbyterians built a church of logs at the site. An interim church, built in 1749, burned—to be replaced in the nineteenth century by the landmark Greek Revival First Presbyterian Church. The Doric-columned end of the church faces a long green or commons flanked by mostly nineteenth-century shops and homes. Behind the church is a graveyard with eighteenth-century markers and the Basking Ridge Oak, a white oak eighteen feet in diameter, a hundred feet tall, and perhaps five hundred years old.

Presbyterians, Methodists, Congregationalists, and Unitarians of the time were devoted to personal freedom. To those worshipers the Greek form expressed liberty, and the quiet dignity of the buildings exemplified democracy and independence. The reverence for independence was profound. In New England and New York a bronze plaque at the church door might identify the building as "The Unitarian Church, Formerly the First Congregational Church." Congregational churches are governed by their congregations. If a majority of the members voted to ally themselves with another form of worship, the church building then became home for the adopted creed.

While the surrounding counties of Basking Ridge had

Plate 11   *Basking Ridge Greek Revival*

few Greek Revival homes of modest size, the state had a good share of Greek Revival churches. Neighboring towns are quite small, but most can boast a Temple Style church of generous size.

I painted the Basking Ridge church in late February when the last of the snows were melting. In the center of the pediment a Christmas wreath still circled the delicately mullioned round window.

Plate 12   *Sag Harbor Federal*

Sag Harbor Federal

The Long Island, New York, community of Sag Harbor gained its original prosperity during an age when whaling was its chief industry. That era of prosperity coincided with the Romantic epoch's revival of Greek and Egyptian architecture. While the Whalers' Church is the only Egyptianate structure to survive, there are, in the lovely harbor town, many examples of the Greek Revival mode.

The painting might appear to represent a modest Greek Revival house, but the hasty observer, new to the mysteries of architecture, must be cautioned against superficial observations. The fluted columns and linear aspect of the doorway would lead some to attribute the subject of the painting to the same Greek Revival style of many of its Sag Harbor neighbors; but to do so would be a mistake.

An educated guess places the origins of the house somewhere between 1815 and 1820—too early for the Greek Revival. The most telling element of the architecture is a pleasant Adamesque doorway. The dotted tracery of the side lights and transom lights suits the Adamesque–Federal Style admirably, but it is unusual and probably the work of a gifted local craftsman. The columns are of slender Roman origin rather than of the robust, often squat, Greek heritage. Those characteristics are enough to warrant the conclusion that the house is a Federal, despite subsequent additions.

At some later Victorian-era date, the brackets at the eaves were attached in acquiescence to a changing mood. Purists would give low grades to the accessories, but credit must be given to the carpenter who kept the delicate brackets in scale with surrounding details.

Though its colonial hinges and the Victorian pierced-wood boards are technically at odds with the overall Federal theme, the gateway fits quite happily in its setting. The storm door with a single square pane set atilt is, with the brackets and gate, expressive of later owners' desire to give the house a more relaxed, more country look.

The Sag Harbor Federal is our only architectural example set outside the Romantic years. The original elements of the house are restrained and fall within the limitations imposed by Classicism.

Greek Revival Crossover

The old owners of this Greek Revival mansion, which features a Victorian door, insisted that no other door had ever preceded it. Their belief is probably true, as the interior of the Asbury, New Jersey, Doric structure is Victorian in every aspect. Apparently the original builder desired the restrained refinement of a Classic exterior but felt the urge for a contemporary interior. Pier mirrors, butterfly-manteled white marble fireplaces, and ceiling rosettes testify to the builder's wish to update.

Asbury is a small and attractive town in a rural setting. In the past several decades it has attracted painters, sculptors, writers, and a modest group of retired people. The presence of a Greek Revival mansion in that pastoral area came as a pleasant surprise. When I painted the doorway the house was badly deteriorated. The columns showed rotting, the outbuildings were collapsing, and the grounds were overgrown. The place has since been bought by a brave woman and her son who, with other family members, have worked tirelessly to restore it. The results are gratifying to anyone who understands what a great contribution such a restored place makes to a community.

Restoration presents many problems. Houses have been denatured, ruined, made valueless, and otherwise embarrassed by overzealous restorers and modernizers who had no knowledge of architectural styles. A question arises with the Asbury Greek Revival: in the process of restoration should a door true to the Greek Revival Style replace the non-Classical door originally supplied, or should the present door act as a bridge between the

Plate 13   *Greek Revival Crossover*

Classical exterior and the Victorian interior? Neither of the alternatives would be a serious breach of taste, but a present-day consensus seems to be that to honor the intentions of the builder would be the most appropriate choice. The moods that gripped the builder are now only dimly understood, and an effort to be *authentic may easily disturb a subtle balance perceived by a planner keenly attuned to his time.*

Although the door of the painting is undeniably Victorian, it belongs to no special substyle of architecture. "Victorian Baroque" is perhaps the most suitable stylistic description.

IV. The Gothic Revival

IN THE PAST, when printers set pages by hand, type came from foundries. The foundries published specimen books to exhibit their type faces, woodcuts, and ornaments. A typical specimen book, published in 1841 by William Hagar & Co. (corner of Fulton and Gold Streets, New York, New York), is printed on a fine-laid, beautiful paper. The ink seems especially black, and the hundred or so woodcuts show meticulous engraving.

The woodcuts are noteworthy because they depict social themes of the time. Eagles wearing starred and striped shields on their breasts, grasping arrows in their talons, and gripping streamers in their beaks clearly symbolize patriotism. The farmer and his plow superimposed on a richly flowing cornucopia illustrates a pride in agriculture, while canal barges, paddle-wheel steamboats, and tiny locomotives hauling iron-wheeled carriages suggest the enormity of the opened land. In these representations there is an enthusiasm and an ebullience that befits the expansive spirit of the 1840's.

But another more somber kind of pictorial theme intrudes as counterweight to the themes of optimism. Throughout the same type-specimen book the weeping willow shelters an Empire-gowned maiden with downcast eyes. Skulls and crossbones harmonize with engravings of wind-bent trees arched over neglected gravestones. One engraving shows a vine-strangled signpost pointing the way to a landscape so dreary that it can only portend horror and doom. These lugubrious and naive depictions were as much in keeping with the times as the optimistic symbols of the young nation. Mournful sensitivity to sorrow, combined with a shuddering enjoyment of the macabre, were sentiments that colored the perceptions of all literate Americans. We were at least twenty years behind the European enthusiasm for the ghastly, but with Hawthorne and Poe setting the pace, we were catching up fast. Even though Mary Shelley had written *Frankenstein* in 1818, twenty-seven years before Poe wrote his "Raven," the works were in perfect tune to the Romantic mood, which came in time to prevail on both sides of the Atlantic.

No text captures the Romantic gloom of the 1840's better than the beginning of Poe's "The Fall of the House of Usher" (1839):

> During the whole of a dull, dark, and soundless day in the autumn of the year, when the clouds hung oppressively low in the heavens, I had been passing alone, on horseback, through a singularly dreary tract of country, and at length found myself, as the shades of the evening drew on, within view of the melancholy House of Usher. I know not how it was—but, with the first glimpse of the building, a sense of insufferable gloom pervaded my spirit.

If we substitute a carriage for the horse, we can see the English traveler approaching the Gothic pile that was the scene of Dr. Frankenstein's galvanic experiments. Gothic novels and Gothic tales display similar backgrounds; the words and phrases are much the same: bleak walls; rank sedges; gloomy tarns; vacant, eyelike windows; lightning-blasted trees—all setting the scene for the dolorous action to come.

Poe was a master of the mood. His "Fall of the House of Usher" is a model Gothic tale and included most of the totems of the genre. Some quotes: "I shuddered the more thrillingly, because I shuddered knowing not why;" and, "The impetuous fury of the entering gust nearly lifted us from our feet. It was indeed a tempestuous yet sternly beautiful night." Poe's setting for the House of Usher was mandatory. Nothing but a Gothic edifice could suffice: "A servant in waiting took my horse, and I entered the Gothic archway of the hall." At one point, the narrator views a painting. What else could that painting be but a Fuseli, work of the arch-Romantic painter and master of the nightmare?

In reading "The Fall of the House of Usher," a remarkably cogent element emerges. Roderick Usher, in the throes of profound depression, consoles himself with a guitar, 125 years later the instrument of choice for the alienated young people caught up in the Romantic revival of the 1960's. Romantic symbols seem impervious to change.

A delight in the lugubrious and woeful was not in the mid-nineteenth century an unprecedented fashion of western culture. In the sixteenth century, the lutist John Dowland came into fame and fortune with his "Lachrimae," instrumental works guaranteed to bring tears to the eyes of the sturdiest Elizabethans. Again, in the years of the Great Depression a large segment of the public thrilled to a baleful number titled "Gloomy Sunday"—although the suicides attributed to the piece may have been caused more by its repetition than by the influence of its content.

In the earliest Middle Ages the Carolingian, the Ottonian, and the Romanesque churches and monasteries were the evolutionary stages contributing to the glories of the Gothic. The Gothic style was the climax of the evolution. The original style flourished from the thirteenth to the fifteenth century, although the Abbey Church of St. Denis, outside of Paris, remodeled between 1137 and 1144, has buttresses, the pointed arch, rib-groined vaults, and the general airy and weightless character of the mature Gothic style. These elements necessarily figured to greater or lesser extent in the revival of the style in Europe, its eventual transplantation to America, and its transmutation to American forms.

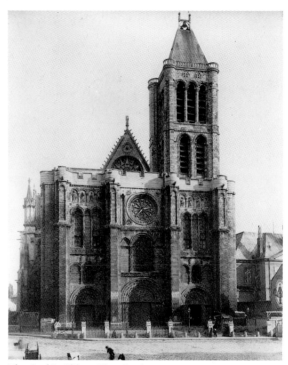

The Gothic Abbey Church of Saint Denis

"Strawberry Hill," in Twickenham-on-Thames was the first Gothic Revival house. Horace Walpole's "little Gothick castle" was remodeled over the old Walpole home by the architect William Robinson. Walpole directed the design, which was innovative, even bizarre.

"Strawberry Hill," a Gothic Revival house

Horace Walpole

certain amount of respect for eccentricity prevails, the folly is a cheerfully endorsed institution. To an Englishman, the word usually suggests a Gothic sham ruin in a landscaped park, intended to enhance a picturesque view. With the reintroduction of the Gothic into England, sham Gothic structures became Romantic necessities for those who could afford them. As early as 1758, one Charles Over had gone so far as to publish a catalogue of ruins, for the edification of landed gentry. The illustrated ruins were designed in the "Gothic, Chinese and Modern Taste." For the especially demanding, the catalogue recommended a resident hermit for the ruins of one's dreams. Mr. Over failed to mention a source for hermits.

Strawberry Hill became an attraction during its building, which took nearly thirty years (1749–1777). The exterior has lancet windows, pointed arches, windows in the form of trefoils and quatrefoils (representing the trinity and the cross), a battlemented keep, and a cone-topped tower. The walls are castellated, and the chimneys are grouped in Tudor fashion.

Walpole had begun a trend that would become a major influence throughout the world. The new Gothic style became a favorite during the heyday of the colonial era. In Singapore, Haiti, South Africa—almost anywhere under the sun, some version of the Gothic exists. Colonial administrators claimed that the style had a civilizing effect on the natives, and, of course, it was considered a form of Christian expression.

The Gothic Revival was pre-eminently the age of the "folly." In architecture that word's meaning differs from the version usually given by dictionaries. As applied to architecture, and in American usage, "folly" has a pejorative connotation such as might be applied to the Natchez, Mississippi octagon extravaganza known as "Nutt's Folly," or to Mrs. Trollope's arabesque vision in Cincinnati. In England, by contrast, where a

"Nutt's Folly," Natchez, Mississippi

The most excessive sham building in all of England was built by a singularly outrageous gentleman named William Beckford (1760–1844), whose great fortune came from the slave labor of the West Indies. Like Walpole, Beckford had a penchant for building, and like Walpole, he had a talent for writing. Beckford's *Vathek*, first written in French, is, in its English translation, considered a masterpiece of the Gothic novel form.

The story of Beckford's folly, "Fonthill Abbey," is as extraordinary as the miasmatic fantasy of *Vathek*. In 1796 Beckford commissioned James Wyatt to design a ruined convent at Wiltshire. The chapel parlor, a dormitory, and a cloister alone were designated as enclosed living areas. The main hall was 120 feet high, the cathedral ceiling was braced with Gothicized wooden arches decorated with medieval escutcheons, and the pointed-arch fenestration reached to a lofty eighty feet. The rest of the immense aggregation was exposed, in the best tradition of a ruin. A Gothic-decorated octagon tower was added, and wings four hundred feet long flanked the mostly Gothic pastiche. The "abbey" was enclosed by eight miles of twelve-foot-high walls. The whole construction was meant to be seen at a distance and to be, above all, *picturesque*, that being one of the leitmotifs characterizing the remaining Romantic years.

The accounts of the building of Beckford's Fonthill Abbey are legion and legendary. Five- or six hundred workmen were employed to work around the clock. In the freezing winter nights, they worked by the light of huge bonfires. Beckford's impatience at finishing his fantasy led to slipshod and dishonest workmanship. Wyatt, the architect, was unable to control structural quality, and an overall instability plagued the project from its inception.

Beckford's quixotic nature soon caused him to tire of Fonthill and to sell the sham abbey to the eccentric Mr. John Farquhar. (Besides, some unsavory behavior at Fonthill during the Christmas season put him in bad odor with neighboring moralists.) Beckford thought it wise to leave the country for a while, but before he left he heard the deathbed confession of Wyatt's clerk of the works, who, it developed, hadn't been altogether vigilant in seeing that the contractors met the provisions of their contracts. The dying clerk of the works confessed that the solid foundations specified by Wyatt that should have been laid to support the central tower were never provided. There could be but one result. In 1825 the

A Cottage Orné

tower simply subsided into the turf with hardly a trace. Today nothing remains of Fonthill Abbey.

The mania for shams, ruins, instant grottoes, and other picturesque follies continued to the middle decades of the nineteenth century. A cousin of the sham was the English cottage orné. By 1810 it had become fashionable to build cottages that were patently picturesque, quaint, or rustic. They were designed in asymmetrical forms with decorative weatherboarding, rough-hewn columns and, typically, rather overdone thatched roofs. Somehow the cottages ornés managed to incorporate Gothic overtones. Originally they were meant to lend picturesqueness to the landscape or to serve as colorful laborers' shelters, but increasingly they became chic hideaways for the leisure set (and seats for scandal). The interiors

Fonthill Abbey

became luxurious, often decorated with the newest and most expensive wallpapers from Paris. An entire village of cottages ornés was built by John Nash (1752–1835), the greatest architect of the Picturesque movement, at Blaise Hamlet in 1811.

By 1830, builders in the Gothic Revival had turned to more serious purposes than shams, ruins, and follies. The new Gothic was almost universally fashionable, and in 1836 the architect Charles Barry won a competition to rebuild the fire-ruined Houses of Parliament in the Gothic style. Around the same time that most decent of early Victorians, Sir Walter Scott, elected to build his house, "Abbotsford," in the Gothic mode, his gesture of continuity with the past.

It is important to understand that the link between revival and original Gothic was never quite broken. During most of the seventeenth century, traditional Gothic church architecture continued to find favor in rural areas of England. Gothic Revival was the reincarnation of an almost moribund style to new uses and new forms. A new class had risen in England. The wealth that came from industrial, mercantile, and other entrepreneurial activity (as distinct from the landed wealth of the gentry and aristocracy) could now express itself in a new, yet ancient form. The new rich built their villas and secular buildings with energy and, often they built with taste, although the occasional monstrosity attracted more attention than all the charming Gothic villas combined. The classic English detective novel is an intriguing form of entertainment, but a distasteful element of snobbery invariably intrudes. Not only must the heroine have gray eyes and be related to an archbishop or an earl, but every reference to "Gothic" or "Victorian" must be preceded by "awful" or "horrid."

Some memorable names in English Gothic Revival architecture: Augustus Welby Northmore Pugin (1812–1852) is usually credited with the revitalization of the style. John Ruskin (1819–1900) wrote the influential book *Stones of Venice*, a celebration of Gothic archi-

tecture. Batty Langley (1696–1751) wrote the book on Gothic architecture (1742) which was the guide and inspiration for America's first Gothic building, St. John's Cathedral in Providence, Rhode Island (John Holden Greene, 1810). In France, Eugène Emmanuel Viollet-le-Duc (1814–1879) was the foremost Gothic architect.

The Gothic style in America had a difficult beginning. In church architecture, objections to "popery" were commonly raised, while in domestic architecture an association with "Englishness" alienated potential builders who complained that the style elicited undemocratic aspects too close to rich men's whimsies. As the style made gradual inroads, objections to its pretentiousness, nonconformity, and eccentricity were voiced. To offset the criticisms, defenders pointed out that the popular Greek style was based on pagan temples, while the Gothic was of Christian derivation.

Other influences gradually began to operate to aid in the acceptance of the Gothic Revival. A kinship between the Gothic revivalists and writers like Thoreau and the painters of the Hudson River School helped the new form's cause. The Gothic was also thought to be more natural than the Greek Revival. Gothic revivalists railed against temples painted white, white, white. They offered "natural" colors—colors of the earth. Andrew Jackson Downing, in his *Architecture of Country Houses* (1850), offers Sir Joshua Reynolds' advice to home builders: "If you would fix upon the best color for your house, turn up a stone, or pluck up a handful of grass by the roots, and see what is the color of the soil where the house is to stand, and let that be your choice."

The word "natural" is often used both in defense and in attack on styles of architecture. The pro-Greeks termed the Temple Style natural because the columns represented hewn tree trunks. They referred to the Gothic style as unnatural. The Gothicists replied that their interior columns represented whole groves of trees in their natural state, branching out to form roofs and ceilings. Gothicists considered the Temple Style entirely unnatural.

To add fuel to the debate, Gothicists noted that Sir Walter Scott had built his Abbotsford-on-the-Tweed in the Gothic manner. To the American reading public, Scott was a hero. Being a Scot, he was not quite English and therefore more acceptable to contemporary Americans. The fact that he had paid off the huge debts of his bankrupt publishing firm also appealed to his American followers, and it didn't hurt that his books, dealing with lovely ladies in distress, black knights, castles, and grottoes, were marvelously romantic. The castellated form of the Gothic experience came on the scene a little later in the century than the vogue for Scott, but each castle was, in some way, a tribute to Sir Walter.

There is no doubt that the Greek Revival style had severe architectural limitations. Dormers, loggias, balustrades, bay windows, and verandas were impossible within the Temple Style. The desire of the neo-Gothicists was to break out of the architectural envelope that the Greek style required. The Gothic Revival, with infinite opportunities for variation, represented "functionalism" and "structural morality"—rationally conceived—at least in the eyes of Romantic philosophers. Beyond the philosophic elements, technological advances made possible new forms of framing that encouraged expressions of lightness and space suited to the aims of the Gothic builders.

The Architecture of Country Houses introduced Downing's readers to such pleasing variations on the Gothic theme that much of the resistance to the style was swept away. By 1850 the country was ready for change. Architectural fashions, like fashions in clothing, decor, and behavior, are allotted a limited life span. The change that came was dramatic; soon towns were graced with Americanized versions of Gothic tracery, pendants, finials, hood moldings, trefoils, and quatrefoils. The pointed, steep roofs of the Gothic played counterpoint

to the low-pitched roofs of Greek neighbors. Tudor chimneys, adopted by the Gothicists, seemed suddenly correct, while the anachronistic chimneys of the Greek Revival houses looked as inappropriate as ever, Greek temples never having had chimneys, or, for that matter, windows.

Too often, the vision of a Gothic house is that of a "cocked hat" house, afroth with gingerbread. The house that A. J. Downing proposed was a house similar to the one shown in plate 14. This handsome "cottage" is in Llewellyn Park, part of West Orange, New Jersey. Llewellyn Park was America's first planned suburb and is the site of Thomas Alva Edison's home. The house has all the elements of the Gothic except the gingerbread bargeboards. It was designed by Alexander Jackson Davis, Downing's collaborator in *The Architecture of Country Houses*. The proportions of the Llewellyn Park house are more harmonious than the proportions of Davis's more famous Rotch cottage in New Bedford, Massachusetts.

Rotch Cottage, New Bedford, Massachusetts—A. J. Davis, architect

Diamond-paned casement windows that reach to the floor should not go without notice. Ever since the advent of the noble savage of Romantic literature, an increasing feeling toward the outdoors, nature, and the natural created a change in attitude toward the home. In England, for generations in the large houses of the gentry, outside stairways led visitors to second-floor reception rooms. The first floors had entrances at the sides and at the rear and were reserved for servants and what the English call "lumber rooms"—rooms for storage. With the advent of a sensibility to nature, new houses were built to provide direct access to the outdoors—a feature of the Gothic Revival. Gardens and lawns that seemed to flow into welcoming parlors became fashionable. Typically two parlors flank the central entrance way, which is flawed by a storm door. To give a sense of vertical ascent, the board-and-batten siding in our Gothic was favored by builders, its production made possible by the new steam-driven saws.

Occasionally there was a concentration of houses that were Gothic touched or Gothic inspired, sometimes the result of a concentration of craftsmen who could lavish their skills on the intricacies of the Gothic. In southern New Jersey, below the Mason–Dixon line and on Delaware Bay near the mouth of the Maurice River lies Mauricetown. The natives pronounce it "Morristown." The area, distinguished by Gothic or Italianate houses adorned with wonderfully elaborate carpenter's lace, has lost most of its inhabitants to more promising areas, and thus, many of the houses are deteriorating. In its Civil War boom-town days, however, Mauricetown was a shipbuilding site which attracted many skilled shipwrights. In the waning days of the industry the craftsmen stayed on and applied their skills to the monuments they left behind them.

Cape May, New Jersey, near by, was once the summer residence for well-to-do southern families. The families and their servants arrived for the summer season at a community that to this day is a living museum of Gothic-inspired architecture. Although there have been losses to fires and to real-estate developers and property owners without the sense or taste to leave the town alone, Cape May is, architecturally, a mid-nineteenth-century village. In chapter twelve, the painting of the porch of the Republic guest house (plate 58) gives some idea of the love and labor lavished on buildings meant

to create a happy and carefree ambience. (The house also shows the kind of architecture that A. J. Downing deplored.) The Republic guest house is by no means the most lavish of the Cape May belles. It is, in fact, among the more modest examples. Although well-maintained, when I saw it one late September, it conveyed a poignant and faded expression in keeping with season's end. Perhaps the rocking chair facing that uncertain interior accounts for the mood.

Gothic Revival houses were also concentrated at camp-meeting sites. The complete capitulation of church groups to the Gothic/Stick Style is illustrated in the little camp-meeting house at South Seaville, New Jersey (plate 19). By the mid-nineteenth century, the wild, emotional revival meetings (so distasteful to Mrs. Trollope), had been tamed into peaceful summer rituals. Families too poor to afford a summer vacation could join church groups for inspiration and relaxation in rural settings, sheltered by tents and the kind of cottage in the painting. The South Seaville camp-meeting place is now a summer retreat for Methodist ministers and their families, who arrive each summer with paintbrushes and tools, and with the desire to refurbish themselves and their tiny Gothic cottages.

In a cemetery in Millburn, New Jersey, stands a little Gothic that is the caretaker's home (plate 15). It is isolated from neighbors by the graveyard and by ancient trees. It has the features of a style of Gothic sometimes called Chalet Gothic. The cottage was designed as a gesture of friendship to the Episcopal community of Millburn by James Renwick, who built the Gothic Grace Church and St. Patrick's Cathedral in New York, as well as the Smithsonian Institution in Washington and a few buildings at Vassar College in Poughkeepsie, New York. Also in Millburn stands the St. Stephen's Church rectory (plate 16), which displays most of the elements of the Gothic Revival. The bargeboards are particularly rich and prominent, with quatrefoils cut in deep relief. The heavy pendant and finial, the pointed eaves and the pointed arch, and the hood-molded windows are in

Grace Church, New York City

keeping with the style. I chose to paint the end of the building away from the street, as it shows a portion of the battlemented and quatrefoiled side porch. The siding of the rectory is at odds with the board-and-batten treatment of St. Stephen's Church, which stands next door. I suspect it was altered at some time.

It appears almost impossible for the protagonists of architectural history to lead prosaic lives. The life of Andrew Jackson Downing, one of the chief exponents of the American Gothic Revival, is a case in point. He was born in Newburgh, New York, on the Hudson River, in 1815, the son of a nurseryman. His father died while Downing was a child. In time, with his brother Charles, he revived the family business, and in his day-to-day contacts developed a clientele of wealthy New Yorkers whose estates lined the Hudson. Downing went beyond the role of nurseryman and became a largely self-taught landscape architect in the tradition of the Regency landscape planners. In his books he was aided and encouraged by Alexander Jackson Davis (1803–1892), who drew all the pictures, but they were never able to join in an architectural partnership.

In England Downing met the London-born American architect Calvert Vaux (later to be associated with Frederick Law Olmsted in the planning of Central Park in New York City), and back home, the two formed the firm of Downing and Vaux. It was short-lived. On a hot summer's day, Downing and his wife, Caroline, were cruising the Hudson on the steamboat *Henry Clay*, which encountered a rival steamboat, the *Armenia*. A race ensued, a boiler overheated, fire broke out, and frantic passengers jumped into the river. Downing ran to the upper deck, and, to the end, threw deck chairs to his fellow passengers in the water below. Caroline survived, but Downing died a hero's death on July 28, 1852.

Downing, like Edgar Allan Poe, was deeply sensitive to the Romantic mood of his time. In *The Architecture of Country Houses*, a single statement embraces the motivating components of the picturesque, the noble savage, and the mysterious:

> But let another person . . . gifted not only with common sense but imagination live amid such scenery as meets his eye daily . . . and he will often feel that a commonplace square house is an insult to the spirit of all that surrounds him. In such bold scenery, nature overpowers all and suggests all. . . . It is in such picturesque scenery—scenery which exists in many spots in America besides the banks of the Hudson—that the picturesque country house or villa is instinctively felt to harmonize and belong to the landscape. It is there that the high tower, the steep roof and the boldly varied outline seem wholly in keeping with the landscape—because these forms in the building harmonize—either by contrast or assimilation—with the pervading spirit of mysterious powers and beauty in romantic scenery.

As the Gothic Revival style became more and more acceptable, the rich and the very rich built increasingly in the form. In America the greatest house in the Gothic style is unquestionably "Lyndhurst," overlooking the Hudson near the Tappan Zee Bridge. It is one of the

"Lyndhurst"

glories of our architectural heritage. The construction and enlargement of Lyndhurst spans the entire Gothic period from the late 1830's to the era of the industrial tycoons after the Civil War. The house was designed and built by Alexander Jackson Davis, beginning in 1838. The original owner was General William Paulding, a veteran of the War of 1812 and once mayor of New York City. The general's neighbors were skeptical of the new form rising beside them, and the house was quickly labeled "Paulding's Folly." Paulding's detractors would have been startled to learn that the house would become the supreme example of the style once known as Hudson River Gothic.

The working relationship between Paulding and Davis was warm and cordial. Paulding left all the details of the furnishings to Davis. A letter from General Paulding to his architect reads, "You will oblige me by inspecting the mantels before they are sent up. If you see anything offensive to your gothick eye, put your veto upon it. They are extremely elegant and I wish them to be correct specimens of the style. How the ladies will dote on them!"

Lyndhurst was bought by a wealthy merchant named George Merritt who, with good sense, had A. J. Davis enlarge it to double its size. A new wing to the north, a porte-cochere on the east, and a tower to the west brought it to the state of picturesqueness required in 1865. The addition worked so well that by its com-

pletion, the ensemble was recognized as a masterpiece of composition.

In 1880 the railroad tycoon and financier Jay Gould had Lyndhurst rebuilt and restocked without altering its essential forms. When Gould died in 1892, the house was lived in successively by his two daughters, Mrs. Helen Shepard and Anna, Duchess of Talleyrand–Périgord. Each occupant of Lyndhurst left his or her imprint on the house—yet never by any drastic tampering or break with the past. The house underwent a gentle, tasteful evolution, so that we can still distinguish those separate layers of life on the Hudson, each with its own mood: the Gothic style laid down by Paulding, Merritt's Gothic and High Victorian Gothic together with the Beaux–Arts style of Jay Gould and his daughters. They are all still visible in our time as one splendid, harmonious masterwork, now cared for by the National Trust for Historic Preservation, and is open to the public.

When the fashion for domestic building in the pointed Gothic style had all but died (circa 1865), a new form of the style, High Victorian Gothic, came into favor for public building. It was distinguished from the preceding style by being less perpendicular, and, most characteristically, by employing alternate varicolored and varitextured stone.

In the eighteenth century, "character" in architecture carried with it the Classical connotation that a style must be compatible with its functions. The architects of the post-Civil War era deemed character to be the force expressed by the nature of the building itself. It is now very difficult for us to view the efforts of the High Victorian Gothicists and understand what they meant when they asked for "truth, reality and character" in their buildings. I once lived within a block of the Jefferson Market Branch Library in Greenwich Village, New York City. It was impossible to walk by the building without such words as "whimsical," "eccentric," "quaint," "bizarre," and "capricious" coming to mind. Even after painting so many architectural oddities, I am stunned

Jefferson Market Branch Library, New York City

The neo-Gothic styles touch our lives in unexpected places. In New York the Woolworth Building, fifty-two stories high and once the tallest building in the world, is a Gothic. The Brooklyn Bridge is thoroughly Gothic, and traces of battlements, the pointed arch, etc., will survive in newly built schools, churches, and factories until the next revival emerges.

The neo-Gothic Woolworth Building, New York City

by the library's audacity. I hope it will be preserved forever. In most High Victorian Gothics there is a serene strength and a high-born elegance that supersedes any sense of frippery in the structure. Another fine High Victorian is Peter Wight's National Academy of Design, also in New York City.

To the original Gothicists, the Gothic style of architecture had no name. Since it was, to them, the only form of building, it seemed unnecessary to give it a name. The Gothicists meant their style to go on forever, and in one form or another, it may. After High Victorian Gothic ran its course, another version surfaced in 1903 when the United States Military Academy at West Point was rebuilt in the Late Gothic Revival style. The form was more perpendicular than the High Victorian and more restrained. In the early years of the twentieth century the Gothic found acceptance in the building or rebuilding of major churches and in the Collegiate Gothic style of Princeton, Bryn Mawr, Duke University, and other schools, which is closely allied to the Late Gothic Revival style.

The American Embattled Style

The "American Embattled" is a tongue-in-cheek name of a substyle of the Gothic more properly called the Castellated. It of course refers to the millionaires' castles that were built by the most romantic of the Romanticists. The castles had to be reasonably huge, and to have any presence at all, they had to be built on a height. They were, like their originals, draughty, and they were dark, for the requisite lancet windows, originally built for defense, admitted very little light. Roofs were flat, and the bartizans, machicolations, (slits built out from the battlements through which hot oil was poured on attackers), and battlements were nonfunctioning and costly to maintain. For these reasons we have very few lonely survivors of the American Embattled. The castle in plate 18 was razed a few years ago to make way for another road. The Vanderpool family first built a wooden castle in Summit, New Jersey, which was consumed by flames shortly after completion. In 1882 it was rebuilt in stone and brick. The Vanderpool Castle was long the subject of local speculation because of the uniformed policeman who patrolled the perimeter of the estate for decades. The lone survivor of the Vanderpool family remained as the sole occupant of the castle for thirty years.

The inspiration for our American castles can be traced to Sir Walter Scott's *Ivanhoe, Kenilworth, Waverly*, etc., books that captivated American audiences. In fact more of Scott's works were printed and read here than in Great Britain, although Charles Dickens, visiting in America, vehemently complained that American publishers paid not a cent in royalties to Scott or his heirs.

In its time the castle represented the utmost status symbol. The interiors were cluttered with coats-of-arms, bogus linen-fold paneling, and huge manorial fireplaces bearing all the lord-of-the manor trappings of medieval liege lords. Chances were that the occupant was a generation removed from a log cabin and Jacksonian democracy, but the style gave him a chance to live out a dream, and for a few generations it gave our skylines the Romantic quality of Scott's fiction.

Vestiges of the castellated form carried into the twentieth century in the form of government buildings and National Guard armories, although in the last quarter of the century, the building of castles is the concern only of daydreamers, Disney Worlds, and hamburger emporia.

By 1884 Mark Twain, America's reigning iconoclast, had had enough of the mournful pictures and dolorous literature that so dominated American cultural life in his time. In that year he had completed *The Adventures of Huckleberry Finn* (published 1885), which was set in a time "forty or fifty years ago"—nicely located in the Gothic mood. In the chapter titled "A Visit to the Grangerford's," Twain destroyed the vestiges of Gothic sentimentality just as Charles Dickens's works had replaced the European Gothic novel. Huck Finn, an admirable realist, described the Grangerford home and noted the pictures on the wall:

> They was different from any pictures I ever see before; blacker, mostly, than is common. One was a woman in a slim black dress, belted small under the armpits, with bulges like a cabbage in the middle of the sleeves, and a large black scoop-shovel bonnet with a black veil, and white slim ankles crossed about with black tape, and very wee black slippers, like a chisel, and she was leaning pensive on a tombstone on her right elbow, under a weeping willow, and her other hand hanging down her side holding a white handkerchief and a reticule, and underneath the picture it said "Shall I Never See Thee More Alas." Another one was a young lady with her hair all combed up straight to the top of her head, and knotted there in front of a comb like a chair-back, and she was crying into a handkerchief and had a dead bird laying on its back in her other hand with its heels up, and underneath the picture it said "I Shall Never Hear Thy Sweet Chirrup More Alas."

There was one where a young lady was at a window looking up at the moon, and tears running down her cheeks; and she had an open letter in one hand with black sealing-wax showing on one edge of it, and she was mashing a locket with a chain to it against her mouth, and underneath the picture it said "And Art Thou Gone Yes Thou Art Gone Alas."

Huck's description of the prevailing bathetic pictures is totally accurate. Twain's readers didn't miss the pointed satire. What had been pleasantly dolorous became ludicrous—even hilarious.

Yet if the Gothic's sentimental gloom has passed on, some essence of the true Gothic spirit remains alive. In September of 1982, amidst great ceremony, work was once again begun on the world's largest Gothic structure, the Cathedral of St. John the Divine in New York City. Construction had been halted in 1941 because such work was deemed irrelevant in wartime. But times and moods change. In recording the resumption of the building of the cathedral, the architectural historian Paul Goldberger wrote in the *New York Times*:

> The seriousness with which the cathedral's officials, Mr. Bambridge and his crew of apprentices approach the job inevitably invites comparison with Gothic precedent—and raises the obvious question as to whether the erection of a Gothic building makes any sense in this city at this time. It is a question that would almost certainly have been answered negatively a decade or so ago, when the creation of any building other than a purely modern one seemed a foolish anachronism. Now, however, modernism has lost not a little of its appeal, and we are seeing a substantial return to classical styles in both public and private architecture.

Picturesque Gothic, Chalet Gothic, Carpenter Gothic, High Victorian Gothic, Collegiate Gothic, Late Gothic Revival, and the Pointed Style are variant terms and variant modes based on the original concept. As no other architectural form provided so deep a well of heritage and tradition over so great a bridge of time, no other style inspired so many spiritual descendants.

Alexander Jackson Davis Gothic

Of all the literary-architectural bonds, no stronger one can be found than the link between literature and the Gothic Revival style. The fact that the energetic Horace Walpole built the first Gothic Revival structure and wrote the first Gothic novel is in itself a remarkable connection.

When eighteenth- and nineteenth-century Gothic novels are examined, modern readers must wonder how Romantic readers could be beguiled by themes so patently melodramatic. An answer is that Gothic literature suited the mood of the times. In 1775 a critic named Aiken published a book titled On the Pleasures derived from Objects of Terror and an Enquiry into the Kinds of Distress which

Plate 14   *Alexander Jackson Davis Gothic*

excite Agreeable Sensations. *The title gives a clue to the Gothic sensibility.*

Writers of the period rose to the task of providing objects of terror. The sovereign adjectives of the Gothic novel included, among others, murky, melancholic, dreary, dolorous, brooding, tempestuous, lugubrious, and woeful. The props *included weeping willows, howling storms, pitfalls, nitre-encrusted crypts, catacombs, bats, rats, secret passages, ruined monasteries, niches, recesses, flambeaux, and tattered tapestries. The cast was never complete without lemon-eyed wolves, evil monks, deformed servants, and beautiful, bewildered, and orphaned maidens with gray* eyes and impeccable lineage. A bleak November was a favorite month, the thirteenth, the preferred day, and midnight the appointed hour.

All this seems a heavy burden to place on a house that seems visually removed from the themes expressed above. Yet all the elements of its Gothic heritage are combined to make the Llewellyn Park, New Jersey, cottage an admirable model of Gothic Revival architecture. The house was built (circa 1853) for landscape artist Edward Nicholls and later became the boyhood home of Charles Follen McKim, of the great architectural firm of McKim, Mead and White. The architect who planned the cottage was Alexander Jackson Davis, who lived out his declining, embittered years in the house he conceived as a young and successful architect.

Llewellyn Haskell, who planned Llewellyn Park, the first major residential real-estate development in America, had as his goal the creation of "a retreat for a man to exercise his own rights and privileges." Architectural historians have observed that the Gothic Revival style expressed elitism and snobbery, motives seemingly consistent with Haskell's plan. In his inspirational Images of American Living (J. B. Lippincott, 1964), Dr. Alan Gowans noted that the Gothic Revival Style was also an expression of a serious "intellectual class" in American society who felt that the often irregular style blended with, rather than opposed, nature. That its first occupant was a landscape painter would support Dr. Gowans' contention.

One hundred and twenty years after its planning, Llewellyn Park remains much as Mr. Haskell envisioned it—full of "cascades, flower gardens, winding roads and rambles."

Chalet Gothic

At sundown a traveler stumbling on this lonely cottage might well feel transported to the Black Forest. Local legend insists that James Renwick, the great architect of St. Patrick's Cathedral and Grace Church, New York, and The Smithsonian Institution in Washington, among others, planned the caretaker's lodge for St. Stephen's Cemetery in Millburn, New Jersey. It is a variation on a Gothic theme variably called "Chalet," "Swiss," or "Switz" Gothic. The patterned, varicolored slate roof is unusual for a cottage of its size as the weight of the slate requires heavy supporting members.

While the lodge has many of the characteristics of its Gothic Revival compatriots, it is distinguished by the cantilevered, projecting dormer, reminiscent of Alpine or Black Forest houses. The understated bargeboards at the eaves of the dormer are foliated. Bargeboards are also called "vergeboards" and come, generally, festooned, foliated, or cusped. The finials, pendants, picturesque chimneys, and diamond panes are all part of the Gothic lexicon.

Renwick was one of the rare Gothic architects who made a successful transition from Gothic and Italian modes to the styles of the High Victorian era. Alexander Jackson Davis, an advocate of the antebellum styles, felt hostile to the changes that were to come. It was not that he was incapable of change—he was a pioneer in the development of cast-iron storefronts—he simply could not tolerate the overburdened qualities of the newer creations. While Renwick continued to receive prestigious commissions until his death in 1895, Davis faced inactivity and a world that cared little for his past triumphs. Davis, like Augustus Welby Pugin, believed that an architect who could adopt any style was as unworthy of honor as a priest who could accept any creed.

The painting of the caretaker's lodge at St. Stephen's cemetery brings A. J. Davis to mind. But for its height, it is very much like a "Bracketed Cottage" drawn by Davis for Andrew Jackson Downing's Country Houses of 1850.

Plate 15   *Chalet Gothic*

Gothic Rectory House

It was Davis's drawings in Downing's books that popularized the pointed Gothic. In fact Davis was formally trained in drawing and only informally trained in architecture, yet in his partnership with Ithiel Town, he shared with Town the foremost architectural firm in New York.

St. Stephen's rectory house in Millburn, New Jersey, is alongside one of the finest examples of Carpenter Gothic church interiors to be found. I chose the back view of the rectory house to illustrate the easy relationship between the castellated battlements of the porch at the left and the Gothic motifs of the house.

The bargeboarding is exceptionally rich and heavy, and eaves at the gable end extend to achieve dramatic ef-

Plate 16   *Gothic Rectory House*

foils, pendants, and cusps on fireplaces and stairways. The pointed arch is a repeated motif in extensive paneling.

Several distinctions have been made between Gothick architecture and Gothic architecture, but the sense of amateurism and frivolity surrounding the Gothick seems to be its own explanation. English architects of the earliest Gothic Revival period had few accurate illustrations of medieval models until the publications of John Britton and the elder Pugin appeared. The resulting Gothick structures tended to be whimsical, picturesque, and archaeologically incorrect, but they were expressive of a new mood or, at least, a new point of view. Later in the period Gothick frivolity was studiously avoided, and castellated components were freely mixed with the Gothic. By the 1830's the English admitted that the details of their new Gothic churches, schools, and universities were, at last, literate.

The employment of the Gothic mode in England was limited largely to public buildings and to the country seats of the aristocracy and royalty. It was in America that the Gothic found expression in modest homes, as typified by A. J. Downing's examples. Some areas resisted the Gothic Revival in both domestic and ecclesiastical forms. I. T. Frary's 1936 book, Early Homes of Ohio (Garret and Masie, Inc., Richmond, Va.), finds houses of the Federal and Greek Revival persuasion to be praiseworthy but has this to say of the Gothic Style:

fects of light and shade. The joined ovals of the bargeboards frame elongated quatrefoils. Between the paired dormers, sections of the roof project more to create a picturesque effect than to pitch water away from the siding. The pointed arches in the dormers are offset by trabeated windows capped with hood moldings. Finials, pendants, and Tudor chimneys round out the decorative Gothic elements essential to a building that in basic form is not especially Gothic. (The basic mass or form of a house is called the "carcass" by builders.) Horizontal siding and overall form place the rectory house late in the Gothic tenure.

The Millburn rectory's interior uses trefoils, quatre-

These windows reflect the approach of a Gothic Revival which, at a slightly later date, closed the classic episode and begat a numerous family of weird churches and other buildings as well on which scrawny, emaciated buttresses, pinnacles, tracery, battlements and other pseudo-Gothic masonry details were wrought from boards and scantlings by carpenters who were intended by Nature for brilliant careers as makers of stage scenery.

Frary wrote his book in the thirties, when the public was instructed to abhor all things Victorian or Romantic and to admire either the new or the Classical.

Crouse College

Plate 17   Crouse College

The broad route that leads from Binghamton to Syracuse, New York, enters the magnificent Tully Valley some twenty miles south of Syracuse. Beyond, the countryside remains epic as the city comes into view. In the far distance, on the highest hill, a romantic pile dominates the skyline. It is the College of Visual and Performing Arts at Syracuse University. Essentially Gothic, it is joined to the Romanesque and other High Victorian styles. The architect was Archimedes Russell, a disciple of Henry Hobson Richardson. His building stood complete in 1889 and was named the Crouse College for Women. Until recent times it was the Crouse College of Fine Arts. Syracusans call it Crouse.

Sometime in the early 1940's, the interior was modernized. Thirty years later, thankfully, it was handsomely restored to its golden, wooden elegance. A full-scale replica of the Winged Victory of Samothrace dominates an intricately balustered stairwell. The details of the place are pertinent, but the significant thing about Crouse is the aura. No one who ever attended Crouse can forget the gallimaufry of sights, sounds, and fragrances of the place. Fixative, turpentine, linseed, walnut, and poppy oils furnished the redolence. Harps, voices, organs (there were three or four practice organs in the underground portions of Crouse and a vast pipe organ in the beamed and crossbraced auditorium), strings, and brasses provided accompaniment for the winds soughing through the crockets and recesses of the spires. It was all heady stuff, and it produced some of the nation's outstanding artists, composers, and musicians.

John R. Crouse, the donor of the building, took direct interest in its construction and supervised as endless cartloads of red Longmeadow sandstone were laboriously inched up the hill. Sadly, he died a few months before his college was completed.

The original pipe organ has been replaced by a Classical organ, but the restoration was otherwise complete and true to the landmark building as it stood in 1889.

American Castellated

The Vanderpools built their first castle in Summit, New Jersey, in 1877. It was wooden and remote, two factors that made the castle especially hospitable to the flames that consumed it two years later. In 1882 the family moved into their new masonry castle and found it a pleasant retreat from the heat of New York City. The last of the Vanderpools lived here through the years as a recluse and wrote a brilliant history of New Jersey. He had been educated as a lawyer, was involved in one case, won it, and retired from the profession.

The text in the chapter on the Gothic Revival, above, refers to the policeman who patrolled the limits of the Vanderpool Castle. In my youth I was fascinated by this lonely patrolman endlessly making his rounds. At that time he had a sentry box for shelter, his uniforms were blue, and he was quite military in his bearing. But as the years passed the shoulders of his uniform grayed and his posture edged on the woebegone. The last time I saw him (in the thirties) gray predominated, and the poor fellow's pace was sadly resigned.

The presence of the guard was of great interest to the young people of the surrounding communities, and the castle itself gave rise to wild imaginings and rash rumors. During World War II security guards replaced the lone sentry, and strange blue lights in the castle accelerated speculation as to what might be going on behind the battlements.

The site of the Vanderpool Castle met all the requirements the Romantic ideal set for an American gentleman's castle. It overlooked an antique turnpike (New Jersey Route 24 is still known as the Morris Turnpike, and the alternate road is referred to as the Shunpike) and hundreds of acres of patterned farmland. At the downside of the castle a willowy stream flowing from a bosky dell provided the country sounds and the uncultivated "wilderness" that was such a delight to city dwellers—and to Sir Walter Scott's readers. Flower gardens were graced with statuary, an iron gazebo, and wandering paths interspersed with flagstone steps. Two miles away the Delaware, Lackawanna, and Western offered swift, regular, and elegant transportation back to the city.

The interior of the Vanderpool castle has been described as austere. Paneled walls, high ceilings, massive fireplaces, lancet windows, a circular staircase to the tower, and Tudor ornamentation gave legitimacy to the rooms.

In 1967 New Jersey's Highway Commission replaced this invaluable landmark with a stretch of highway.

Plate 18 *American Castellated*

Plate 19   *A Camp-meeting House*

A Camp-meeting House

The camp meeting was entirely an American institution. Mrs. Trollope took a dim view of the emotional exhortations, shrieking, and holy rollings she witnessed in Indiana forest clearings. Her contempt for the proceedings was complete, and it brought wrath upon her from the questionable segment of the clergy that profited from the events.

By no means were all camp meetings scenes of religious excess. Most were of a very different nature. They were well organized and utterly sincere in purpose. The camp meeting served not only as a place of religious reinvigoration but also as a place of escape from city life in summer. For nineteenth-century families too poor to afford summer vacations, the meetings were an ideal retreat.

Tents were available to families and cooking areas provided. While religious activities predominated, singing, swimming, hiking, and baseball provided healthy recreation. Whole congregations in wagons loaded with camping equipment traveled in a haze of dust from the heat of the city to the camp, often in a wooded area near a clear stream.

As years went by the camps became permanent establishments. Central meeting houses were built, and a few small cottages to house the clergy were added to the perimeter of the grounds. In Chautauqua County, New York, a very famous camp meeting developed. It was originally a camp for the study of the Bible, but it evolved into an institution to sponsor concerts and lectures ranging over all things intellectual. The lectures were called "Chautauquas" and attracted distinguished speakers from all over the world.

If the term "Stick Style" hadn't been invented, we would be forced to describe the camp-meeting cottage of our painting as Gothic, for the suggestion of pointed arches is there, and a finial and pendant are present. The cottage is in South Seaville, New Jersey, north of Cape May. It is quite unknown to the public. A walk from the highway through the pine woods to the enclave is a walk through a time warp to the nineteenth century. But it is not a dream or a movie set that confronts the visitor—it is a group of buildings unaltered since the 1870's. The elaborate carpenter's lace and pierced wood indicates a kinship to the craftsmanship and ingenuity of the Cape May builders to the south.

South Seaville has seen more than 120 annual camp meetings. Methodist ministers on vacation from southern New Jersey parishes arrive with paint and tools, roll up their sleeves, and become carpenters, masons, and painters. The results are spiritually and aesthetically uplifting.

Kingscote—A Gothic Cottage Orné

The Preservation Society of Newport County, Rhode Island, describes "Kingscote" as a Gothic cottage orné. Richard Upjohn was its architect, and the original owner was George Noble Jones, of Savannah, Georgia, one of many southerners who had ties to Newport. From the beginning the board-sided house was painted to represent stone, and the façade remains unchanged since completion in 1842.

The Civil War brought an end to the prosperity of the Jones family. Kingscote was sold to William Henry King, a China trade merchant, who, unfortunately, lived in the place for only two years. For thirty-one years after, he lived in hospitals. Kingscote then became the home of a succession of Kings. In 1881 Stanford White planned the huge annex that stands behind the original picturesque silhouette. It was a mistake. The barrackslike addition spoiled the asymmetry of the Gothic concept and added nothing but bulk to what had been a pleasantly scaled building.

The bargeboard eave at the left of the painting has battlements that serve as a porch over an oriel that extends to the base. The heavy molding over the windows is a hood molding. Pendants, finials, and pointed-arch windows are all hallmarks of the Gothic.

The interior of Stanford White's dining room was a daring adventure in its time. The room incorporates unusual materials including cork, glass, tile, and rare woods against a backdrop of oriental screens and decorations.

George Noble Jones showed daring, too, when he introduced indoor plumbing, gas lighting, a bathroom, and an aviary in 1842!

Unlike other houses of this book, Kingscote is, during the season, open to public viewing. The volunteers of the Newport County Preservation Society are the tour guides, and the interior of the building is filled with reminders that the King family was in the China trade.

Plate 20 *Kingscote—A Gothic Cottage Orné*

Plate 21   *Jocky Hollow Gothic*

Jockey Hollow Gothic

The domed glass structure at the right of the painting is an orangery. The orangery has been a symbol of wealth and status since Mansart built his magnificent orangerie for Louis XIV at Versailles in 1685. Mansart's structure was over 500 feet long and 42 feet wide with side galleries 375 feet in length. It held 1,200 orange trees and 300 other fruit trees. The orangery attached to the Gothic McAlpin house in the painting is adequate for that size house, but some were 50 feet high and sheltered a variety of exotic plants including palm trees. Citrus fruits were expensive and not readily available in the northern regions of Victorian America, although the nutritive value of the fruit was well known. An orange was special enough to be considered a lavish treat at Christmastime.

The McAlpin house is at the entrance of the Jockey Hollow National Park near Morristown, New Jersey, where General Washington's troops spent three of the War of Independence's most heartbreaking years.[4] The house

4. More battles were fought and more blood was spilled in New Jersey during the Revolution than in any other state. Cornwallis admitted to Washington that the war had been won on the banks of the Delaware. By 1779 ten thousand American troops were stationed near Jockey Hollow.

was of great interest to the local children because a somewhat mysterious but genuine princess lived there for thirty years until the post-World War II period.

The elements of pedigree are extensive in the Gothic house of the painting. Tudor chimneys, a robustly framed trefoil window in the principal gable, deeply dimensional bargeboarding, pendants and finials, windows with pointed arches, windows with rich hood moldings, and a balustrade ingeniously provided with interlocking trefoils complete the list of Gothic components.

The McAlpin place was built late in the Gothic tenure. Its masses are more conventional than the massing of the Pointed Gothic style of an earlier period. The house itself, if stripped of the cosmetic Gothic effects listed above, would be indistinguishable from any standard form.

The shapes of the bodies of the early Gothics, such as the Alexander Jackson Davis House in plate 14, were distinctive and could be identified without the ornaments associated with the style. Incidentally, the most recent owner of the McAlpin house has chosen to paint the brownstone white.

By the time the McAlpin Gothic was built, architects were beginning to be licensed. In reading architectural history it is revealing to learn that medieval architects of the great European cathedrals were master masons. In another instance, much later, a pharmacist became a master builder: Thomas Rickman was the planner of St. George's Church in Birmingham, England, completed in 1821. It's considered a successful example of the Perpendicular Gothic Revival style.

Point of Rocks Depot

At midpoint in the Victorian century, a group of unusually talented Englishmen joined in architectural ventures that were to lead to a style developed as much by an art theorist and critic as by any architect. The inspiration for the ventures was provided by the English critic John Ruskin (1819–1900), whose Romantic conception of the artist as a prophet and teacher became a motif of the idealistic members of the Pre-Raphaelites, a brotherhood of dedicated painters and sculptors. In 1849 Ruskin wrote his influential Seven Lamps of Architecture, urging architects to study the Italian Gothic. His Stones of Venice, which followed, further exhorted planners to regard the medieval, polychromed Venetian structures as exemplars. In 1850 the first High Victorian Gothic church, All Saints', was built in London. The architect, William Butterfield, employed horizontal bands of alternating red and black brick to achieve the principal hallmark of the style, polychromy. Other examples followed, and the artists of the Pre-Raphaelite Brotherhood, whose views early coincided with Ruskin's, participated to some degree in the planning

Plate 22   *Point of Rocks Depot*

of the churches that followed. Edward Coley Burne–Jones and others designed stained-glass windows, and the remarkable William Morris (1834–1896), whose studio produced tapestries, wallpapers, furniture, and beautifully handcrafted books, contributed carvings and other details for the polychromed interiors of the new Gothics. Other members of the Brotherhood, Dante Gabriel Rossetti and John Everett Millais, made material and aesthetic contributions to the burgeoning style, as did the painter Ford Madox Brown, who never joined the Brotherhood.

The contribution of the Pre-Raphaelites was but an interesting sidelight to the development of the High Victorian Gothic style, but credit for its inspiration must still go to Ruskin and the architects who, ultimately, controlled the design of the churches.

Almost as soon as the High Victorian Gothic churches were built, they were seriously criticized. The word "strident" was at the forefront of the criticism, but the style had its ardent admirers whose defense of the style ensured its tenure for at least three decades.

The High Victorian Gothic came to America soon after the Civil War. One delightful example of the style is in Point of Rocks, Maryland. Point of Rocks is close to the Potomac and not far from Leesburg, Virginia. It's west of the nation's capital and an important freight junction. The depot has been a landmark and a visual pleasure since the late 1870's. It's a favorite subject for artists and a diminutive example of the Victorian. The alternating red and cream panels over the ground-level windows, the horizontal sandstone bands that encircle the building, and the bands of cusped slate in the roof and tower set the style as High Victorian Gothic. The huge quatrefoil in the tower and the windows of the dormers that form a trefoil are Venetian touches. The style is alternately called "Ruskinian Gothic" and "Venetian Gothic."

V. Ways and Means

IN ARCHITECTURAL TERMS the Romantic era spanned the seventy years from 1830 to 1900. The dates are not exact limits, as the earliest Greek Revivals appeared well before 1830, and some Romantic era architecture carried into the twentieth century. The dates coincide roughly with the reign of Victoria and encompass unprecedented changes in the fabric of men's lives. Woven into that fabric was James Watt's invention of a practical steam engine, which revolutionized industry, travel, and building. In fact a successful steam engine had been developed by the 1780's, but it took almost fifty years to develop the means for foundries to produce machinery sufficiently advanced to manufacture efficient engines for building and travel. By the late 1830's paddlewheel boats were traveling the Hudson, and steam-driven locomotives were heralding the demise of just-completed canals.

Inventors tended to apply the energy of steam engines to the motions and implements of man-powered conveyances and tools. The earliest steam-driven vessel was not a paddlewheeler, but a boat equipped with rows of oars propelled by a driving arm that gripped all the oars in a simultaneous stroke. It didn't work very well, and necessity mothered the paddlewheel.

The impact of steam power on building cannot be underrated. Traditionally beams were hewn from logs with broadaxes and "planed" to approximate size with the adz. Boards were sawn from rough-trimmed timbers. This operation involved two sawyers, one who stood at the bottom of an eight-foot-deep pit pulling a seven-foot-long pit saw, and his partner, who stood atop the timber and raised the saw. The saw tended to buckle, so an improvement called a "sash saw" was invented which braced the blade with flanking boards, adding considerable weight. Inhaling all that sawdust didn't add much pleasure to the grueling task of sawing boards. Trees had to be felled nearby and seasoned within hauling distance of the building site. Building techniques were necessarily tied to these laborious and slow-moving elements of supply. Building a house took a long, long time and a lot of labor.

With the advent of the steam engine, mills sprang into being wherever there was enterprise and demand. The early mills used steam energy to imitate the up-and-down motions of the saw, producing sawtooth marks at right angles to the length of the board. This fact is significant in the dating of early houses. The boards in the earliest houses clearly show the rest marks, the shifting of the sawing angle as the saw encountered the resistance of knots, and other inconsistencies of the hand-sawn product, while the steam-driven up-and-down saw showed a consistent right-angled marking throughout the board.

When beams and boards could be cut to very accurate and consistent dimensions, the entire approach to construction changed. Railroads or steamboats were able to transport pre-cut lumber from mills to whatever outpost was linked to rail, river, or canal.

From the colonial era until 1825 treenails (wooden dowels), clinched mortise-and-tenon joints used in the heavy framework of house construction. Iron nails were made one by one by blacksmiths and were used only where absolutely necessary. A settler moving westward often burned his buildings to retrieve the nails. (The governor of Virginia gave migrating families as many nails as the house contained to encourage settling and discourage burning.) In 1825, with smelting furnaces able to produce $\frac{1}{8}$-inch-thick pieces of sheet iron for steam boilers and other needs, a new way to turn out great quantities of nails emerged. Sheets of the iron $2\frac{3}{4}$

inches wide were fed into mill-operated cutters similar to the paper cutters used to trim books. By feeding the cutter at a slight alternating angle, the shaft of the nail could be tapered. A crimping device, also operated by water or steam power, put a head on the square nails. Like boards, nails enable us to set a date on our older houses, for the mill-cut nail dates from 1825 to about 1850 when the wire nail, at first imported, was found to be even more practical and economical.

In a symbiotic masterstroke, a third invention, dependent on the steam-driven saw and the mill-cut nail, came to the rescue of a furiously growing nation. In Chicago in 1833, either George Washington Snow or Augustine D. Taylor invented the balloon house frame. Authorities disagree about the originators, but they do agree that the first balloon-framed structure was St. Mary's Catholic Church in Chicago. The lumber, presumably cut by steam-driven saws, was hauled from St. Joseph's, across Lake Michigan. The total cost of the church was $400! The house-building revolution was underway.

The essentials of balloon framing have not changed. The system employs pre-sawn two-by-fours (now 1¾ by 3½ inches), with heavier corner posts. Horizontal two-by-fours frame out windows and doorways and eliminate the complexities of heavy-timber joinery. Joists to support floors and ceilings were of heavier dimension and helped stabilize the structure. The balloon system met with scorn from traditional builders, who insisted that the first good storm would lift the new buildings into Lake Michigan—thus the derivation of the term "balloon." The practicability of the system soon proved to be undeniable, however, and the techniques of balloon structure spread like the wildfire that consumed so many balloon-framed houses in the great Chicago fire of 1871. On August 27, 1980, a wrecking crew with a permit arrived at a wrong address and mistakenly destroyed the Rinker House, the second oldest house in Chicago. It was a balloon-framed, bargeboarded, board-and-batten Gothic which had survived the 1871 holocaust.

The new framing technique required few of the skills of the mortise-and-tenon joiners. In the great boom of building accompanying westward expansion, unskilled laborers were suddenly carpenters. A saw, a hammer, and a rule were their principal tools. The balloon-frame house became as vital to the winning of the west as the covered wagon, the iron horse, or Colt's revolvers. The technique was quickly adopted by other nations. America had made its first major contribution to architecture. That contribution was to be a signal to the growth of the architectural styles that were to come.

In the nineteenth century, as today, most building did not involve formal architecture. The houses we have discussed, noteworthy for their style, represented only a minority. The majority of buildings were indigenous structures—barns, cabins, warehouses, and houses that, through need or prosperity, grew from crude shelters to more habitable houses. Building contractors were local men able to enlist skilled hands and build whatever was required. As cities grew, however, the population multiplied, and building became an industry complete with the speculative professional builder. At the time architects were still not licensed, but simply acquired their title by skill and reputation. Not until 1865 did William Robert Ware found the first school of architecture at the Massachusetts Institute of Technology.

The subject of ventilation was quietly ignored by polite company prior to the 1840's. Then, somehow, the topic became of paramount interest to the magazine writers of the times. Readers were warned of air rendered impure "by respiration, the exhalations of the skin," etc. Andrew Jackson Downing alarmed his readers with the following passage in *The Architecture of Country Houses*:

The want of attention to ventilation arises from the fact that the poison of breathing bad air is a slow one, and though its effects are as certain as those which follow from taking doses of prussic acid, yet, they are only observed remotely, and little by little. Nature does not immediately protest against slightly impure air as against want of food and water, and, therefore we go on from day to day, suffering the accumulated evils resulting from ignorance, and only wondering at our want of physical health and spirits.

The raising of levels of awareness to the evils of poor ventilation ran head-on into new systems of heating that the availability of sheet metal had made possible. "Hot sheet metals scorch the air, rendering it unfit for breathing," said the conservatives, who maintained that the fireplace, which forced impure air up the chimney and brought in fresh supplies (through the cracks and crevices of the house) to feed the fire, was the only decent way to heat a home. Progressives answered that noxious gasses escaped from open fires, while stoves and furnaces contained the gasses and flames and radiated only healthful heat. In turn the conservatives claimed that the tenants of houses in Scandinavian and other forest countries, where the houses were loosely built and wood fires were made in large, open fireplaces, were much more healthy than the inmates of tight, modern-built (i.e., balloon-frame), houses. Any other method of heating would bring ill health, paleness, and often consumption. The rebuttal indicated that fireplaces, unable to supply adequate heat, encourage everything from pneumonia to frostbite.

Other than stoves and fireplaces, the only alternative for home heating was something new called the "hot-air furnace." Downing's description of the hot-air system, and his endorsement of the innovation, were clear in *The Architecture of Country Houses*:

Hot-air furnaces offer a very complete means of warming a house of any size, since, by means of hot-air pipes and registers, one fire, in the lowest part of a house, may be made to warm a large column of heated air, which, with its natural tendency to rise, may be distributed to every room in the house. . . . But most of the hot-air furnaces hitherto used are open to the strongest objections, on account of their unwholesomeness. They are so constructed as to heat the air by means of a surface of heated iron, raised to a very high temperature—often quite red-hot. Dr. Ure has correctly remarked that as "cast-iron contains, beside the metal itself, more or less carbon, sulphur, phosphorus, and even arsenic, it is possible that the smell of air passed over it in an incandescent state, may be owing to some of these imperfections; for a quantity of noxious effluvia, inappreciably small, is capable of affecting not only the olfactory nerves, but the pulmonary organs."

For twenty years prior to the Civil War, the arguments of the ventilationists and the advocates of central heating caromed back and forth in the national press. Even the pulpits engaged in the debate with comments on the loss of the hearth as a unifying element of the home. Never before was the time so right for experimentation. Inventive minds created technological advances, challenged by increasing demands for higher standards of living. It was an age utterly fascinated by the potentials of the new-found forces science had unleashed. The most romantic observers predicted a Utopian future, while pessimists warned that, like Mary Shelley's galvanic monster, science was a mindless force that would one day rise to destroy its creators. The all-too-frequent explosions of steam boilers bore them out and must have had a sobering effect on the public, but there was no stopping technological and industrial progress.

The Means

The cost of building in the northeast of the 1850's was low in terms of the prevailing middle-class income. Labor costs, to the modern mind, are hardly conceivable. Twelve-hour days and six-day weeks were considered respectable. In one project, to lay the floors of an eight-room house cost $8 including the nails. The 1,600 feet of flooring required cost $24. The framing for the entire house cost $42, or $10 per 1,000 feet of framing. (At this writing we pay $240 per 1,000 feet.) The eleven windows of our 1850's house cost $38.50. For the least expensive window available today we pay $90. The entire roof of an 1850 house cost $40.25 including labor. Today, a square of cedar shingles costs $225 installed, and eighteen to twenty squares are needed to cover the roof of an eight-room house without dormers or extra valleys. The cost, at eighteen squares: $4,050.

The 1850 eight-room house from which the aforementioned figures were obtained cost $573.86 complete—complete without closets, plumbing, electricity, air conditioning, or central heating. By 1860 some plumbing, tentative central heating, and even indoor toilets would arrive in the most progressive homes. It is safe to multiply all 1850 costs by 120 to arrive at today's figures.

Away from the northeast, excepting the frontier boom towns, building costs were often less than those detailed. Near Whitecastle, Louisiana, not far from the ruins of the once-magnificent "Belle Grove" of Greek Revival fame, stands "Nottoway," a mansion that is a blend of Greek Revival and Italianate overlooking a

"Belle Grove," a Greek Revival

sugar plantation. Nottoway was built in 1858, and the records of its construction still survive. Specifications called for four coats of paint inside and out. Bath water was to be supplied by two 1,000-gallon tanks installed in the attic. The contractor's fee to build the sixty-four-room house, with a slate roof and twenty-two enormous columns, was $650. The charge for carpentry came to $3,800, while the plastering, including elaborate friezes and medallions, came to $1,901. No figures were given for a total cost, but it is reasonable to assume that the entire cost did not exceed $10,000—or, in today's money, over one million dollars!

In the colonial era, goldsmiths and silversmiths acted as caretakers for the coins of their customers. They were also money lenders to a select group of qualified borrowers. Beyond goldsmiths and silversmiths, businessmen and merchants established a loose system of deposit and lending that served as a banking entity for approved clients. The system was exclusive and contributed to a shortage of ready money for those outside the favored circles. It helped to have friends or a rich uncle.

In 1781 Robert Morris, who worked tirelessly to finance the Revolution and was privileged to languish in debtor's prison from 1798 to 1801, founded the first national bank with a loan from France of $450,000 in

"Nottoway," a Greek Revival and Italianate blend

gold and silver coins. Oxcarts delivered the money from quayside to one Tench Francis's building on Chestnut Street in Philadelphia. From such a precarious beginning and such informal systems, banking institutions developed that would soon be chartered by Congress. The very successful Bank of the United States (privately owned and delivering a return of 8 percent per annum to its investors), under Greek revivalist Nicholas Biddle, thrived until in 1833 Andrew Jackson introduced a decentralized "pet" banking system by withdrawing the government's gold and silver from Biddle's bank and distributing it to pet state banks. Now each state could print its own money. The results were chaotic and led to bank failures and lack of confidence in printed money. A poor harvest and financial crises in England, which led to the recall of gold and silver from American banking institutions, brought on the panic of 1837. Six years of financial instability and hardship followed. Every sector of the economy suffered, but the need for building continued. New lending groups and methods evolved based largely on some sort of a mortgage agreement. Religious groups, fraternal organizations, trade guilds, unions, and grange societies endeavored to assist the builders of the new nation financially. Inevitably, unscrupulous lenders gave rise to the caricature of that villain of melodrama who joyously forecloses on the widow and orphan. But somehow, despite depression, crop failures, foreclosures, fly-by-night speculators, and other assorted disasters, houses continued to be built in increasing numbers. Many of them were worth building.

Jeff's Barn

In the 1960's and '70's, a dream of many young men was to buy a few acres of countryside in Vermont, the Berkshires, Virginia, or the Carolinas. On the two or three acres would be a wonderful old barn, sturdily built with hand-hewn timbers and aromatic with timothy. The taxes would be low, and a nearby stream would provide clear water and trout. On weekends, so went the dream, steady progress would be made in making the barn into a year-round retreat. A few wise but inexpensive craftsmen would supply any necessary know-how and fill in on some of the rough spots. In the end the labors would provide a picturesque retreat for family and friends in sylvan surroundings. The dream was quintessentially Romantic: a return to the earth, a love of crafts—especially those crafts that showed the signs of the hands of man rather than the marks of machinery—and a yearning for solitude, are elements of Romanticism.

Those few who found such a place also found difficulty at every turn. Shortages, roads impassable in rain and snow, poison ivy, oak, and sumac, bee stings, rising costs, surly contractors, failed deliveries, disputed titles, stolen tools, splinters, mismeasurements, and exhaustion were part of the struggle. For those very few who held on to the dream and saw the project through, however, the rewards were infinite. To be close to nature and to feel the seasons change, to watch a low September sun make magic in those fields of timothy—those were the rewards of a dream come true.

My son Jeffrey had just such a dream, but a burgeoning career shunted his dreams elsewhere. One of the barns he found in Hunterdon County, New Jersey, is the subject of the painting. The purpose of his figure in the painting is to give scale to the massive timbers framing the structure. The purpose of the painting is to remind viewers of the labor and ingenuity that went into nineteenth-century rural construction.

Jeff's Barn is the only painting in the book with a figure. In the Cape May storefront (plate 60) I at first painted a woman walking into the doorway in abbreviated costume appropriate to the season and the seashore; but somehow the painting was no longer an architectural portrait. The eye was attracted to the figure, and the Cape May storefront became subsidiary. So I painted her out and replaced her with an antique barber pole in the store's interior. Once again, it's an architectural portrait.

Plate 23   *Jeff's Barn*

Plate 24   *The Balloon Frame*

The Balloon Frame

The house in the painting near Newport, Rhode Island, was dismantled some years ago. The framing shows it to have been a house built early in the balloon-frame era, perhaps as early as 1840. The two-by-fours are 2 inches by 4 inches, and not the present-day 1¾" by 3½".[5] The corner posts are generous, hearkening back to earlier post-and-beam buildings. Another echo of previous construction is the mortised corner posts accommodating a cross member of the eave-end structure.

As the balloon frame became more and more acceptable, the transitional, vestigial elements disappeared that linked it to post-and-beam days. Heavy corner posts were succeeded by several two-by-fours clinched with sturdy nails. Skilled carpenters turned to cabinetry and interior finishing, as now the unskilled could handle the framing

with a saw, nails, and a hammer. Wood butcher's kits were sold by mail-order houses to young men working their way westward. The false-fronted buildings of the western frontiers were knocked together almost overnight by an entrepreneurial foreman and his crew of overworked wood butchers.

The sheathing of the Newport house (seen at the left end of the house) was a good 1½ inches thick. Today's standard is ½-inch plywood for the sides of a house and ⅝-inch for the roofing. Until the 1920's sheathing boards were often applied diagonally. The custom increased costs, but builders felt the triangular construction thus achieved gave buildings increased rigidity.

The care with which the Newport structure was being dismantled indicated either that the house was to be re-erected elsewhere or that the lumber was destined for another purpose.

_____

5. *In some areas the size has dwindled to* 1½" × 3½".

VI. The Italianate Style

THE LEGEND OF THE ORIGIN of the Italianate style of architecture is *almost* true, but selectively colorful lapses into fancy deny the story the dignity of history. Good myths and legends grow from historic truths. A few imaginative alterations to truth shift history to myth.

The legend: Visualize the jacket of a modern Gothic novel: a grim Gothic mansion, and the word "patroon" somewhere in the title. In front of an enormous fireplace in a great, cusped-and-paneled room stands the patroon. Facing him, her lineage subtly reflected in the magnificently sculptured planes of his own face, stands his daughter. She wears her hair parted in the middle and severely drawn to a chignon at the back. Her lovely face shows all the determination that the generations of the Vanderveers have bred into her. Now determination turns to frustration, and tears well in those exquisite gray eyes. Seeing her emotion, the old man, torn between love for his only daughter and a devotion to stern practicality, finally relents and agrees to send Rachel on the fashionable Grand Tour of Continental Europe. Of course there will be chaperons and suitable traveling companions and dozens of round-topped, ribbed leather trunks. But the trip will be broadening. (Vassar hadn't been invented yet.)

In late summer our heroine arrives in Italy, the Mecca of the privileged young people of Western society. The cream of the young English gentry is there also, and, best of all, so are Keats, Byron, and Shelley, the superstars of the generation. Among other exotic sights, Rachel remembers the Tuscan plains, dotted with picturesque and haunting villas. The campaniles and the asymmetry of the buildings are picturesque and unforgettable.

All too soon the idyll ends and, back in Washington Irving's not-too-sunny Hudson River Valley, Rachel faces the stern realities of earnest America. She marries the handsome, or mysterious, or slightly older, worldly young man who has also known Italy. In time, finding the home of generations of Vanderveers too oppressive, they build a Tuscan villa for their beautiful young family (they all have gray eyes) to recall those heady, superbly romantic days in the Italy of Lord Byron. Presumably their Tuscan transplant didn't look out of place on the shores of the Hudson, as their friends all seemed to have shared the same idea.

Rachel's is a nice story, and everyone lives happily ever after, but it's woefully anachronistic and neglectful of the English origin of the Italianate style.

Edith Wharton referred to the style as "Hudson River Bracketed." Nineteenth-century contemporaries called it the "Tuscan Villa" style, and the English knew the villas as "Rural Italians." Under whatever name, the style made a formidable imprint on taste and architecture in America even though it came here via England where societal adjustments had made the Italianate a welcome change.

Since 1750 the intelligentsia of Europe had become openly critical of Europe's aristocracy. Men of intelligence rankled against the privileges of inheritance and they let the world know about it. In the *ancien régime* scientists depended upon the handouts of the upper classes to further their research. Musicians and composers were regarded as servants and dressed in livery. The peasantry was ready for physical revolt. Merchants, manufacturers, and those in the trades were awakening to a sense of personal importance and bridling at the demeaning social status imposed on them by an aristocracy whose own value to society was becoming less and less apparent.

In their hostility against the titled, the emergent

groups had powerful allies in the legal profession. Primogeniture—the system of the mandatory and exclusive succession of the eldest son to title and estate—brought about its own downfall through the practice of sending second and third sons to the universities to be educated in the professions. These sons, *sans* title, *sans* estate, often chose the law and in time became the judges who would rule on matters of property and succession. Reminded of the inequities in their own experiences, those judges, ruling favorably for more equitable disbursement of property and privilege, further weakened the absolute dominion of the ruling class.

The intelligentsia came up with a new class, the meritocracy. The members of·this new class gained wealth on their own merits by intelligence, pluck, talent, or enterprise, not through the accident of birth.

In England change was slow to come, but when it came, it came with impact. It was becoming more and more obvious that the aristocracy had little genuine *raison d'etre*. The idea of mutual protection ("touch my servant and you touch me") and the responsibility of land owners to ensure tranquility for their dependents, were dissolving in the societal changes of the eighteenth century.

By the 1820's criticism of the English upper classes by the emerging middle class grew to such an extent that the ruling groups, very much aware of the violent revolution across the channel, were prepared to make social concessions, some of them real. The tight grasp on civil-service jobs and sinecures was relaxed to admit the middle class. Other, hitherto upper-class perquisites, were modified or enlarged to placate critics and reformers. In this climate the nobility and the landed gentry made, or were advised to make, efforts to overcome an image of arrogance, immorality, and inefficiency.

Some early public-relations man reminded his aristocratic clients that architecture speaks out on certain attitudes of buildings' owners, and architecture's permanence and prominence can be an implacable reminder of those attitudes. To the average Englishman the architecture of castles and other militant Gothic expressions appeared to speak menacingly of the arrogance that the upper classes were striving to disown. For some undetermined reason, however, towers had a different symbolic effect. Towers, it seemed, quietly symbolized dignity without arrogance, and the new Rural Italian style villas had not only towers, but an inborn dignity and an innate affinity to the earth.

That affinity was attractive to the upper-class builders of the early nineteenth century. Closer ties to nature, which had become modish through the efforts of Rousseau, Chateaubriand, and their literary comrades, changed the habits of the gentry. Eighteenth-century landowners considered the journey from London to their country seats an onerous obligation, and visits to their country seats were perfunctory and tinged with distaste. By the nineteenth century, through literature, a great change in outlook had occurred. With the help of new and safer roads and bridges, with enlightened views of agriculture which made conversations about land use and husbandry acceptable in the drawing rooms of London, the upper classes began to know and appreciate the country. The draining of fields through ditching and other agrarian techniques improved the land, and to the delight of the landowners, their efforts became highly profitable. Landowners now felt that stays of six months in town and six months in the country were not only economically warranted but had the added benefits of being spiritually and socially uplifting as well. Country-house parties became so popular that new houses were purposely built to accommodate them. The sense of the country became an element in that building. Communion with nature and accessibility to the outdoors all figured in the plans of the new structures.

The new-found mysteries of country life fascinated the recently initiated, and the writers of the early nineteenth century hastened to supply agreeably exciting touches to monstrous tales dredged from bucolic sages. The great god Pan, half goat, half man, sometimes evil, sometimes benevolent, became an arcadian obsession—

although Pan had roved the lower depths of English consciousness for centuries. The poignant chapter in Kenneth Grahame's masterpiece, *The Wind in the Willows* (which places Pan in the animal realm and outside the understanding of man), gives a cameo view of the late-Victorian reverence for that deity.

The new appreciation and sensitivity to country life even changed the nature of contemporary painting. Eighteenth-century paintings of manor houses were alive with figures of servants and the squirearchy, while early-nineteenth-century paintings limned a pastoral simplicity. Human intrusions into the idyllic settings were limited to a distant plowman or a remote and lonely horseman.

Young people of the upper classes *did* make the Grand Tour of continental Europe and, having tasted Paris and roamed the Rhine, they fell under the spell of the Italy of the poets, returning to England with dreams of Tuscan villas. The Romantic mood seized them and, in time, they built their towers and the picturesque asymmetrical villas. Browning captured the feeling young Britons had for that land when he wrote: "Open my heart and you shall see . . . graved inside there . . . Italy."

A campanile is a bell tower. The leaning tower of Pisa is an unusual bell tower in that it is cylindrical; most are four-sided. While not serving as bell towers, the campaniles of the Italian villas, fascinating to travelers, are common to the style. The irregular mass of the villa, so attractive to a generation saturated with the symmetry of Classical architecture, was accentuated by the tower and by the informally placed additions built on to the villas over the years. The towers had very low-pitched roofs and extending eaves supported by decorative brackets. Brackets should be visualized as supports similar to the supports that hold up bookshelves. They usually extend farther down the wall than outward under the eaves. By contrast, the kind of eave support indicating an extension of rafters through the wall is called a *modillion*. Windows in campaniles were round

topped and unadorned. The original villa itself was characterized by extreme simplicity, relieved only by sheltering eaves and generous brackets. Most windows and doors were round topped.

An example of a campanile in Princeton, New Jersey

The Italian style suited all the new philosophical requirements of the English builders at the beginning of the nineteenth century: accessibility to the outdoors, a picturesque silhouette, an affinity to the earth, a Romantic break with tradition . . . and not a breath of aristocratic arrogance in the entire conception. Now the builder could break out in any direction that need dictated, and in so doing add to the picturesqueness of the whole.

The style presented so many easy solutions to previously difficult problems that it is surprising that villas did not become anything approaching a national style in England. Italianate was reasonably popular, but there was too much competition from demilitarized Gothic variations and a host of other styles and nonstyles. Few English public buildings grew from the Italianate mode. Most of the Rural Italians were built as country seats (although there was some speculative building in the style), and those that remain constitute a minority form of architecture in England. For the record, John Nash, of Picturesque fame (and George IV's favorite architect), built the first Italianate at Cronkhill, near Shrewsbury.

The vernacular builders of the Tuscan farmhouses would have been amazed to see the interpretations of their handiwork in the green English countryside. What Americans did with the style would have dumbfounded them.

In the 1830's the Protestant Episcopal Bishop of New Jersey was George Washington Doane. In architectural history his name is remembered because in 1832 he commissioned John Notman to build "Riverside," the first Italianate structure in America. No firm correlation between colorful characters and original buildings has ever been proved, but surely some relationship exists, as Bishop Doane's career suggests. It seems the bishop, a decent and dedicated clergyman, liked to have himself shipped around in crates. The details are unavailable, but there is an account of at least one such event. Doane was also distinguished as the first American to preach in England after the American Revolution. It took Parliament sixty-five years to repeal an act that forbade any American to man an English pulpit. In celebration of the occasion, Wordsworth devoted three sonnets to Bishop Doane in his *Ecclesiastic Sonnets*.

Bishop George Washington Doane

What Doane had in mind for his Burlington, New Jersey, house, was something Gothic. Notman thought of his creation as a practical variant of Gothic Revival

"Riverside," Bishop Doane's residence, built by John Notman

architecture. The interior of Riverside was pure Gothic, and the library was considered a masterpiece of interior Gothic design. In England the Italianate style was understood to be a sophisticated variant of the Classical style, and in later buildings, Classical elements were incorporated into the design. In America, however, from the outset, the style was interpreted as a variant of the Gothic. The American view may have helped to make the Gothic respectable again, as builders were trying to move away from the criticisms that regarded the Gothic images as not only alien but as obvious medieval throwbacks.

For a time, the new style was called "Rural English" and even "Norman." James Renwick, after completing his Gothic Grace Church in New York City in 1846, plunged into the planning and construction of the Smithsonian Institution in the new mode. He called the style "Norman." Others felt it was Italianate because of its random asymmetry. Today the term Italianate indicates variations on the theme that include the Cube Style, the Campanile Style, and the big city Brownstone Style. The massing of the three modes is different, but they all share the flat or low-pitched roofs and determined brackets of the Italianate. Excepting the rectangular (*trabeated*) windows that are sometimes placed just below the eaves, most windows are rounded (*arcuated*) or have arched hood moldings. Columns are distinctive, and the painting on page 90 shows the rather simple stop-chamfer

The Smithsonian Institution—J. Renwick, architect

posts and plain or scrollwork capitals. The painting of the Cape May guest house (now a gourmet restaurant) on page 117 shows how elements of the Italianate manner carried even into the Victorianism of the 1870's.

The Italianate Cube style was, as the name implies, one massive block, crowned by a cupola or belvedere. Cupolas and belvederes served chiefly as a decoration and, occasionally, as recreational rooms. For the latter use, of course, the weather had to be quite perfect, the temperatures inside cupolas ranging from freezing to roasting with hardly a pause between.

With the new freedom of arrangement afforded by Italianate asymmetry came loggias, oriels, balustrades, galleries, porches, and any number of elements unsuited to previous styles. Walls could be stone, board-and-batten, brick, stucco, or conventional clapboard siding. Quoins, even quoins of alternating colors, were acceptable in the style. The Italianate fit city streets and suburban lanes.

The picturesque quality of the irregular forms was framed and enhanced by something new—lawns. Lawns had a civilizing effect on the nature of homes. Before the lawnmower, grass near houses was cut with scythes or cropped by sheep or other grazing animals. The lawnmower was invented in the 1840's, and the velvety, rolling lawns that then flourished gave a formal setting to the informal lines of the Italianates. For those who sur-

vived the panic of '37, the new style and the smooth lawns that went with them were a tempting investment.

As the Italianate style grew, its components were introduced into firehouses, town halls, railroad stations, and churches. Churches in the Italianate style were called "Norman Lombard." Campaniles were ideal for churches for the purpose originally intended, but they were such an architectural godsend for fire-engine houses that they continued to be built until well into the twentieth century. Hardly a city or town in America lacks an Italianate firehouse with an accompanying campanile, whose chief purpose was to provide a tall space in which woven cotton fire hoses could be suspended to drain and dry.

Andrew Jackson Downing's *Architecture of Country Houses* was devoted to cottages, lodges, farmhouses and villas largely in the "pointed" (Gothic) style. At the two-thirds mark in his book, however, a new style is introduced to the reader in a casually ambivalent manner. In his heart of hearts, Downing was an elitist. His talents and instincts, his journey from modest origins to easy association with the loftier echelons of talent and society made him so. To Downing the Gothic style represented the ultimate in character and taste. Yet by the late 1840's, the Gothic style was firmly categorized as an aristocratic expression, and Downing recognized the Italianate innovations as a graceful transition to a more acceptable form. Downing understood the importance of the new style and how very well it suited the mood that permeated the art, literature, and music of his time. He wrote:

> It addresses itself more to the feelings and the senses and less to the reason and judgment than the Grecian style, and it is capable of a variety of expression quite unknown to the architecture of the five orders. Hence, we think it far better suited to symbolize the variety of refined culture and accomplishment which belongs to modern civilization than almost any other style.

In presenting his first Italianate, Downing introduced the style with some reluctance, but he warmed to it as his work progressed:

As a rural style, expressing country life, the Italian is inferior to pointed and high-roofed modes. If it is not so essentially country-like in character, it is, however, remarkable for expressing the elegant culture and variety of accomplishment of the retired citizen or man of the world, and as it is capable of the most varied and irregular as well as very simple outlines, it is also very significant of the multiform tastes, habits, and wants of modern civilization. On the whole, then, we should say that the Italian style is one that expresses not wholly the spirit of country life nor of town life, but something between both, and which is a mingling of both.

Downing describes his villa in the Italian Style:

The leading features of this style are familiar to most of our readers. Roof rather flat and projecting upon brackets or cantilevers; windows of various forms, but with massive dressings, frequently running into the round arch, when the opening is an important one (and always permitting the use of the outside Venetian blinds [shutters]); arcades supported on arches or verandas with simple columns, and chimney-tops of characteristic and tasteful forms. Above all, when the composition is irregular, rises the campanile or Italian tower, bringing all into unity and giving picturesqueness, or an expression of power and elevation, to the whole composition.

Downing describes his villa as a modest country dwelling. To modern sensibilities the house seems huge. On the first floor is a porch, a closet, a kitchen, a separate scullery and separate pantry, a dining hall, a library, a drawing room, a veranda, and a vestibule. The second floor consists of a bath, a dressing room, two closets, and five bedrooms. (The bath and the closets were unusual at the time.) No mention is made of any use given to the third floor of the tower. Downing estimated that if the villa were built of brick and stucco, it would cost $4,600. In cheap-lumber districts, it might cost $3,800. In the 1840's it was a very expensive house.

By the late 1850's, therefore, three styles of architecture were alive and competing in America. The Greek Revival style was by no means out of the race, although criticism was mounting, not only from the proponents of the newer styles, but from Classical purists who never seemed satisfied with a capital, column, pediment, or molding and who found fault and error in every new structure.

The Gothic revival builders, for their part, were suffering from the elitist image, the cost, and the building difficulties inherent in the intricacy of the style.

The Italianate, finally, was direct and simple but capable of handling almost any amount of decoration (as later examples proved). The style had a fine dignity, yet expressed a comfortable and democratic informality; its origins were Classical; still, the Italianate qualified admirably as a Picturesque expression. It seemed the ideal architecture for democratic, Romantic America.

The Greek Revival style did not survive the Civil War. The style had passed the zenith of its popularity in the north by the late 1840's, and the ruined economy of the South precluded any future building in the style. The last building of note built within the time span allotted to the original Greek Revival period was the San Francisco Mint, begun in 1867 and completed in 1874. The residential Gothic style, never a front-runner in terms of popularity, passed into obscurity in the 1860's. In ecclesiastical and in collegiate architecture, the Gothic style lasted well into the twentieth century, with elements of the style sometimes incorporated in the most contemporary church buildings.

The Italianate, already by the 1850's a prevailing form, was to attain greater ascendancy in the decades to come. Symbolism had undergone a change. The Greek Revival style specifically evoked Liberty, and the Gothic,

Faith. With the Italianate, it was understood that architecture was to invoke not an idea, but a *mood*. Nothing specific or overt—just a mood—perhaps prompted by nebulous historical allusions.

The early Romantic era architecture incorporated interior accouterments that reflected the nature of the exterior. The Temple Style brought with it the Empire style of furniture—as Greek as the houses themselves—and the Gothic Revivals housed Gothic furniture, which, with quatrefoils, trefoils, cusps, pendants, and finials, echoed the character of the house itself. Furniture in the 1860's broke with architecture and took on a life of its own that somehow nevertheless contrived to blend harmoniously with the Italianate. The formal name for the highly decorated, curvaceous furniture is "Victorian Rococo Revival." The style is better known as simply "Victorian" and has had a remarkable revival of its own in the late twentieth century. A good John Henry Belter piece of Victorian Rococo Revival now sells for more than a good-sized house sold for in the 1850's.

Art historians trace the Italianate movement through a number of phases, and some segment the general style into substyles such as North Italian Renaissance and High Victorian Italianate. The broad acceptance of the style and its longevity produced so many variations that categorizing the miscellaneous themes destroys the straightforward and easily identifiable character of the Italianate. The late-Italianate style is more baroque, more decorated, and more intricate than the earlier style, but the natural evolution of every style parallels the Italianate progression.

Often the earliest examples of a style remain the finest. The temptation to embellish, to caricature, to exaggerate, and to push elements of a style beyond the limits of practical or aesthetic judgment cause a style to sicken and die. The kind of Italianate that Charles Addams made into a symbol of eerie obsolescence, with iron cresting, varicolored slates, and a wind-whipped campanile, represents the final phase of the style as the assimilation of Louis XIV and other unsuitable elements transformed the Italianate into a commercial burlesque of a once-honest design.

If one visualizes the front of a big-city brownstone as one side of a campanile, it becomes obvious that these town houses are Italianate. Brackets support projecting eaves, the roofs are flat, the windows arcuated, and the *consoles* (ornamental brackets of compound curve that support the overhang of a doorway) are baroque. The Italianate brownstone replaced Federal town houses. In the 1860's and '70's, at a time when the need for city housing was growing at an unprecedented rate, the style was fashionable and, because of its relative simplicity, was suited to mass production. Hundreds of thousands were built in cities large and small, and the differences among the houses were generally confined to interiors and to width. Height rarely varied—four stories was the norm. Buildings that looked Italianate but were taller and more massive were built as tenements, not town houses. The Italianate brownstones were wood framed, brick sided, and surfaced at the front with brown sandstone or with brown-stained imitation masonry in stucco. (Stucco is usually thought to be a highly textured surface, but it is actually any cement-plastered surface.)

One of the great advantages of the brownstone row house is that the longest sides of the dwelling share the walls of neighbors, resulting in minimal heat loss. If the climate is not severe and if a brownstone dweller chooses to victimize his neighbor, play the parasite, and wear thermal underwear, it is actually possible to get through a mild winter without providing one's own heat. Likewise, during the hottest of summers, that same sandwiched house can be maintained at reasonable temperatures by its adjoining air-conditioned neighbors. The prototype brownstones have only one set of outside stairs, which serve the upper levels. The ground floor is served by its own ground-level or below-ground-level doorway set beneath the balustered main stairway. In the original town house, the below-level ground floor was a kitchen, a dining room, and a pantry, while the shallow top floor, the only floor without fireplaces, provided generally uncomfortable quarters for servants. The heat that drifted up from the lower floors was deemed adequate for the domestics above. Owners usually furnished the second floors as a parlor and a library. The next two floors were bedrooms, baths, etc. An 1859 brownstone was often 14 feet, 6 inches in width. By 1879, 16 feet, 8 inches was a standard width. Twenty feet was considered a maximum span.

Because of the economics of the 1980's, owners of brownstones often live in the first or first two floors and rent out the rest. The top two floors can accommodate up to four separate studio apartments. A brownstone floor-through on the East Side of Manhattan rents at $2,400 a month, and a single room can command $1,800. A brownstone town house that sold for $30,000 in 1950 sold for $500,000 in 1980 and for $1,100,000 in 1988. The original cost, depending on the quality of the interior, was probably as low as $1,600 exclusive of land.

Of all the brownstones in New York City, I chose to paint the lonely one in plate 25. On the extreme right is an Italianate that has been denatured with a textured stucco and stripped of all the Italian features. Between it and our brownstone is some designer's idea of modern architecture of the late 1940's, possibly influenced by the paintings of Piet Mondrian. Behind are the ubiquitous 1970's office buildings.

The word "chauvinism" derives from a soldier named Nicholas Chauvin, whose highly exaggerated devotion to Emperor Napoleon, even after Napoleon's exile and loss of public support, led to the derisive character given the term through a series of 1830's vaudeville skits. The word *campanilismo* has a similar connotation. The cost of building a campanile placed a burden on an Italian community. Those who felt compelled to build ever-taller campaniles, for purposes of prestige or in competition with rival towns, were scornfully termed *campanilismi*. In the post-Civil War years, the spirit of campanilismo jumped the Atlantic, and

American campanilismi built ever-taller campaniles. In time the practice was recognized as conspicuous display and contributed to the arsenal of jokes that bring about the downfall of any style, be it in architecture or Edsels. For all the expressiveness of the campanile and its contributions to the cause of the Picturesque, it at last fell victim to a new reasoning that saw the towers as excessive, impractical, uneconomical, and pretentious. For a while the campanile would be combined with the Mansard (or Second Empire) style, as in the impressive Waverly, New York, house shown in plate 38, but increasingly, the country Italianate was built in the Cube Style, eliminating the campanile.

An Italianate in Washington, D.C. before and after the wrecker's ball

From "Riverside," the original Italianate villa built overlooking the Delaware River in 1832, to the High Victorian Italianates, the style lasted more than sixty years. No other nineteenth-century style came close to that tenure. Unfortunately Italianates seem a favorite target of the wrecker's ball. Greek Revivals are less prone to destruction. They still inspire respect and convey a patriotic impression of the Early Republic. Gothic dwellings, now a rarity, are regarded as precious antiques. Italianates, however, now too often associated with the inner-city blight, are unprotected by notions of history, patriotism, or religion. To younger generations it seems inconceivable that the Italianates were ever thought attractive. Only the campaniled mansions hold any fascination for the young, and then only when seen through the eyes of Charles Addams or Alfred Hitchcock.

At the end of a late September afternoon, when the last golden rays of sunlight pass windows that reach to the floor and cast the deep, undulating shadows of rich, ornate brackets, the Italianates are at their romantic best. Their interiors, with easy access to the outdoors, baroque marble fireplaces, high, medallioned ceilings, and mahogany or rosewood newel posts, still create a charm and warmth that succeeding styles have failed to match.

Italianate Brownstone

What was once a row of brownstone Italianate town houses on Third Avenue in midtown Manhattan has now been reduced to a single representative of the style. The blue glass and stainless-steel restaurant, reminiscent of a Mondrian painting, is all that is left of the brownstone's original companions. The building at the far right is so denatured as to have lost all contact with its origins. The skyscrapers that surround intimidate the lesser buildings. They seem to cower in the shadows.

The dynamics of a great city generate great change, and today we are witnessing the beginnings of a new sensitivity towards architectural compatibility. The nationwide acceptance of the glass-sided skyscrapers of the International Style played havoc with any conception of neighborhood harmony. New York's Park Avenue has suffered from the insensitive juxtaposition of fifty-story glazed grids with, among others, Renaissance Revival buildings. There are glorious exceptions. Somehow the Seagram Building is scaled to be comfortable with its neighbors, and Lever House has a two-story adjunct in contemporary style which happily separates it from its Classical compatriots. Most of the Park Avenue contemporary constructions,

Plate 25   *Italianate Brownstone*

however, have so little in common with the architecture around them that the composition has become unsettling.

On other Manhattan avenues, where entire blocks of earlier construction have been replaced by glass skyscrapers, the results have clearly shown a dehumanization of the area, and even the most ardent proponents of Mies van der Rohe's architecture admit that the imitators of that genius have done a disservice to architecture and a greater disservice to the people who must survive in those forbidding surroundings. Philip Johnson, for one, has shown sensitivity to the challenge of joining our past with the present. It will be fascinating and, I hope, rewarding to watch what may happen in our cities as new construction is expected to harmonize with old.

Although the windows of the Third Avenue brownstone are not arcuated, the bracketed moldings above the windows provide the curve essential to the Italianate style. The projecting eaves, supported by robust brackets, are unmistakable hallmarks of the Italianate. The brackets were occasionally masonry, but more often they were fashioned from sheet copper or other malleable metals to reduce their weight. The brownstone is easily identified as an Italianate. The face of the building is essentially one side of an Italian bell tower—a campanile.

It still comes as a surprise to remember that trees and ivy survive in the tiny plots of unsurfaced soil behind the 1880's brownstones.

High Street Italianate

The word villa originally described a large Italianate mansion on its own estate. In time the term came to denote any detached dwelling used as a summer retreat so long as there was some Italianate identification. Some early English and American examples indicate that the style, which freed planners from the restraints of symmetry, was an excuse to indulge in exotic excursions. These excursions resulted in the loss of any connection with the Italianate except the picturesque aspect of the style. An outstanding example of such an excursion into fantasy is P. T. Barnum's "Iranistan," built in Bridgeport, Connecticut, in 1847. The Italianate form overcame the limitations imposed by previous styles and led to Picturesque Romanticism—a theme which would persist throughout the Romantic era.

In theory the Italianate form was adopted because of its adaptability to varied natural settings. In England the asymmetric masses of the mode were eminently suited to the picturesque landscapes, sometimes created especially for a villa. America abounded in picturesque settings that seemed ready-made as settings for the style. Soon the Italianate became stylish, and successful examples were simply copied and built without regard to how well the style might suit its surroundings. By the 1870's the Italianate style embraced every possible type of structure from the detached villa to the urban brownstone to the elegant town house of the painting, part of which is shown here.

High Street, Newark, New Jersey, angles off the city's main street and ends in a mile or so at the New Jersey Institute of Technology. The leading families of Newark

Plate 26   *High Street Italianate*

once made their homes here. Some of the houses were spectacular. The Krueger mansion has a five-story tower, but its marble fireplaces are being stolen, and its future is bleak; indeed, the mansion is a source of anguish to those citizens who have worked so hard to bring Newark back to its former status as New Jersey's number-one city.

The house in the painting remains and is occupied, but many of its neighbors have been victims of arson, vandalism, foreclosure, and neglect. The interior of the High Street Italianate is typical of its style: high ceilings, white marble fireplaces with butterfly mantels, sliding doors, rich moldings, and inlaid floors give the interior its Victorian pedigree, while the arcuated doorway and windows, the columns, and the flat projecting eaves of the porch complete the Italianate effect. The decorations along the balustrade and under the eaves relate to no particular style, but they are undeniably Victorian and would be so costly to duplicate that replacement of them is out of the question. Any substitution or elimination of those ornaments would denature the entire structure.

Italianate Tuscan Villa

I could hardly ask for a better example of a modest Tuscan villa than the one I found in Plainfield, New Jersey. The campanile is ingeniously handled so that the topmost segment suggests a belvedere. It is a well-designed building with carefully related decorative elements that contribute to a picturesque outline and an integrated whole. The house would look as comfortable on a dozen acres as it does in its suburban setting.

The little window in the frieze below the eaves is in colonial houses called an "eyebrow window" and is usually bottom hinged to open inward. It is an unusual feature in an Italianate. The paired windows in the gable are arcuated, and the horizontal, bracketed eaves that stop short of the windows are called "returns." The siding has been replaced and the porte cochere simplified, but the house is otherwise as it was built in the 1870's, with some flowing elements that were in advance of its time. I refer to the joining of the second-floor gable window frames that flow into the roof of the bay window and the stepped integration of the gable end of the house with the campanile and the end of the house at the left. Windows of the bay are trabeated, but the arch connecting the pilasters in the bay conveys the sense of arcuation. The finial over the arcuated eaves is crowned by the topmost element called an epi. (Finials and epis often appear in crossword puzzles.)

Because of the long tenure of the style, Italianate houses are difficult to date. It began in America with Bishop Doane's "Riverside" in 1832 and continued in favor until the late 1880's. In the eighties the popularity of the detached house in the Italianate mode faded, but the enthusiasm for the Italianate big-city brownstone was just about at its peak. Through all those years the style variations remained quite constant, with the Cube Style and the simplified forms gaining preference over the irregularly massed forms that featured campaniles.

The last Italianates to be built are the most sought after today. For one thing they are smaller and so more convenient than their predecessors. The exteriors are simpler, with ornamentation concentrated on brackets and generous window dressing. The first-story windows that reach to the floor, three or four marble fireplaces, high ceilings, parquet floors, ceiling rosettes, generous moldings at doorways and windows, hot-air ducts and registers ideal for the most advanced pulse-jet gas furnaces, and the presence of trees in full maturity all contribute to the value of such residences.

Plate 27
Italianate Tuscan Villa

Hunterdon County Cube Style

The green of the roof is the oxide of copper—a cherished color in parts of the country, though the oxidation process is slow. When copper roofs are newly completed, the red-orange deepening to browns and black is not the most harmonious of hues, especially when combined with brick. Solutions are applied to hasten oxidation, but the acids can seep into crevices and weaken the roof's seams. Patience and air pollution do the best job.

The standing-seam roof of the house in the painting has become a rarity in domestic building in the northeast, but in Maryland and Virginia it is still a viable roofing choice. In most instances aluminum, painted white, has superseded the traditional copper. For farm buildings the standing-seam roof is still almost universal. A composition-shingle roof may last thirty years, but a copper standing-seam roof is good for seventy to ninety years.

A Cube Style Italianate differs from the earlier Italianate in that it is chiefly symmetrical, lacking the campanile or other masses intended to produce picturesque asymmetry. The style almost always includes a belvedere—Italian for beautiful view—or cupola. The painting illustrates a belvedere, as the structure is large enough for human occupation. The Victorian builders meant the belvedere to be used for viewing, and it was with pride that the owner of a house invited guests to enjoy the view from his housetop. In Neshanic Station, New Jersey, a cube Italianate's belvedere once housed a mother-of-pearl-inlaid billiard table, indicating that the structure was provided with heat as well as a vista.

The curved break in the roofline is called a "segmental arch," and while it may harbor a rounded window, it was designed to please the eye. The round-topped windows gave rise to still another name for the Italianate: the "Round Style."

Plate 28   *Hunterdon County Cube Style*

VII. The Octagon Style
A Classical House in a Romantic Era

THE STORY OF NINETEENTH-CENTURY American architecture would be less colorful without the Octagon Style. For one thing the style represented rebellion. At almost dead center of the Romantic mood in America, this Classical expression rose to challenge the Romantic, Gothic, and Italianate modes of building. And, excluding the tepee, the hogan, and other forms of the original Americans, the Octagon was the first genuine style of architecture "made in America."

Many octagonal structures were built before the Octagon Style became a style. Palladio built octagonal wings on his neoclassical structures. James Gibbs designed a three-story octagonal addition in the early eighteenth-century Twickenham-on-Thames, near the home of the literary arch-Classicist Alexander Pope and not far from Horace Walpole's "Strawberry Hill."

In England a late-seventeenth-century octagonal cottage survives in lush greenery (plate 29). The picturesque thatched roof and Gothic details are not at all what the author of the American Octagon Style had in mind, however. In colonial America the Dutch built an octagonal trading post in 1630, while in 1714 an eight-sided arsenal was built in Williamsburg. Thomas Jefferson designed "Poplar Forest" as a mansion in the octagon form.

The style, which became a rage in the 1850's, was the inspiration of a remarkable American, Orson Squire Fowler (1809–1887). A famed phrenologist and lecturer on a wide range of subjects, Fowler was born in upstate New York. At Amherst College, he became a classmate of Henry Ward Beecher, another intellectual adventurer. Fowler's posthumous fame rests chiefly in his book titled *The Octagon House: A Home for All*.

Much has been written of Fowler. He was considered one of America's leading eccentrics. There is a lot

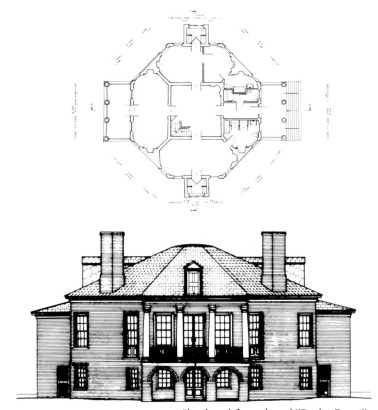

Sketch and floor plan of "Poplar Forest"

of eccentricity in those who have written about him as well, for the accounts of his life vary widely. One account insists that he started his own publishing company when he learned that the publisher of his original book on the pseudoscience of phrenology earned more than its author. The firm, Fowler and Wells, attracted few authors, however, and in desperation, so the story goes, Fowler wrote his *Home for All*. In light of the innovative and technologically advanced ideas set forth in his book, however, it seems unlikely that Fowler produced the work as filler.

Beyond the central theme of the octagon as a shape favored by nature, Fowler offered his readers many forms of advice. Houses of the forties and fifties had no closets as such. Yet the octagon, said Fowler, had natural closets in the triangular sections left over from squared rooms within the octagonal form. His plans called for rooms that would accommodate standard-sized rugs, and he embraced the use of glass as a natural roofing and flooring material. Fowler also advocated fresh air and ventilation, a novel suggestion in its time.

A Home for All had a powerful influence on the young and adventurous. Fowler's mathematical assurances that an octagon contains a fifth more room than a square of comparable size really concerned economy: much more space can be contained with fewer bricks in an octagon plan than in a square. An octagon presents more surfaces to be warmed by sunlight than a square or rectangle. Fowler's book argued that steps were to be saved in that geometric form.

In Fowler's own home, in Fishkill-on-the-Hudson, New York, built in the octagon form of "gravel and grouting" (concrete), the author further scandalized the community by including at least one flush toilet under the stairway in the hundred-room house. He defended the invention in an oft-quoted passage concerning squeamish maidens and their beaux who preferred the rigors of al fresco conveniences.

Despite the modern ideas that Fowler poured into his home, the house had an unhappy history. The speaking tubes, the dumb waiters, the two gymnasiums, the solarium, and the more-or-less central heating didn't add up to what the homeowner of the time was looking for. Debts forced Fowler to sell at great loss to his daughter, who sold the house to a school for young military aspirants. In turn it was sold to a girl's school and finally to a woman who had hopes of making it into a boarding house. Sadly, she had the same name as a notorious murderess, and there were few applicants for her establishment. A typhoid epidemic caused by seepage from a gravel-and-grouting cesspool into a gravel-and-grouting well, and a reputation for ghosts, finally spelled finish for Fowler's dream. The authorities in Fishkill ordered it destroyed. One writer enthusiastically claimed that it

took a hundred cases of dynamite to raze the place. More recent reports indicate a single charge brought the house down from its ninety-foot height. A house meant to stand for generations lasted just forty-nine years.

Yet for those young and venturesome souls, Orson Squire Fowler's ideas made sense. His octagonal plans mocked elaborate architectural detail, which the brave new generation of the 1850's found excessive. There were plenty of arguments in defense of the style: the octagon adapts to a central stairwell to give easy access to all parts of the house; the octagon never has cross lights and has no hallway to encourage drafts; the central chimney radiates even heat. One argument Fowler never espoused—although he might have—concerned the aerodynamics of the octagon. Years ago a Sunday rotogravure section displayed an aerial view of blocks of houses leveled by a tornado. The lone survivor was an octagon.

Orson Squire Fowler's one-hundred-room Octagon home in Fishkill, New York

A Home for All went into nine editions and inspired the building of schools, factories, churches, and barns in the octagon, hexagon, dodecagon, or circular form. The octagon shape itself seems to have intrigued the public. Octagon gazebos, mourning houses, and bandstands dotted the landscape. The octagon gazebo in plate 30 was a gift to Mark Twain from his sister-in-law. It stood at the head of the Chemung Valley near Elmira, New York. Twain loved it. While writing *Huckleberry Finn* he could watch great storms gathering and booming in the hills. Twain's gazebo now resides at Elmira College.

The story of the Octagon Style is hardly complete without noting the anomalous turn of the octagon tide. What Fowler had in mind was the form-follows-function house shown in plate 31. This pure Octagon was built for the postmaster of Hackettstown, New Jersey, at the waning of the style. The house is straightforward and unadorned except for decorative balusters. An additional chimney at the side, to accommodate a fireplace, is the only alteration to the house since its building. In the yard the kiln which made the bricks still exists.

The house cost $450 in 1865, more than a hundred times less than its value today and inexpensive even in its own time. Fowler had envisioned a "home for all" and clearly succeeded in realizing his vision. He was a true sympathizer of the common man and was one of the first to direct his efforts toward that audience rather than exclusively toward the American gentry. Indeed, his choice of editor for his firm, also a man of the people, verifies his intentions, for it was none other than Ralph Waldo Emerson.

Given its author's democratic instincts and intentions, the Octagon Style had a strange development. Those who could afford to do so built their Octagons in the Romantic style. The wealthy and fashionable were inextricably caught in the mood of their times, and though attracted to the new form of building, they built in a fashion suited to contemporary feelings. Excesses were encouraged by the 1852 book of architect Samuel Sloane, who, steeped in Romanticism, proposed the Octagon as an oriental villa. The result was, among others, "Longwood," at Natchez, Mississippi. It is Romantic in every sense—totally decorated and impressively domed in Islamic flamboyance. It can best be described as an architectural confection with oriental yearnings.

More restrained, but handsomely Romantic, the Armour–Stiner house, in Irvington-on-Hudson, New York, is better known as the "Bonnet House" (plate 32). This domed Octagon has seen some pleasant and timely alterations over the years. The porch and window treatments show Italianate influences, and there is some sur-

An example of the effect of the Romantic style on classic Octagon expression

face Stick Style decoration. The enormous bonnet now sports a steel cable that engages the circumference of the dome at its base. Every month the Bonnet House's present owner, restoration architect Joseph Pell Lombardi, takes a few turns in the cable's turnbuckle to inch the base back to its original spread. It's only one of the many labors in restoring the house, recently saved from ruin by the National Trust for Historic Preservation.

Before the Lombardis and before the National Trust, the house was owned by Carl Carmer. His books on the Hudson River area are twentieth-century classics. Carmer loved his Bonnet House and wrote lovingly of it, of Orson Squire Fowler, and of the beautiful French Lady whose ghost still haunts the grounds in Irvington.

The Octagon Style was born out of its time, yet it has survived to be valued once again. In an energy-concerned age, Fowler's Octagons are, in Bauhaus terminology, efficient machines for shelter. Fowler himself survived his debts, married three times, and went on to write books on marriage, sex, and tight corseting (to which he was opposed). His book entitled *Matrimony; or Phrenology and Physiology Applied to the Selection of Congenial Companions for Life* contained the following epigraph: "Natural waists or no wives." After his death the firm of Fowler and Wells limped on, producing periodicals and journals on phrenology. The company lasted into the twentieth century, where it bumped into the realities of a new Classical era. The rising generation ridiculed the occult and the pseudosciences. Fowler's contributions to the rethinking of the American home were forgotten, and he was relegated to the dustheap of crackpots and charlatans.

Since the 1960's and the swing to another Romantic mood, the occult, science fiction, and the pseudosciences have once again flourished. Incredibly, people seem genuinely delighted with the lore of Capricorns and Virgos. In 1970, Fowler's book on phrenology was reprinted in a handsome oversized edition, and again people seem concerned about sloping foreheads and amative lobes. At the same time the writings of preservationists and architectural historians have placed Fowler in a more favorable perspective. *A Home for All* is recognized as a remarkable forerunner of ideas that are only now reaching maturity.

In the simplicity of its original conception, the Octagon Style was more Classic than Romantic. Orson Squire Fowler was not the only Classic holdout in the midst of the Romantic era.

Horatio Greenough's sculpture of George Washington in Roman garb. Formerly located on the East Plaza in Washington, D.C., it is now in the basement of the Smithsonian.

Horatio Greenough (1805–1852) was the neo-Classical sculptor who is credited with the creation of the term "form follows function." Greenough championed that philosophy, yet it was he who sculpted George Washington in a Roman toga. His defense was that he had likened General Washington to Cincinnatus, who had deserted the plow to lead his country in war. The Classicist Greenough forgot that looking backward to recreate the past is a very Romantic action.

English Octagon

I have no information on the origins of this colorful English thatched Octagon. It may have originally served as an oast, or kiln, for hops. The Gothic windows give no indication of its age: because of the unbroken tradition of the Gothic in England, it is not certain whether the Gothic element is of the revival age or older. The friend who kindly gave me the photograph from which I made the painting, thinks the Octagon is somewhere between Surrey and Essex. The English people have long had a penchant

Plate 29   *English Octagon*

beams, the rough bricks and braces, and the wooden planked floors are appealing to a generation confined to the slick, untextured, unnatural materials of a plastic culture. The spaciousness of lofts and warehouses, the unaffected colors of old brick and massive timbers pierced by tie rods headed with bolts of epic proportion—all these elements are reminders of the energies of nineteenth-century Americans.

On a less monumental scale, carriage houses, barns, and other agricultural outbuildings have found reuse as residences. Again, interior structural members are exposed to give warmth and texture to interiors that fifty years ago would have been disguised beyond all recognition.

Elmira Gazebo

The structure in the painting can hardly qualify as a house; it is an enclosed gazebo meant to resemble a steamboat's pilot house. It was built to be a study for Mark Twain by his sister-in-law, on her farm near Elmira, New York. The gazebo was a perfect gift. Twain spent some of his happiest and most creative hours in its snug confines. The little Octagon was built in 1874 on a hillside overlooking the grand Chemung Valley. Twain loved to watch flashing storms rumble up the valley and relished the cozy security of his hideaway as the winds lashed all about him. At least parts of Huckleberry Finn *and* Tom Sawyer *were* written here.

The eaves decorations somehow allude to the Gothic. The same treatment is seen on whistle-stop railroad stations, bandstands, and other small buildings of the late nineteenth century. The Stick Style ornamentation beneath the windows are called cross bucks. The beveling on the sticks is called a stop chamfer—*a widely used finishing effect. Corner brackets groove into corner posts terminating as finials. The brackets are open to suggest the Stick Style. Every detail is lovingly finished, and the Octagon shows the high state of carpentry at the time. In 1962 Twain's*

for the picturesque, the arcane, and the eccentric. This trait has stood them in good stead, as their carefully maintained follies, shams, and antiquities are never-failing attractions for tourists.

The adaptation of buildings originally meant for industry or agriculture by transforming them into residences and places of business is relatively new in America. Seaport cities from Portland, Maine, to Charleston, South Carolina, have made abandoned warehouses and textile mills into attractive, income-producing business sites. Shops, restaurants, schools, and offices occupy areas that lay idle for decades. The "honesty" of huge exposed

Plate 30 *Elmira Gazebo*

gazebo was moved to the campus of Elmira College.

Mark Twain was a fine craftsman with a genius for cutting through cant and hyperbole. He used his satirical talents most cuttingly on the lecture platform and punctured many a Romantic/Victorian dogma. Huckleberry Finn was Twain's street-wise spokesman, speaking in Classic realism. The windbag preacher, the parvenu, and the quack all fell before Twain's pen. Things Gothic were a special target. Huck Finn simply could not understand the pleasures of Romantic sorrow or sentimentality. He had experienced too much brutal tragedy to enjoy the luxury of sorrow or the pleasures of mourning.

By the 1880's, at the height of Twain's career as the nation's leading writer and lecturer, the demise of the Romantic era was in the wind. Twain contributed to the demise with what was recognized as a fresh and clear vision of conventions and responses that had become stale, pompous, overblown, and meaningless. Every age, every mood breeds its iconoclasts. Samuel Clemens and Charles Dickens were the nineteenth century's best.

The Octagon House

This Hackettstown, New Jersey, house is precisely the house that Orson Squire Fowler had in mind when he wrote The Octagon House, A Home For All. *In fact his book has an illustration of the house so close to the house in the painting that it is almost certain the carpenter-builder followed the illustration exactly. Sometime later on the chimney at the left of the house was added to accommodate a fireplace in the parlor. Late for the style, the house was built in 1865 for the postmaster of the crossroads town. The bricks were made in a kiln on the lot.*

Brick was only one of the materials used in construction of the Octagons. Houses were built of stone walls covered with stucco, of board-and-batten siding, of rusticated stone, of gravel and grouting—and in Madison, New York, a Classically detailed Octagon is built of cobblestones.

In recommending gravel-and-grouting wall construction, Fowler was scornful of bricks. "A proud English lord [he wrote] spent an immense sum in erecting a magnificent manorial mansion, and invited another noble lord to examine, and say what he thought of it—proud to exhibit his riches and his taste. As his opinion was solicited, the visitor replied: 'Well done for a mud house.'"

In defense of gravel and grouting, Fowler wrote:

In 1850 near Jaynesville, Wisconsin, I saw houses built wholly of lime, mixed with coarse gravel and sand found in banks on the western prairies and underlying all prairie soil. I visited a house put up by Mr. Goodrich, the original discoverer of this mode of building, and found his walls as hard as stone itself, and harder than brick walls. I pounded them with a hammer, and examined them thoroughly till fully satisfied as to their solidity and strength. Mr. Goodrich offered to allow me to strike with a sledge, as hard as I pleased, upon the inside of his parlor walls for six cents a blow, which he said would repair all damages.

What Mr. Goodrich had reinvented was concrete of a sort. In 1872 an English mason invented Portland cement, which is the binding material in modern concrete.

The chapter devoted to the Octagon Style made allusion to squeamish maidens who resisted indoor plumbing. Having just submitted the case for and an explanation of the function and the functioning of an indoor water closet to be placed under the stairs of his Octagon house, Orson Squire Fowler wrote:

To squeamish maidens and fastidious beaux, these points are not submitted, but matrons, the aged and the feeble, are asked, is not such a closet a real household necessity and a luxury? Yet it need to be used only in cases of special need, the one generally used being outside, as usual.

Plate 31   *The Octagon House*

Plate 32   *Romantic Octagon*

Romantic Octagon

Unlike most of the houses in Portraits of American Architecture, *the Armour–Stiner house is a famous example of its kind and it is discussed in the chapter on the Octagon Style. The Octagon form in America was meant to be a form-follows-function Classical house with a minimum of ornamentation and strict observance of Classical dogma. The Octagon was born in a time when most Americans were feeling the influences of Romanticism and were building in the Italianate, Mansard, or Gothic Revival forms. The Octagon form appealed to daring builders who wanted to step away from consensus expressions to declare individuality. At almost dead center of the Romantic tenure the modest "Home for All" had made its debut. What can happen to an idea born out of its time is illustrated by the subject of the painting.*

A Statement of Significance for this building from the Historic American Buildings Survey (HABS No. N.Y.-5620) has this to say about the Armour–Stiner house:

> In addition to eclectically incorporating Gothic, Stick Style, Second Empire and Eastlake detail, this house is one of the two domed octagonal residences in the United States. Its siting, design and heating-plumbing systems reflect the contemporary mid-19th century architectural philosophies of Orson Squire Fowler, noted phrenologist, sexologist, amateur architect and author of the popular The Octagon House: A Home for All.

The significant statement omitted was that the Armour–Stiner house was, unlike other Octagons, a Romantic Octagon: the dome, a monumental addition, was not a simple, straightforward roofing solution, nor was eclecticism acceptable to Classical tenets.

Recent investigations have indicated that the original house was an Octagon two stories high with undecorated sides and a cupola-crowned eight-sided Mansard roof. Paul J. Armour, a banker and broker, was its first occupant in 1860. In 1872 Joseph Stiner, a Hungarian tea merchant, bought the house and added the dome and present cupola. It is conjectured that Stiner's tea-trade connection with oriental imagery may have inspired the dome, but some credit for its construction must be given to the Romantic eclectic mood into which it was born.

The Armour–Stiner house is popularly known as the "Bonnet House" and is in close proximity to Washington Irving's "Sunnyside" and A. J. Davis's fabulous "Lyndhurst."

Vermont Octagon

In search of the circular schoolhouse in Brookline, Vermont, I came on the unusual winged octagon in the painting. The far wing is a duplicate of the structure nearest the viewer. I can only guess that it was intended to be a form of a New England continuing barn with living quarters in the octagonal section. I have never met anyone who knew of the place, and I sometimes think I dreamed it, but I like to believe it belongs to a young family who needs plenty of room to spread out.

The variations developed on the Octagon form are impressive, given the ten short years the style was in vogue. At least a thousand Octagon houses were built in that period, along with dodecagons, churches, barns, and schoolhouses. The ideas put forth by Fowler's book, which started it all, had a lasting effect on American home builders, although as in the case of Mr. Fowler's 1848 water closets, the ideas took time to catch on. Forty-one years later, in 1889, The White House installed a single bathroom. Speaking tubes, hot-air furnaces, and dumb-waiters eventually became commonplace, but glass as a roofing and flooring material—advocated by Fowler—had little acceptance in residential building circles.

A section of The Octagon House is titled "Comparative Beauty of the Gothic, Square and Octagon Forms." In that section Fowler makes a comparison of human forms with architectural forms and presents the modern reader with a very different idea of beauty than today's ideal of super-slender human forms. He asks, "Why is it that a poor animal or a lean person is more homely than the same animal or person when fleshy?" In the same vein, and in an obvious reference to the Gothic, he continues, "For one, I cannot consider cottages or wings handsome. They always strike me as unsightly and well-nigh deformed." He further describes a Gothic cottage roof as "full of sharp peaks sticking out in all directions." These pronouncements are all in defense of the ideal spherical form, which Fowler claimed was approached by the Octagon. In his references to wings Fowler was referring to any style that used the square as the essential form in building. He concluded his defense of the Octagon in favor of other styles with the following:

> Since, then, the octagon form is more beautiful as well as capacious, and more consonant with the predominant or governing form of Nature—the spherical—it deserves consideration.

Plate 33   Vermont Octagon

Murray Hill Octagon

Fowler's The Octagon House, A Home for All (*1848*) did more than promote a form of architecture. In many ways it projected the prevalent spirit in contemporary America. Permanency was essential to the American dream of the time:

Let others [wrote Fowler] spend their money on balls, rides, fashions, etc., but let me expend mine on home, in annually adorning and improving it, till in life's decline, I shall have erected for myself and family A PERFECT HOME; surrounded by as many means of

Plate 34   *Murray Hill Octagon*

comfort and even luxury as possible, my land rich, trees yearly loaded with every variety of the choicest fruits, and provided with every thing conducive to beauty, utility, and comfort.

Fowler felt his book would be incomplete without an essay each on greenhouses, shade trees (he insisted they bred mosquitoes), fruit trees, strawberries, black and red raspberries, blue and whortle berries, cherries, peaches, apricots, plums, pears, and apples, most of which he approved. His book also held some strange notions. He wrote: "The ruins of Pompeii contain only two houses (and those of rulers) above one-story high—humanity then being little developed." And he maintained that the true builder was one who was endowed with strong phrenological organs of Inhabitiveness and of Constructiveness.

In Murray Hill, a section of New Providence, New Jersey, the space-age Bell Laboratories dominate the landscape, but nearby a complete mid-nineteenth-century village was planned to house a variety of shops. Today it is called Historic Murray Hill Village, although its history is limited to a decade or so. Nevertheless it was built with integrity and authenticity and is a joy to anyone interested in nineteenth-century architecture. Near the center of the village is one of the newest buildings—an 1850's Octagon house complete with central chimney and eight-sided belvedere. It was adapted from a Chenango County, New York, Octagon. As Octagons go it is of good size. The smallest Octagons are of pre-Fowler vintage—law offices and other nonresidential buildings. The smallest residential building inspired by Fowler is a one-story circa-1870 house in Syracuse, New York. The sides are ten feet by ten feet.

Excluding the two existing domed Octagons, the largest house in the form was built in Watertown, Wisconsin, in 1854. For some time it was the largest residence in the state. The triangles resulting from laying out squared rooms within the octagonal perimeter were large enough to accommodate bedrooms. The two most acute angles of the triangles became closets, which were unusual features in those days.

Round Schoolhouse

Octagon, dodecagon, and round structures are labeled by many architectural historians as "eccentric," even though the principles behind the forms are sound. Like good antiques, Octagons survive in surprising numbers, and round barns are regarded as treasures. While not exactly eccentric, the round schoolhouse of the painting certainly has an unusual raison d'etre.

The schoolhouse was built by the town fathers of Brookline, Vermont, at the suggestion of one Dr. John Wilson, who had come on their rather remote scene in 1821. (Orson Squire Fowler, prophet of the Octagon Style, was eleven years old.) Wilson was a tall and imposing figure of obvious education who was said to have arrived from Boston. Although he was eagerly and gratefully accepted in the community as a schoolmaster, a peculiar reticence arose when the subject of his past was broached. Yet he occasionally alluded to travels in Scotland, Ireland, and the West Indies. Years later, Dr. Wilson, whose conduct as a teacher was exemplary, left the school to engage in the practice of medicine in nearby Newfane where he developed an excellent reputation as a physician.

During Wilson's residence in Newfane, a Boston newspaper printed the confession of one Michael Martin, alias Captain Lightfoot, who had recently been hanged for a crime in Boston. The confession detailed Lightfoot's infamous career and his partnership with a notorious English highwayman, Captain Thunderbolt, whom Martin described in such a manner that Dr. Wilson found Newfane no longer to his liking. In 1836 he moved to Brattleboro, Vermont, and built a place more like a hideout than a home. At Wilson's death, years later, an old bullet wound was discovered in his leg, and by his bed were found three English double-barreled guns, three pairs of brassbound pistols, several swords, and, most incriminating, ten heavy gold watches. They explained his insistence on an easily defended circular schoolhouse, and also his restless habit of pacing round and round the schoolhouse peering apprehensively up and down Brookline's only road.

Plate 35   *Round Schoolhouse*

The schoolhouse was brick, roofed with hand-hewn timbers to support the conical roof. Because the timbers exerted tremendous outward pressure an iron rod, 120 feet long, girds the building just under the eaves. The building was originally heated by a sheet-iron stove in the center of the room, which was furnished by oak benches for girls circled around the stove. Individual chairs were placed in an outer circle for the boys. In 1910 the shed was added.

In the years before the Civil War, Brookline was a busy agricultural area surrounded by such settlements as Grassy Brook, Lily Pond, and Hedgehog Hill. At the end of the Civil War many Brookline youths who had served the Union cause and survived saw a better future elsewhere than that offered by their birthplace. The schoolhouse has stood empty since Depression days, because of a dwindling population.

VIII. The Mansard or Second Empire Style

A MANSARD BUILDING is the most easily identified of all the nineteenth-century styles; its distinctive roof alone sets it apart from its neighbors. I have chosen to call the domestic buildings "Mansard" and the public version "Second Empire," although the styles are essentially the same. Opponents of the Second Empire style of public buildings gave them still another name, "General Grants," a pejorative appellation referring to the building era in Washington during President Grant's administration. Washington and other capitals have many General Grants, but these public buildings are now fiercely defended by a new generation who regard them as landmarks worthy of preservation.

PERSPECTIVE.

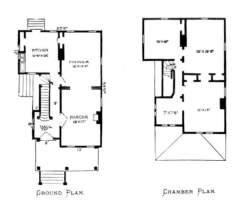

GROUND PLAN.   CHAMBER PLAN.

A Mansard house plan

If the low-pitched roof of an Italianate house were removed and replaced with a high Mansard roof, the result would be a Mansard house. The Mansard style refers especially to a form of roof with steep and curved sides interrupted by dormer windows set in ornate moldings. The elements of the bodies of the Mansard houses were essentially Italianate with some emphasis on the baroque character in the moldings over doorways and windows.

The residential Mansards which populated most cities from 1855 onward were typically two stories with a habitable third story contained in the attic. Windows were arcuated or trabeated with heavy moldings. Beneath the final outward thrust of the Mansard roof area were flat, projecting eaves supported by bold brackets in the Italianate form. The sides of the Mansard roofs were concave, convex, or S-shaped. They were sometimes broken by decorated arches, as shown in the Hopewell railroad station (plate 36 & 37). Other variants included truncated campaniles whose Mansard roofs were incorporated into the main structure. In an age when eclecticism was becoming acceptable, a dominating campanile with a Mansard roof became still another variation—a sort of Franco–Italianate compromise. The imposing Waverly, New York, house in plate 38 is a fine example.

Public buildings, built in such profusion following the Civil War, developed into richly decorated wedding cakes and reintroduced Classical elements to already overburdened façades. Freestanding Roman columns, loopings, garlands, modillions, and anthemia battled with baroque themes beneath the crowning Mansard roofs. Cast-iron cresting or a decorative curb surmounted the flat roofs to soften the abrupt cutoff.

The Mansard style's name goes back to the French

A heavily decorated public building in New York showing a blend of numerous architectural styles

Classical architect François Mansart (1598–1666) who, though identified with the roof, did not originate it. Mansart was a respected architect—innovative, idealistic, and not too careful with his clients' wishes or money. He spent his last twenty years without any commissions, having torn down the entire façade of a chateau he had just completed because some obscure details offended his eye. His patron, shocked at the waste, made certain that the news of Mansart's whimsical and costly

New York Central & Hudson Railroad Station, N.Y.: A fine example of Mansard roofing.

ways was well circulated. Mansart was thus effectively removed from the architectural arena despite his work at the Duc d'Orléans's chateau at Blois, which was considered a masterpiece of rebuilding. Beyond that his church of the Val de Grace in Paris was to influence architects for generations. Christopher Wren's St. Paul's Cathedral is a direct descendant of Mansart's Val de Grace church.

The impressiveness of Paris owes much to François Mansart and his great-nephew Jules Hardouin Mansart, if not directly, then through the renaissance of architecture and city planning during the Second Empire, the reign of Napoleon III (1852–1870). In the best of public-relations tradition, Paris, the undisputed world capital of art and fashion, held two international expositions, in 1855 and 1867, to introduce the world to the splendors of the city. Visitors must have been impressed, for architectural imitations of the Second Empire architecture appeared in the major cities of North and South America as well as Europe. For the first time America adopted a style with an eye to international fashion rather than out of a romantic affection for the past. The forms and the rich details of the Mansard and/or the Second Empire lent Romantic aspects to the style, and the Romantic allusions to historic France assured the style a wide acceptance in a nation that was beginning to assume some airs of sophistication. The Mansard rage lasted from the late 1850's to the early '70's, neatly bracketing our Civil War.

Fifteen years is not much of a span for a major architectural style, but the Mansard fashion rose and fell in that short time. The Franco–Prussian War (1870–1871) was a severe blow to French cultural prestige and to French influence in general. Some architectural historians link the loss of France's cultural leadership to the demise of the style in America. That explanation seems, perhaps, conveniently circumstantial in view of the practical nature of the style. The Mansard roof offered usable attic space with obvious advantages over the traditional slanted roof. The Mansard area also

A portion of the Duc d'Orleans' chateau at Blois—François Mansart, architect

St. Paul's Cathedral, London

provided quarters for domestics; indeed, during the years of its popularity, the Mansard roof was a status symbol precisely because it suggested the presence of servants. For the less affluent the area served as an income-producing apartment. Another explanation of Mansard's fall from favor held that the disrepute surrounding General Grant's presidency was closely linked to that style which flourished during Grant's tenure. The style was derisively dubbed the "General Grant Style." Critics of the early twentieth century referred to the distinctive roof as "a crowning indignity."

Perhaps the best explanation for the Mansard's short reign was the restlessness of America in the post-

Val de Grace Church, Paris, France

Civil War period and the changing character of builders. Automobile makers of our time offer three or four distinctive models with as many body variations. Similarly the public in the 1860's had become accustomed to change and demanded more of the same. Architectural firms, then well established in major cities, competed with one another in offering not only major architectural styles but all the eclectic variations on them that their clientele required. Nowhere was this development more obvious than in the plan books, or house-pattern books, that had become so popular.

In England since the 1830's, increasing industrialism and materialism were contributing to a decline in taste in the decorative arts. Mass-produced furniture, machine-made fabrics, excessive ornamentation, and bulging forms brought condemnation from A. W. N. Pugin in his *Contrasts* (1836) and thirteen years later from Ruskin in *Seven Lamps of Architecture*. Periodicals, such as *The Queen* and *The Young English Woman's Magazine*, rose to shape the tastes of the affluent middle classes. Coupled with articles on aesthetic interiors, the magazines published notes on morality, religion, and how to avoid social errors—the choice of the wrong house furnishings being considered one of the gravest of gaffes. Despite all the breast-beating, however, the 1851 London Exhibition provided viewers with such an olio of household disasters that Ruskin described it as the depth of moral and artistic degradation. Across the channel the French reacted to the exhibition much as they might to an inferior champagne. Naturally the failure of the exhibition brought criticism to the exhibitors and manufacturers.

Shortly thereafter Marlborough House, (a philanthropic institution that encouraged the arts and crafts of England), in an effort to educate the public to a greater sensitivity, mounted a display of objects from the 1851 exhibition that were deemed to be in excruciatingly bad taste. A little later "principles of good taste" were printed in poster form and distributed to every art school in the country. In 1862 a second London Exhibition was a tremendous success. Even the French admitted that they now had a rival.

Much of the credit for the revival of good design must be given to Charles Eastlake (1833–1906). His articles in the *Cornhill Magazine* altered public thinking and directed designers towards "simplicity." Other writers and designers expressed such dicta as "truth is the essential element of all beauty," and "the well-executed is good art."

American magazines reprinted or aped much of the English output, and our interest was whetted for style and for variety. Our architects, designers, and manufacturers saw profit in the public's interest and bent to the task of providing new ideas and new leadership. All this public stimulation, and the dislocation and unquiet feelings following the Civil War, contributed to the desire for more and faster change. The public's attention span for styles in architecture, as for so many other things, would become shorter and shorter.

The Plan Book House

Some of the new prosperity that abounded after the Civil War found its way to people unaccustomed to making building choices. Recognized architects were concerned with public buildings and thus sought commissions for them and for houses larger and more expensive than the new class of home builders could afford. Although standard plans for prosaic houses were available, the new homeowners and builders wanted something more distinctive and suitable to their expanding needs and tastes.

In the late 1860's, innovative architects became architect/publishers and reached the new builders through mail-order systems. Some provided catalogues; others advertised plans of modest houses in newspapers and magazines. The more enterprising firms offered plan- or pattern books, house plans with a choice of details and interchangeable floor plans. The buyer could take developed plans to his local builder and feel assured that his house would be both structurally sound and fashionably correct. The system also worked well for the contractor. On the basis of cost analyses provided by the architect/publisher, he could now conveniently supply cost figures backed by the authority of the publishers—and the publishers were canny enough to embody modest profit margins for the building contractor and to allow for often considerable cost variations. Costs were affected by distances from railheads and ports, by the availability of materials, and by the rates of labor. A. J. Downing's *Architecture of Country Houses* generalized the variant cost factors by suggesting "the cost of materials and labor in the interior of the State of New York may be taken as about a fair average for the country at large." In one estimate for a nine-room "Bracketed Cottage, With Veranda," Downing wrote, "The whole cost of this cottage is estimated at $1,356. Of course, in portions of the country where timber is more abundant, the cost would be from 15 to 20 per cent less." Downing may have understated the differences. The twenty years that followed the 1850 publication of *Country Houses* found a rapidly developing midwest and a far west beginning to build and populate. Cost variations were considerable, with the highest costs occurring in frontier areas where labor and materials were scarcest.

An advertisement from a nineteenth-century mail-order catalogue for pre-fabricated dwellings

It was inevitable that the subjects of the earliest pattern books would change from the designs for the most modest houses to those for the more affluent middle class. By the mid-1870's, catalogues contained plans for houses that ranged from seashore and lakeside cottages to "artistic dwellings" suitable for millionaires.

Most notable of these mail-order enterprises was a firm headed by an architect who had begun his career as a carpenter. George Palliser and his brother Charles published twenty pattern books between 1876 and 1908. The Palliser brothers not only supplied plans, they also rendered adjustments to plans required to suit topographical variations. After all details were discussed with their client via the mail, the Pallisers returned a set of working drawings with sketches and elevations. Fully armed and satisfied with all decisions, the client presented his builder with the customized plans, some money, and the go-ahead to build.

With many thousands of the Plan Book Houses built in the seventies and eighties, their impact on the architectural scene was immense. The general styles utilized by the Pallisers' plans were the Queen Anne, Roman-

esque, Stick, and Shingle. Under Plan Book influences, eclecticism became an accepted and almost standard form. Plans showed elements of Gothic, Italianate, Mansard, Queen Anne, and Shingle styles in one elevation. Whether the Cape May vacation house in plate 40 was a Plan Book House is uncertain, but it is quite certain that a number of styles were inspired by Plan Book

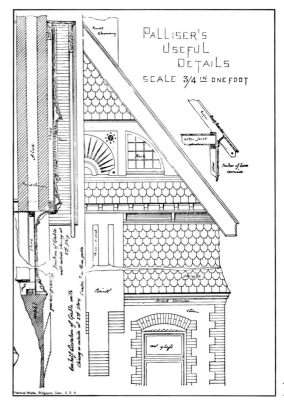

A house sketch from a Palliser pattern book

ideals. Indiana, Ohio, Missouri, and Michigan were in their rapidly developing stages when the Plan Book Houses were in greatest demand. Throughout those states the variety and the surprising detail of many of the structures still surviving can be traced directly to the Pallisers and their associates.

In Knoxville, Tennessee, George Barber, who also began his career as a carpenter, took mail order architecture one step further than the Pallisers. Barber offered to provide materials as well as plans. Barber house kits included intricate millwork, hardware, and all other interior and exterior details not easily acquired at the site of building. Barber's success can be measured by the fact that he sold three hundred kits of one design alone, and his houses graced almost every state in the Union. Barber also endorsed the eclectic ideals and produced houses that could boast of Renaissance, "Colonial," and Beaux Arts elements.

The Pallisers and Barber were not the last purveyors of plan books. Several other smaller firms were in the business, and by the turn of the century the plans and materials for an entire house could be ordered from a Sears and Roebuck catalogue and shipped by rail to almost any place in the United States.

If a house is not a pedigreed Queen Anne, if it's not a pure-bred Romanesque, if an Italianate has sprinklings of other styles—it is probably a Plan Book House.

Chances are that it was shown in one of Geo. Palliser's, Wm. Comstock's, A. J. Bicknell's, or George Barber's catalogues or bought from Sears.

Of course there was an outcry over the departure from traditional building procedures. One architectural authority complained that the Plan Book Houses were "so commercially wrought as to be an affront to public decency" and insisted they would lead to "the disestablishment of all standards and reason." Actually many of the Plan Book Houses made very decent little homes indeed—well planned and often designed with restraint and charm. But for the plan books, thousands of families might never have realized a crucial part of the American Dream—to own one's own home.

Plates 36 & 37   *A Mansard Depot*

A Mansard Depot

There are many crossovers of styles in High Victorian architecture. Elements of Second Empire and High Victorian Italianate provided the opulence that characterized the era, but the Hopewell, New Jersey, depot was built with restraint and was meant to be practical as well as impressive. When the Reading Railroad built the station in the 1880's, there were great expectations for growth and prosperity in the region. The planners envisioned the development of a downtown commercial district that would eventually envelop the depot. Princeton was only a few miles away, and the Garden State's truck farms were thriving. Hopewell prospered after a fashion, but the town never grew to dimensions anticipated by its planners. A hundred years later, Hopewell is quite unchanged, and its eighteenth- and nineteenth-century houses make it one of New Jersey's most attractive communities.

In the 1880's American railroads were prideful empires competing for patronage and prestige. Every American boy went through some phase of wanting to be a railroad engineer, and the railroads did their best to live up to an image of brawn and indomitability. The Lackawanna Railroad maintained three greenhouses to supply flowers for its dining cars, while other railroads' dining-car systems provided bone china and silver service for its travelers. (A Pennsylvania Railroad demitasse with saucer from an 1880's dining car is now valued at over $200.) Parlor cars, for those who could afford luxury travel, were paneled with rosewood, mahogany, and walnut and were marvels of the cabinetmaker's art.

The House at Waverly

In 1852 Louis Napoleon, in an era of turmoil and political indecision in France, reinstituted the hereditary empire and adopted the title Napoleon III. The Second Empire of France lends its name to architectural styles that evoked a glamorous image of Paris during the reign of Napoleon III. The Second Empire was a period of overt prosperity, and the remodeling of Paris was the symbolic display of that prosperity. Under the supervision of Baron Georges Eugène Haussmann, old city walls were replaced by boulevards, great railroad stations were located in a circle outside the old city, and decrepit buildings were razed to make plazas for public buildings, theaters, and monuments. The city's roads were paved with asphalt, and buildings of architectural worth were restored. Paris became the greatest attraction of the era. In 1855 the Exposition Universelle brought visitors from every point of the globe, who were as much impressed by the city as by the Exposition. At the same time French Renaissance detail and the Mansard roof became a reigning fashion in the Americas, although in the United States, the reign was short.

The glitter of Paris was camouflage for a nation beset with internal and external difficulties. In 1864 Napoleon provided Mexico with an unwanted emperor, Ferdinand Maximilian, brother of Emperor Francis Joseph of Austria. From the beginning the rule was a disaster. The United States, engaged in a Civil War, took a very dim view of the French expeditionary forces sent to bolster the tottering throne of the New World emperor. Because of dire conditions at home, Napoleon III withdrew French troops, sealing Maximilian's doom. In 1867 he fell to a Mexican firing squad.

Food riots, the Franco–Prussian War of 1870–1871, and the siege of Paris brought French prestige to its nadir. French styles, including architectural styles, no longer represented the enlightenment, sophistication, and effervescent charm evoked by the comic operas of Jacques Offenbach. Those who mark epochs by the artists whose works per-

Plate 38   *The House at Waverly*

sonify the times cite the death of Offenbach in 1880 as the date of the demise of the gilded Second Empire.

The portrait is of an imposing house that dominates a hilltop in Waverly, New York, a neighbor of Elmira. It could be classified as an Italianate, but the Mansard struc-

ture capping the campanile and details identified with French Renaissance buildings rules out a single classification. I think of it as Second Empire Franco–Italianate and very Romantic.

Mansard House

I first saw this house in Berkeley Heights, New Jersey. The lighting had placed the old Mansard in a setting so Romantic it seemed almost contrived. Yet each time I returned to the house, I failed to recapture the impact of my first viewing. Then, on a June morning at six o'clock, I drove one of my children to rendezvous with her classmates for the traditional class trip and at last saw the house as I remembered it. There is a perfect time of day and season of the year for each old house. Stalking them for optimum effect is part of the enjoyment for the old-house connoisseur.

In the 1920's this building became a golf clubhouse. It was later sold for a dollar during the Depression. Finally it was restored, and once again it's a residence.

Plate 39 *Mansard House*

A Mansard roof, peculiar to the style, makes the Second Empire the most easily recognizable of all styles, but the body of the building may have traces of Italian and French Renaissance and of other baroque influences. The ornate style introduced the High Victorian era of architecture.

The enthusiastic acceptance of the Second Empire Philadelphia City Hall of 1869 and the overwhelming success of Philadelphia's 1876 International Centennial Exposition indicated profound social changes. The Centennial Exposition was designed to illustrate a century of progress, but its ten million visitors sensed more than progress. Inherent in the exposition also was an awareness of internationalism and of a cosmopolitan outlook. Second Empire buildings had just the urbanity to express this nation's departure from the Age of Innocence to post-Civil War ideals that endorsed worldliness.

The tenure of the domestic Second Empire style was limited by the decline of French influence and other historical events harmful to the image the style represented. But Second Empire public buildings in the form of state capitols and post offices continued to be built after interest in the domestic style waned. The Washington, D.C., building originally called the State, Navy and War Department Building (1871), now the State Department, is the quintessence of the Second Empire style. Washington wags refer to similar buildings as "General Grants."

Cape May Vacation House

Indoor plumbing had a good deal to do with architectural eclecticism. The Dr. Henry Hunt house in Cape May, New Jersey, is an example. The house was surely picturesque enough at the time of its construction in 1881, but in 1890, with the advent of indoor bathrooms, fanciful additions were built to accommodate the new convenience. The additions were generally added in what was a current style. At the time they were built, consistency in domestic architecture was no longer felt to be essential. Decades earlier campaniles were tacked on farmhouses to make them fashionable, and Mansard roofs replaced ordinary roofs to make room for boarders or servants. (Trabeated windows in Mansard houses are the giveaway that the roof is not original.) The difference between the Cape May vacation house and the "Roselawn" house at Flemington, New Jersey (plate 69), is that the former was conceived as a conscious eclectic entity and made more eclectic by other style additions within a very limited time span. The house at Flemington grew during a hundred-year time span and arrived at its present form in an ingenuous fashion.

The sharply pointed eaves at the right are of Gothic inspiration, and the decoration at the point of the eaves is a scissors truss, an element used widely in the Stick Style. The truss is repeated over the window, which is part of the Mansard element. The decoration above the Mansard roof is called cresting, and the imbricated shingles of the roof would be called fish-scale shingling if the shingles were rounded. (Queen Annes have fish-scale shingles.) The first-story bracketed porch is Italianate, and the conically roofed gazebolike structure, with the cusped pierced-wood decoration, shows oriental influences.

Dr. Hunt's vacation house now stands on what was part of the vast lawn that swept from the venerable Congress Hall hotel, a landmark of landmarks in America's most Victorian city. The present owner of the Dr. Hunt house is dedicated to restoration. His summers are spent on ladders, scraping, sanding, and painting. The house is no longer white but is wonderfully picked out in colors

Plate 40   *Cape May Vacation House*

*made famous by the "painted ladies" of San Francisco.
The results of the owner's labors are beneficial to his community, to dazzled visitors to Cape May, and to the heritage he preserves.*

IX. Some Working Buildings of the Victorian Age

TO IGNORE THE FACTORIES, mills, stores, railroad stations, and other working buildings that were at the heart of American industrial efforts in the nineteenth century would present an incomplete view of Victorian ingenuity. Though the service buildings that Victorians built were Classical in nature, the nineteenth-century builders nevertheless contrived to inject Romantic elements into any aspect of their structures that could support decoration.

Buildings that serve a purpose also serve to display the character of a people. A barn in the Pennsylvania Dutch country will reflect the nature and heritage of the German immigrant descendants who built it. As architects were rarely involved in the planning or construction of older working buildings, folk know-how replaced sophistication to lend rugged charm to those structures.

Pride of ownership found ready expression in the factories and farms of nineteenth-century America. Factories and foundries were adorned with turrets and other castellated embellishments, and niches were provided for the standing statues of the founder of the enterprise. The statues, often cast in concrete, became perches for pigeons, to the delight of the workers.

The cupola was regarded as a status symbol for barns and carriage houses. A cupola had no function other than to dignify a vent allowing grains to expel accumulated heat. Yet a farmer, whose buildings were otherwise rigidly functional, indulged himself in that eye-pleasing but intricate appurtenance. And it *was* an indulgence. From the ground, cupolas and weather vanes may seem no great size, but to be proportionate to their buildings, they must be of generous dimensions. There are few things more offensive to the eye than the pinheaded look of a stinted cupola. The golden arrows of a weather vane may be six feet long. The gilded horses

endlessly trotting into the wind were often five feet and longer depending on the height of the building. The cupola on a fair-sized barn may be as large as a single-car garage. A *belvedere* is similar to a cupola. Placed on a house, it provides ventilation and a view. Cube Style Italianates often wore belvederes. (*Bello vedere* is Italian for "beautiful view.") A *lantern* is a cupola that sits atop a dome.

A cupola and weather vane

Carriage houses, when reflecting the architecture of the houses that they served, *were* designed by architects, although most were carpenter-planned along very practical lines. Carriage houses were typically three stories high, the lower floor often built into a hill so that the back wall was windowless. Here the horses were stabled. The second story was on the up side of the hill to shelter carriages and provide room for harness and a finished room for the groom. The top floor stored grain. At the front side of the top floor a projecting beam and pulley were used to hoist bags of oats and bales of hay. Behind the hoist, built into the opposite wall, was a chute which coursed the grain to the stable below. Heat for the groom was a wood- or coal-burning stove. Grooms drank a lot.

Water-powered mills in the east are largely holdovers from the eighteenth century. The nineteenth century saw revolutionary retooling of mills for purposes undreamed of by eighteenth-century builders. Because mills were substantially built and because they occupied sites at waterfalls, their evolution was internal. The exteriors were generally unaffected by changes within. Water power did not always appeal to nineteenth-century industrialists. The clean energy provided by the weight of water had its vagaries. Heavy downpours carried limbs of trees and other flotsam to foul the mill wheels. In times of drought the mill could be totally immobilized. Industrialists inevitably turned to steam as engines became more practical. Now the manufacturer could locate in areas where no water mill had ever existed. Yet the water-powered mills continued to produce linseed oil, to process grain (grist for livestock and flour for human consumption), to grind gypsum to replenish overworked soil, and to mill indigo and woad for dye. Lime, graphite, and talc were transformed into marketable commodities by the grinding machinery. The eighteenth-century cams and gears, fashioned from wood, were eventually replaced by the iron gears of the nineteenth century. Iron works facilitated the stamping, perforating, and forming of other metals.

The Clinton, New Jersey, mill (plate 41) was first built in 1763 and rebuilt in the nineteenth century to meet changing conditions. It served its community well into the twentieth century, providing electricity for Clinton's first electric lights. With most of its wooden machinery intact, the Clinton mill is now a museum. On the opposite shore, across a branch of the Raritan River, another mill serves as the community art center. With the exception of an Octagon house, Clinton has examples of every architectural style prevalent in the nineteenth century. The twentieth century has not yet overcome the nineteenth-century ambience that gives the town its grace and character.

The icehouse was once a familiar outbuilding across the northern half of the country. Although pollution and

Washington Irving's residence, "Sunnyside," with its chapel-like icehouse to the right

electric refrigeration have all but eliminated this once ubiquitous structure, every large home, from colonial times until the 1930's, had an attached icehouse. Thomas Jefferson's, at Monticello, was built in the ground and covered by an earthen dome. Washington Irving's is mostly underground, but the above-ground structure resembles a chapel with a cupola topped by a spire.

Most icehouses looked like Dr. Physick's in Cape May, New Jersey (plate 42). Frank Furness, who designed the house to which it is attached, also designed the marvelous High Victorian Gothic Pennsylvania

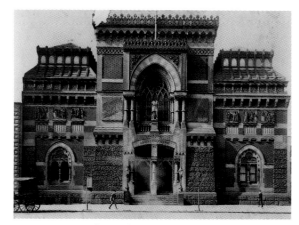

Pennsylvania Academy of Fine Arts, Philadelphia

Academy of the Fine Arts in Philadelphia. There is nothing about the Cape May icehouse that is architecturally interesting, but the construction is unusual. The walls are doubled to contain about a foot's width of sawdust. The roof was equally sheathed and insulated. Cakes of ice 24 × 48 × 72 inches were cut from ponds and lakes to be hauled and hoisted into the windowless buildings. The chunks of ice were separated by layers of sawdust and could remain unmelted through the heat of two summers.

According to Mrs. Trollope, crystal-clear ice was one of America's greatest enticements. Every hotel and wayside inn had mountains of ice to be shaved, cracked, or mashed in drinks or desserts. At first Mrs. Trollope was offended by the American enthusiasm for ice, but in time she became thoroughly addicted. In her prosperous and honored retirement years in Italy, Mrs. Trollope wrote that the only thing that was missing to make her life complete was sparkling American ice.

In 1805 Frederick Tudor, later known as the Ice King, sent a cargo of ice from New England to the West Indies. The venture was a financial disaster, but Tudor was a determined man, and despite ridicule, eventually developed methods of stowing ice in such a manner that by 1833 he was able to successfully deliver a cargo to Calcutta, India. By the 1850's his clipper ships were delivering ice all over the world—146,000 tons in one year alone.

In large cities fire-engine houses were almost always built in architectural harmony with surrounding structures. In suburban communities the campaniled Italianate was by far the most common choice for firehouses, for reasons noted in a previous chapter. Many urban engine houses were originally carriage houses altered to accommodate fire engines and living quarters. In the nineteenth century, moveable hooks were set in the ceiling of the ground-level floor to drop patented automatic harness on waiting horses at the sound of an alarm.

The Brooklyn Heights, New York, fire-engine house (plate 66) is in the Renaissance Revival style, which enjoyed a modest popularity in the last years of the nineteenth century. The style demanded that each floor have a different set of Classical details, some Greek and others Roman. Present-day fire-engine houses resemble the ubiquitous ranch colonials of suburbia. No longer do they boast impressive towers; electronic communications have eliminated the need for lookouts, and fire hoses are dried by blowing them out with machines that resemble giant hair driers.

Although Americans never quite matched the English when it came to eccentric architecture, we have had our moments—most of them commercial. England has a long-standing tradition of amateur architects who were whimsical enough—and rich enough—to build wondrous gazebos, cottages ornés, mock Gothics, etc. Our eccentric architecture has involved some ruined castles and outlooks, and some fantastic monuments and sculptures, but most of our eccentricities have been commercially inspired: attention-getting landlocked ships, brown derbies, huge sitting ducks, and a much-loved elephant.

Lucy, the Margate, New Jersey, elephant was the brain child of Philadelphian James V. Lafferty, who in the 1880's built three metal-skinned pachyderms to resemble Jumbo, P. T. Barnum's great attraction. Lucy's

A fire house

Lucy the Margate Elephant in 1973 before restoration

sister, at Coney Island, was a victim of fire, while her other sibling, at Cape May, was swept out to sea. Lucy, completed in 1885, was fitted out with "mementos worthy of any bazaar" and could boast that more than two million people had visited her. By 1963, when the painting of Lucy was completed (plate 44), she was on her last legs. Neglect and the storms of the Atlantic had brought her to the brink of extinction. By 1970 she was a wreck.

Sylvia Carpenter was the first to deplore the lack of imagination and the indifference that had allowed Lucy to deteriorate. Josephine Harron, convinced that

In 1976 the exterior restoration was complete and she was placed on the National Register of Historic Sites

Lucy represented a great deal more than a derelict eyesore, joined forces with Mrs. Carpenter and began a campaign to restore the pachyderm. The struggle of these two determined women to prevent the destruction of a symbol of innocent delight reached epic proportions and was marked by comedy and monumental frustrations. By 1980, with the help of hundreds of volunteers, an awakened Margate saw Lucy safely placed on the National Register of Historic Sites and her exterior completely restored. Funds from individuals, federal-government grants, aid from corporations, and gifts from the local business community gave Lucy back to a public that had all but abandoned her. With her new hide and a bright red blanket painted under an oriental howdah, Lucy is once again a delight to children and a welcome relief from the spurious sophistication of the casinos in neighboring Atlantic City.

Some of America's most distinguished architects were commissioned to design railroad stations. A proud array of depots, junctions, stations, and terminals once decorated the crossroads of the nation. With the decline of railroad travel, many of the colorful depots were razed or so modified as to render them utterly without character. Perhaps the greatest single atrocity to be visited on American architecture in the name of progress was the arrogant destruction in 1963 of one of the masterpieces of American building, the Pennsylvania Railroad Terminal in New York City. In a contemporary editorial the *New York Times* commented: ". . . we will probably be judged not by the monuments we build, but by those we have destroyed." A more recent awakening to the value of these structures has kept many of the most important buildings safe from the wrecker's ball. Many lesser depots have been pressed into community service as art centers and municipal offices. Railroad stations in cities were, like fire-engine houses, designed to live easily with the nature of the city, but were almost always built in the style of architecture prevailing in the decade of their construction. University towns, for example, were invariably endowed with stations bearing some resemblance to the Collegiate Gothic style.

Railroad stations have a vocabulary all their own. The largest, located at the terminuses of a railroad sys-

A Shingle Style Southern railroad station

tem, are designated *terminals*. At the crossing of railway lines, they are named *junctions*. The very smallest and most local of stations are called *shelters*. Planners tried to project the eventual size of a community and built to that size. The fancy Mansard station at Hopewell, New Jersey (plates 36 & 37), is an example of an overoptimistic prognosis of growth. Hopewell never grew beyond village proportions, much to the pleasure of the inhabitants who cherish its small-town atmosphere.

The Hopewell station itself was a very practical affair. It was both a passenger and freight facility, managed by an agent who lived rent-free with his family on the third floor. The second floor was devoted to business, and the first floor, with its sheltering Stick Style canopy, was for the ticket office and the comfort of passengers. Until recently the Hopewell depot is rented to families who find the location colorful and convenient and the greatly diminished rail traffic no hindrance to their peace. Today it is boarded up.

To younger readers it may come as a surprise that railroads were once quite elegant. The Lackawanna Railroad kept three greenhouses to supply cut flowers for its dining cars. The Pennsylvania Railroad imported ele-

gant china from Austria. The demitasses and other pieces are now regarded as valuable collectibles. The menus for the dining cars and the stations were satisfying to the most fastidious diners. Oysters, a half-dozen or so, sparkling or mineral waters, meat and fish courses, soups and desserts were all offered by the dining-car services on snowy linens with monogrammed silver. And the dining cars themselves were masterworks of the joiner's art—with satinwoods, rosewood, and mahogany, with Tiffany decorations above and oriental carpets beneath.

Stations and terminals had matching elegance. At the head of the marble stairs that led from the passenger level to the arcade of the Pennsylvania Railroad Terminal in New York City, were two handsome bronze figures, considerably larger than life. One was of a Mr. Cassatt, a founder of the Pennsylvania system from Philadelphia. With the demise of his temple, Mr. Cassatt has faded from public consideration, while his sister, Mary, for whom no public monument exists, is increasingly recognized as one of America's greatest painters.

The main arcade of the late Pennsylvania Railroad Terminal in New York City

The Clinton Mill

The red mill in Clinton, New Jersey, is now a museum. The rakes, hoppers, auger lifts, screws, pulleys, chutes, grindstones, crane spouts, wooden gears, combs, sieves, and a host of other devices pertinent to milling are exhibited to the public. For a time the mill generated power for Clinton's first electric lights. Another mill, directly across the Raritan River, is now the Hunterdon Art Center.

Clinton is a postcard town that speaks of Victorian prosperity. Off the main street are Greek Revivals, Italianates, and Queen Annes. The mill itself has undergone many changes, arriving at its present form in the late nineteenth century. In its time its fourteen-foot wheel ground woad and indigo, gypsum to replenish the soil, talc, lime, linseed, grist for animals, flour for human consumption, and, from nearby Asbury, graphite. Mills like this one made possible the mass production of cloth, house paints, varnishes, tools, and lumber products, all of which were

Plate 41 *The Clinton Mill*

previously processed by hand. Mills hammered out huge blocks of white-hot iron in stentorian blows, and they polished gemstones in whispers.

A good-sized mill could establish a town and bring prosperity to an entire area. Early railroads connected to mills to create feed-and-grain centers. That connection attracted other agricultural groups as well as lumber-yards, brickmakers, and related industries. In time the mill that created the commerce was supplanted by more sophisticated technology and phased out. The only mill town in America that has remained unchanged is the textile town of Harrisville, New Hampshire, which still produces woolens. In America's great grain belt, a surprising number of grist mills somehow survive, most powered by diesel engines. In an ironic twist water mills have, in recent years, been resurrected in order to generate the electricity to power those motors which originally relegated the mills to obsolescence.

Windmills are of an era that preceded the Victorian years, but where water was not easily obtained or was undependable, wind-driven mills performed some of the tasks of their water-driven counterparts. Some were built up to the Civil War.

The picturesque qualities of mills now viewed in serene retirement do not tell of the conditions that prevailed in mills, especially textile mills. Early in the nineteenth century mill owners paid young women workers $2 a week and board. The week was a seventy-two-hour week, the work hard and dangerous. As late as 1883 children worked for 30 cents a day and performed their labors in bare feet, as the mill floors were kept awash to humidify the cotton. Respiratory diseases were rife, and mill workers were deafened by the endless clattering of machinery. Young workers soon became undernourished, dwarfed, and alcoholic. According to mill owners pay increases for women were morally wrong because they would elevate women beyond their proper status. Brewers, mill owners, and other employers also felt that the seventy-two-hour week was morally just, as it kept workers away from corrupting influences.

Dr. Physick Icehouse

The modest icehouse in the painting is another determined survivor. I would like to have found an architecturally significant icehouse, but the fact that this one is a building that once served the Dr. Emlen Physick estate makes up for its lack of style. In search of a more impressive icehouse I was repeatedly informed that the specimens I sought had just burned down or had become a garage or an antique shop or, in one instance, a summer theater.

The Physick house is now a Cape May, New Jersey, arts center, but it was planned as a summer retreat for Dr. Physick's Philadelphia family. The builder was Charles Shaw, and it is all but certain that the planner was Frank Furness, one of America's greatest architects. The icehouse was probably built as a convenience somewhat later, as it is inconceivable that the master carpenters who completed the Furness house in 1879 could have been persuaded to build such an unimaginative, unadorned structure.

Icehouses were built with double walls and roofs with, typically, fourteen inches between sheaths. Sawdust from local sawmills was packed between the walls and made an excellent insulation against outdoor heat. In winter ice was cut from lakes, ponds, and rivers by teams of men using saws, hooks, and other specialized tools developed for the work. The men wore spiked cleats strapped to their boots, and their horses were similarly equipped. Blocks of ice, typically 24- by 48- by 72 inches, were placed on sleds, hauled to icehouses, and hoisted to their interior. The ice was placed in layers separated by sawdust. The whole was then covered with sawdust and could be expected to last a year or longer.

Icehouses were built in many forms. Some were built into the sides of hills so that the earth itself was the insulator. Thomas Jefferson built his icehouse beneath a section of covered walk that stretches out from Monticello. It is circular and covered with a deep cone of earth. Washington Irving's icehouse at "Sunnyside" looks like a little chapel that has sunk into the earth. Its sides are board and batten.

Harvard Lampoon House

The Harvard Lampoon *building, in Cambridge, Massachusetts, is the home of a famous collegiate humor magazine and a clubhouse. The building, just outside the Harvard Yard, is whimsically eclectic, embodying pointed arches, stepped gables, and an outsized tower with startled eyes and a mouth expressing eternal amazement. Atop the tower is a hat crowned by a swiveling ibis. Owen Wister, Robert Benchley, Robert Sherwood, and William Randolph Hearst were once staffers on the* Lampoon.

As follies go, the Lampoon *building came late. Though plans for the place were drawn earlier, the construction began in 1909. The style is ambiguous, but the inspiration came from the Holland of the 1500's, and the upper stories owe much to the concept of an English college hall. The main doorway is painted in a diamond pattern, and the last dozen or so coats of paint are blue and yellow, but beneath are layers of the original colors—purple and golden yellow.*

Much of the interior is decorated with eighteenth-century Delft tiles to further the Dutch theme. There is a narthex, a president's room, a public room, and a great hall with an imposing Gothic archway and huge oaken trusses.

At least some of the activities of the building include publishing. The Harvard Lampoon *is a venerable institution (founded 1876) modeled originally on the British* Punch. *From its origin it has prospered through parody, and its issues have provoked often violent criticism. One issue was called "a disgusting example of what can come of too much ink and too little brains." The same issue caused the* Lampoon *building to be shut down for a month and led to the attempted firing of the publication's president, secretary, and treasurer. This action brought about a riot in Harvard Square. Two thousand indignant students forced the reinstatement of the officers and the reopening of the* Lampoon's *home.*

The Lampoon *building stands on a wedge at Bow, Mt. Auburn, and Plympton Streets in Cambridge. The*

Plate 42　*Dr. Physick Icehouse*

To have access to quantities of crystal-clear ice was a great convenience and a luxury in the last century. Crystal-clear ice came from crystal-clear lakes, which were fast disappearing even in the 1870's. There are people alive today who talk of the dark, cool dampness of a country icehouse, the feel of the wet sawdust, and the delight of a splinter of ice in a pitcher of lemonade. Every country hotel had its icehouse before the advent of electrical refrigeration. As icehouses were windowless and posed a fire hazard when dry and no longer used, it was easier to demolish them than to convert them to new purposes.

original building with its land, eighteenth-century tiles, im-
ported oak paneling, massive oak beams, original tile roof,
and terra cotta flooring, cost $46,000.

An Elephant House

I painted Lucy, the Margate Elephant, years before she arrived at such a deplorable condition that neighboring motel operators demanded her demolition. There was little enthusiasm for her restoration at the time, but some preservationists saw a future for Lucy, and an epic struggle against time, deterioration, and motel owners was led by

Plate 44 *An Elephant House*

two dedicated and very determined women. Money was raised, movers found, and a park for Lucy was set aside by the city. Now Margate, close to New Jersey's Atlantic City, has a restored, rehabilitated landmark that attracts visitors surfeited with the glitter of the nearby casinos.

The removal of Lucy from her original home at the seashore to her present location had all the gargantuan qualities of an epic film by D. W. Griffith. The giant pachyderm was placed on flatbed trucks and hauled by tractors made miniature in comparison with their load. Hundreds of ropes, to brace and guide, transformed Lucy into a Gulliver. Throngs of Lilliputians followed in awe as, inch by inch, Lucy was trundled down Margate's main thoroughfare to her new homesite.

In her prime a hundred years ago, two million visitors tramped 350 steps to Lucy's four bedrooms, dining room, and reception room to view the Atlantic from her twenty-two windows. Lucy has been an adjunct to a hotel, and even a home for some private families. Why did they leave? My wife, Wende, suggested that they grew tired of living out of a trunk!

· Lucy is 80 feet around the waist and measures 38 feet from head to tail. Her legs are a trim 10 feet in diameter; her ears are 17 feet long and weigh 2,000 pounds each. Her eyes are 18 inches in diameter, and her tusks are 22 feet long. Statistics provided by James V. Lafferty, who had Lucy built as a colossal real-estate office in 1885, may have been somewhat exaggerated by that Barnum-inspired entrepreneur, but he claimed that "It took a million pieces of timber, 8,560 ribs or arches, 4 tons of bolts and bars and 12,000 square feet of sheet metal to cover it."

Once again Lucy's red-rimmed eyes stare out over the Atlantic, but this time her future is assured by a place in the National Register of Historic Sites. Still, the work of her preservers is not over. Lucy's interior, once "fitted out with studied effort to gratify a curious public" and filled with "mementos worthy of any bazaar," needs replacement. One proposal offered to the Save Lucy Committee suggests that the elephant's interior would make a wonderful children's library.

New Hope Depot

John Maass, an Austrian, came to the United States in 1941 with an eye for the unusual and a mind uncluttered by dicta of the past. He soon found himself caught up in an unlikely preoccupation—a great admiration for Victorian era architecture. In 1957 his classic, The Gingerbread Age (Bramhall House), was published. That book did a lot to make Americans aware of the rich heritage they had in a once-despised period of architecture. Maass's book was an important link in a chain of events that led to today's extraordinary rebirth of interest in Romantic architecture.

To most Americans thirty years ago, the terms of architecture relating to the Victorian era were meaningless. Carpenter Gothic was identifiable to some, probably through association with the board-and-battened house in the background of Grant Wood's American Gothic. Italianate, Second Empire, and Queen Anne had no meaning to the otherwise literate, because examples of the styles seemed destined for oblivion. Maass's book brought his readers to such an understanding of terms and the values of Romantic architecture that a sense of discovery replaced the pejorative clichés concerning Victorian architecture.

Maass did not always adhere to standard architectural nomenclature. In Bethlehem, Pennsylvania, a Mansard-roofed railroad station, with a wide overhang shelter supported by Stick Style trusses embellished with Gothic trefoils, was simply called "Railroad style"—a good name for a building whose function is so obvious and is made up of so many stylistic elements. We say that the little New Hope, Pennsylvania, depot is built in the Railroad style, therefore, as nothing describes it better.

Most railroads could well afford to build attractive shelters for their passengers. At the end of the nineteenth century it was estimated that half of the entire capital of the United States was owned by or in some way involved in railroading. Coal mining and steel production were essentially adjunct industries of railroading. Skilled workers found permanent employment in the vast variety of jobs that kept railroads functioning. Unskilled workers drifted

Plate 45　*New Hope Depot*

*along the expanding rail routes, and, if lucky, eventually
found some sort of berth related to the industry.*

*There were probably more folk ballads generated by
railroad workers than by any other work group with the
exception of a comparatively minor group—the cowhands.
Compare the twentieth century: our trucking industry has
inspired a good number of ballads, but the airlines remain
mostly unsung.*

Plate 46 *Tinicum Barn*

Tinticum Barn

In 1885 eighty-five percent of the American people lived on farms. One hundred years later, eighty-five percent live in cities or suburban communities. Barns, which were once our most prevalent buildings other than houses, are now a vanishing landmark. Barns came in all shapes and sizes—octagon, dodecagon, circular, gambrel roofed, mansarded, and hip roofed. There are Dutch barns, English barns, and Pennsylvania barns, to mention principal types, but there are also connecting barns, tobacco barns, and a whole group of specialized barns. It is a well-known fact that farmers, for the most part, felt that their barns came first and their homes afterward. The farmer's pride was expressed in his barn.

The history of the barn is long and honorable, dating from the prehistoric European barns of cruck construction based on curved heavy timbers to the nineteenth-century barns raised (literally) by the Amish or built in circular form by the Shakers. In the Amish tradition as many as two hundred men were collected to raise the prefabricated, prenumbered sections of the barn. Eighty poles for pushing and thousands of feet of rope for pulling brought the bents, or wall sections, to an erect position. Some barns were large enough to accommodate three or four indoor silos. In the eighteenth century, floors were five- to six inches thick, but in the nineteenth, floors of oak or cedar could be two- to three inches thick and still withstand years of flailing. The floors became so polished from the threshing of the grain that they were slippery. Barns were sided with board and batten and clapboard in a variety of woods, including cypress. The oldest barns have the narrowest clapboard. Rafters were of oak and framing of ash, hemlock, pine, basswood, and walnut.

An architect-built barn is a rarity. Barns, even those of great size, were built in traditional forms with variants supplied from need and only occasionally from a desire for individuality. The greatest threat to barns was fire. Farms were out of reach of fire-fighting equipment, and because of their stored hay and wooden construction, fires quickly grew past control. Destruction was swift, complete, and tragic for the farmers whose animals, tools, and future went up in smoke. The best insurance the farmer had was to own two barns with space between. After fire, the next great destroyer of barns has been the entrepreneur who buys old barns for their hand-hewn beams, for weathered siding to be used in contemporary interiors, and for wrought-iron strap hinges, latches, and bolts.

The barn in the painting is located in Pennsylvania at the Tinticum State Park across the Delaware from Frenchtown, New Jersey. The cupola, which functions only to house a vent or to admit a little light, exemplifies the builder's pride. The Adamesque windows at the gable ends of the barn suggest the status of the prosperous farmer who built this capacious structure.

The last snows of February were melting when I made the painting. In a farm of the size indicated by the barn, the time of the year would mark the beginning of tremendous activities. The barn was the center of it all.

X. Queen Anne

THE TERMINOLOGY OF AMERICAN architectural style is generally stable, except for two recent semantic contradictions. For greater accuracy, but contrary to popular usage, the term "Mansard" has disappeared from strict architectural parlance, to be replaced by the term "Second Empire." With the Queen Anne style the change in name has been the other way around. Queen Anne, the most accepted term, is inaccurate, but replaces "Neo-Jacobean," bowing to usage. Queen Anne's reign, (1665–1714), was dominated by architectural influences of its own, chiefly through the Palladio–Inigo Jones–Christopher Wren line, but they were not the influences that produced Jacobean, or Neo-Jacobean, building.

A small-town home showing almost all of the elements of the Queen Anne style

Jacobus is Latin for "James," and "Jacobean" refers to the time of James I, who succeeded Elizabeth I in 1603 and ruled England until 1625. The architecture that flourished during his lifetime was characterized by variant textures. The surfaces of Jacobean buildings were arrayed with shingles, cut stone, slate, half timbers, and variegated woods that made decorative patterns.

The same houses were alive with turrets and ingeniously contrived corner windows. In Queen Anne's time, such architecture was considered antique. Why the style purveyors of the 1870's and 1880's chose to give her name to what were really Jacobean-inspired buildings is obscure.

More Queen Annes survive today than any other Victorian style. For the new Queen Anne style, arriving in the seventies and eighties, the time was right. The railroads were spanning and interlacing the nation, so that a style emanating from the Atlantic seaboard could find acceptance on the West Coast within months instead of years. Following the panic of 1873, labor, balloon-frame construction, and raw materials were in top-heavy supply. Mass production also contributed to the spread of Queen Annes. Shingles in the shape of fish scales, and in any other conceivable form, were cut out by steam-driven saws. Steam-powered lathes produced spindles and fanciful columns. Mills were able to fabricate complex windows that echoed their Jacobean forebears. The window we associate with the Queen Anne has a centered major pane of clear glass edged by smaller panes of varied colors. Ambers, bottle greens, and cranberry reds were favored.

Queen Anne chimneys are tall, choke-topped, and often paneled. Most Queen Anne supporting columns on porches and porte-cocheres have an upside-down look. They are wide at the top and flared out with decorative brackets. Many of the porte-cocheres that once surrounded the original Queen Annes have been eliminated because of space restrictions and high maintenance costs. Too often the loss has destroyed the horizontal grace of the structure and left the house appearing awkwardly tall. And too often the turrets and other intricately formed portions of the house have been degraded

A Queen Anne with choke-topped chimneys

Henry Hobson Richardson of later Romanesque fame. More important to the success of the style, which was to become a rage, was the Centennial Exposition in Philadelphia in 1876. The Queen Anne style was given impetus by two "honest" half-timbered houses, quite "Elizabethan" in character, which were the offices of the British commission at the exposition. The government of Great Britain felt it necessary to show kinship with the United States to counteract anti-British feeling following the American Civil War. The press was quick to note that the "Elizabethan" houses were the most costly provided by any government. The reaction was enthusiastic.

The British Commission Building at the Philadelphia Centennial Exposition in 1876

with materials more suited to mobile homes. Still, because they were well built, because the ceilings were high, and because they were moderately proportioned, Queen Annes survive in abundance to the satisfaction of a rising generation sympathetic to the ideals of generations past.

Queen Anne interiors reflected motifs of the exterior style. Rounded arches separating halls from rooms were decorated with knobby graduated spindles to hint at the textures and whimsies of the house's exterior. Golden brown was the dominant hue of suburban Queen Anne interiors. Rural Queen Anne interiors were painted white. Stained-glass windows, vaguely Pre-Raphaelite in design, lit golden-stained stairwells. Add to this Eastlake cupboards and sideboards, tiled fireplaces, Turkish rugs, brass gas fixtures, and some exotic flora for a fair picture of 1880's interior decor.

The Queen Anne Revival began in Sussex, England, with a house designed by the leading architect of his time, Richard Norman Shaw (1831–1912). Drawings of his house, "Leyswood," were published in architectural journals, admired, and incorporated into designs by

On the surface the public mood seemed to applaud the "honesty," "simplicity," and "sincerity" of the new style. Beneath these Classical virtues, however, the Romantic mood pervaded the Queen Anne. The financial panic of 1873 had sobered the public to a realism that threatened the dynamics of the Romantic outlook. Yet Romanticism prevailed, and the picturesque qualities of the new style were just what the public needed to enter into a new building era that found Queen Anne the ruling architectural style.

The Centennial Exposition's most significant building, its huge Art Gallery, boasted a marriage of the fine and industrial arts. Great emphasis was placed on the importance of home furnishings as artistic expression. By far the most important pundit of household décor was Charles Eastlake, the nephew of the esteemed painter. Eastlake had written a modest book, *Hints on Household Taste*, which called for honesty, simplicity, and sincerity in the design of furniture, and in 1872 an American edition was published. The edition became a by-word in taste for Americans entering a new era of sensibility. Strangely, however, manufacturers, rushing to meet the demand for "honesty," marketed furniture that remained baroque in form. Only the surface ornamentation was modified. Perhaps the manufacturers knew the public better than the public knew itself. Poor Eastlake was shocked at the interpretations of his taste.

Today "Eastlake" or "Eastlakian" is a rather nebulous phrase describing furniture of the period having an engraved, chiseled, and gouged appearance. When all else fails, antique dealers are especially fond of giving the name "Eastlake" to any heavily carved object. The term also applies to a form of Queen Anne house that has especially ornate, rounded, and gouged elements.

An ad from an 1876 Harper's Weekly *displaying "Eastlakian" furniture from the Centennial Exhibition*

The Queen Anne style worked well with the demand for varied floor plans. A client could state his needs in the layout of rooms and halls, and any irregularities in form adapted easily to the style. Plan books abounded with variations on the theme.

In our time most Queen Annes are painted white, but a growing number are being painted in the original variety of colors, which played so cheerily with the varying textures and ornaments endemic to the style.

Queen Anne mansions were few but invariably spectacular. The Plainfield, New Jersey, mansion in plate 47 stood on a rise above the city that once claimed more millionaires than any in the country. Its irregular silhouette against an uncluttered sky gave it picturesque grandeur. The surfaces are a melange of rusticated stone, scalloped shingles, and ingenious strapwork. The chimneys, paneled and choke-topped, are of massive proportion to balance the tower. Windows are varied and rich in detail and framing.

When the owner of the Plainfield mansion died, the house stood vacant for less than a season before youthful vandals set fire to it. The resulting inferno lit the city below, creating what any film maker might have devoutly wished for the climax to a Gothic film. In the inferno a priceless private library perished along with halls and rooms of imported paneling. The houses replacing this Queen Anne masterpiece are of no architectural interest.

The modest Queen Anne on page 137 is probably plan-book inspired. Variations on it are spread throughout the land. The elements are typical. Upside-down columns flared to support rows of spindles and a cone-topped tower added picturesqueness and the charm of irregularity. Because this Queen Anne was built in the waning years of the style, there is relatively little texture on its surfaces. Fish-scale shingling complements the quieter clapboards, while the tall choke-topped chimney rounds out its pedigree. The multipaned windows survive at the sides of the house.

The Centennial Exposition was a great success. The

Victorian themes of the perfectibility of mankind, morality, and progress were thoroughly propounded. As usual the art displayed in the Art Gallery was the choice of the ruling art establishment. The one great and lasting piece of art at the Exposition was Thomas Eakins's, *Gross Clinic*. Shown at a medical exhibit in a building far removed from the Art Gallery, it was later relegated to almost total obscurity. Richard Wagner's *Grand March for the American Centennial Exposition* is likewise a forgotten opus.

A room in the medical building at the Centennial Exposition. Note Eakins' painting "Gross Clinic" on the back wall.

Queen Anne Mansion

Queen Anne mansions were never plentiful, but they are the rarest of rarities today. Too often they are the victims of neglect, although this magnificent example of the style was the victim of youthful arsonists. I was introduced to this Plainfield, New Jersey, mansion shortly before it burned, by a friend who felt that the place was a huge, tasteless joke and thought I might be interested in it because it was so bizarre. I painted it because it was a rare and wonderful interpretation of that Jacobean and Elizabethan architecture the English call "Jacobethan."

The pendulum swings of taste are sometimes enormous. Lancelot ("Capability") Brown (1715–1783) was one of the greatest garden designers in English history—a great deal of the English countryside owes its appearance to his planning.

He earned his nickname because he thought every plot of ground had the capability of one day being an exquisite garden—if the money and the time were forthcoming.

Brown converted old formal gardens into new Romantic conceptions, designing the gardens for, in all, 140 estates. Typically Brown's estates featured isolated clumps of trees and undulating stretches of grass girt by a belt of woodland. His name rarely appeared in print without being prefixed by "the great."

But Capability Brown was a Romanticist, and when the Romantic epoch was superseded by the new Classical era, his name and his work were regarded with derision. In the beautifully illustrated book titled The Charm of the English Village, *by P. H. Ditchfield, first published in 1908,[6] I came on a startling passage: "Happily this beautiful garden has escaped the devastation of such wretches as Capability Brown, Kent, and such desecrators, who, in cultivating the taste of landscape gardening, destroyed more than half the old gardens in England, and scarcely left us a decent hedge or sheltered walk to protect us from the east winds."*

---

6. *Reprinted in England, 1977; B. T. Batsford, Ltd., 4 Fitzhardinge St., London* W1H0AH.

The gable ends of the Queen Anne in the painting, facing the reader, contain some imaginative elements of the style. The windows below the gable at the left are, in themselves, an exercise in strapwork, the glassed openings being overpowered by the surrounding frames. Strapwork set in slate shingles to the left of the windows is repeated in a variation in the area of the windows of the gable at the right. The dome on the central tower is of a shape peculiar to the Queen Anne style, and the paneled chimneys have the characteristic choke-top configuration.

In England the Queen Anne style is frequently referred to as "Shavian," after Norman Shaw, the most influential proponent of the style during its thirty-five year reign.

Plate 47   *Queen Anne Mansion*

Plate 48   *Westfield Queen Anne*

Westfield Queen Anne

Queen Anne architecture arrived on the scene at about the same time that the plan book became a popular source of building inspiration. The Westfield, New Jersey, Queen Anne in the plate was built circa 1875 by local carpenters from a plan book. Confirmation of dates of houses in the Westfield area is difficult, as records of most nineteenth-century houses were lost in an Essex County Court House fire.[7]

Like the Italianate, the Queen Anne style allowed for a variety of floor plans and the addition of towers, bay windows, and porte-cocheres. The style introduced the spindle to give the jigsaw a rest. The painting illustrates most of the elements that identify the style: there are fish-scale shingles in the gable of the house and an octagon tower attached to its side; the tapering roof of the tower has alternating rows of fish-scale and rectangular slates topped by a medieval ornament; the porch has a frieze of spindles, and the columns have an inverted taper; finally, the chimney is choke topped. Missing is Elizabethan strapwork and windows with small multicolored panes surrounding a larger clear-glass center.

The teams of men attached to contractors and called "shops" in the late nineteenth century did not include shinglers, who are described as drifters following whatever work was available. When a house was framed and enclosed by sheathing, the skilled workers moved inside. The shingler, who needed only a shingle hatchet and a nail apron, then took over, to the annoyance of the skilled men inside who had to listen endlessly to his hammer blows. Also excluded from the shop were lathers, who nailed the inch-wide rough-cut lath to the wall studs in preparation for the plasterers. Lathers were also drifters, and their work came in cold weather when the house was enclosed. The odd ends of the bundles of lath served to keep the lathers reasonably warm, and they spent their nights in the unfinished house. When an old house is razed or restored, empty whiskey bottles, cans of beans, and other sad reminders of the departed lathers are often found between the walls where, unknown to the contractor or the craftsmen, they had been discarded.

The rules set down by the craftsmen in nineteenth-century building trades were strict and were enforced by the craftsmen themselves. A worker calling himself a master carpenter who had no right to do so was soon found out and abruptly exposed. It was best to start all over again in a distant community.

---

7. *Essex County was later partitioned. Westfield is now in Union County.*

Oldwick's Queen Anne

The names of the hamlets and villages surrounding Oldwick, New Jersey, seem to have been invented by a zealous English mystery writer at the height of his powers. Changewater, Cokesbury, Bedminster, Peapack, Gladstone, Lamington, and St. Nicholas Village are part of a lush, rolling countryside that has never lost touch with its eighteenth- and nineteenth-century heritage. Oldwick has its general store, a venerable Tewksbury Inn, and a lovely Queen Anne residence near its crossroads.

In the plate, the section of the house nearest the viewer is an eighteenth-century structure modernized in the 1880's by a wrap-around porch in the Queen Anne style. The tower is pure Queen Anne. Beneath the tower's slate roof, an angled window with a decorative hood added cost to the construction but provided the builder with the stylish form he wanted.

The pierced-wood "ears" at the top of the lathe-turned posts give an upside-down appearance typical of the style. The balustrade provides a singular expression of local talent and may possibly have been a later replacement. The fish-scale and diamond-patterned shingles provide the textured surfaces of the house's Jacobean forebears of the early seventeenth century.

Dentil molding is an unusual accent to the lavish eaves of the house. Such Classical Revival elements were to become more commonplace as the nineteenth century waned and Romanticism fell to resurgent Classicism.

The carefully maintained house graces a lovely country road and serves as a pleasing introduction to Oldwick, a predominantly nineteenth-century town unspoiled by the intrusion of styles incompatible with the regional spirit.

Plate 49   *Oldwick's Queen Anne*

XI. The Romanesque Style

IN HIS LAST YEARS, Alexander Jackson Davis despaired of American architecture. In 1872 he wrote that the Lenox Library in New York City was depraved and that the New York City Post Office was, "a costly, diseased courtesan. . . ." Davis complained that the bedizened expressions of ostentatious eclecticism were concerned with prodigal detail and unconcerned with function and mass. To the older generation of architects the new era of Picturesque Eclecticism, born in the 1870's, seemed infatuated with decoration at the expense of the whole building. Architectural design seemed the work of overambitious draftsmen rather than architects.

The High Victorian furniture designers responded to Picturesque Eclecticism with themes that expressed Baroque, Antique, Renaissance, and Louis Quatorze. Bulges, knobs, finials, pendants, tassels, gouges, and plaques abounded. Today we simply call all such furniture "Victorian," and we are apt to laugh at it; contemporaries, however, felt their ponderous pieces were triumphs of the age.

To the older public—and the older architects—the revolutionary change toward decoration in architectural and interior taste was as undesirable as it was inexplicable. The greatest architects of the pre-Civil War period found themselves unable to cope with the alien demands of the new era. They would not or could not understand the new generation. For thirty embittered years, Alexander Jackson Davis found himself ignored and then forgotten. The master of the Gothic and the Italianate refused to come to terms with the new ideals. He died in 1892 at the age of eighty-nine. The careers of Richard Upjohn and Thomas U. Walter ended as abruptly. The mood had changed, but the change remained well within the Romantic mood.

James Renwick alone (1818–1895), of all architects associated with the pre-war period, was able to negotiate the transition in public taste. Perhaps his travels in Europe had developed insights that his contemporaries lacked. Renwick was easily able to alter his production from the Gothic Revival of Grace Church, New York, to the Picturesque Eclecticism of the Smithsonian Institution and back again to the latter-day Gothic of St. Patrick's Cathedral in New York. His approach was universal, and his practice flourished until the day of his death in 1895.

St. Patrick's Cathedral, New York City

One of the most successful of the Picturesque Eclectic era was Richard Michell Upjohn (1828–1903), son of Richard Upjohn of early Gothic Revival fame. Like most of his thriving associates, the younger Upjohn received European graduate education at the Ecole des

Beaux-Arts in Paris. His best known surviving monument is the State House at Hartford, Connecticut, begun in 1878. It is eclectic from cellar to attic, combining Classical Palladian, Roman, Gothic, and Lombard styles with a salmagundi of keeps, turrets, barbicans, and varicolored stone. In a sense the son took over where the father (judiciously, he thought) had left off. The firm prospered while the senior Upjohn watched in consternation—wondering whatever happened to restraint, understatement, and good taste. But there was little to be argued. Polychromed pinnacles, parapets and gables, multihued varitextured stone, and a Lobscouse of other picturesque elements had joined to become the style of the day.

To the critics of the style, its advocates could quote A. J. Downing's old partner, Calvert Vaux. In his *Villas and Cottages*, published some twenty years before, Vaux had written, "The past should be looked on as the servant, not the master." Conceivably the younger men agreed with William Blake's aphorism: "Prudence is a rich, ugly old maid courted by Incapacity."

But the sophistry inherent in the sentiments of the new breed of architects held within itself the elements of the demise of Romanticism. The winds of change were gusting; the signs of surfeit were all around.

The late 1870's were expansive, brash, and materialistic. For the first time Americans saw themselves as a world power. Dreams of empire and "Manifest Destiny" were finding acceptance in the American consciousness. In fact Europeans were eyeing us with considerable uneasiness. It was an age of twelve-course dinners, of untaxed free enterprise, and of the once-admired rugged individual.

The elegance of the grand hotels and other public places of the east was matched by the viciousness and violence of the newly breached territories of the wild west. At the same time that Mark Twain, in tails and white tie, was regaling an audience of the rich and distinguished, a grubby mob in Tombstone, Arizona, was breaking down a jail to lynch a hapless inmate. Yet in

The State House in Hartford, Connecticut

a decade the sheds, shacks, and shanties of the *Gunsmoke* era would be replaced by courthouses, hotels, and colleges in the "civilizing" styles of architecture current in the seventies and eighties.

A great climax was approaching. A noisy, unbridled optimism and a raucous, lopsided prosperity paraded in public view—and a part of that public became alarmed. The financial panic of September 17, 1873, was only a forewarning of the urgent need for change. In many ways our nation had been on an egocentric binge. Overstatement in the national life generally was nicely symbolized by the excesses that architecture now exhibited. A sick spirit was disguised in decadent and obfuscating finery. A. J. Davis was not alone in his disapproval. The Romantic Movement and the Romantic mood were coming to a gaudy, tottering, and bathetic end.

Henry Hobson Richardson, Louis Sullivan, and Frank Lloyd Wright are frequently named as the greatest American architects. H. H. Richardson (1838–1886) was early affected by the Aesthetic Movement,[3] which advocated the evidence of handwork. Random brickwork, wood shingles, fieldstone, and other elements recalling an earlier America were incorporated in Richardson's late Queen Annes, and in the early examples of the new Romanesque Revival style, to portray an air of quaintness.

A sample of one of H. H. Richardson's late Queen Annes

Richardson quickly tired of these cosmetic affectations, however, and turned to a form of revival unique to the United States.

Every previous architectural revival form had its origins in Europe and had been adopted in this country only later. The Romanesque Revival began here. The style drew its name from forms of architecture that immediately preceded the original medieval Gothic. The English prefer to call the Romanesque style "Norman." The original form reached up out of the Dark Ages, bursting forth into medievalism with such force as to

Alexander Hall, a Romanesque building on the campus of Princeton University

become the first great wave of monumental building since the fall of the Roman Empire. According to tradition or myth, the rough stones of the original Romanesque churches, abbeys, and other buildings were reclaimed from Roman ruins, roads, and aqueducts. In keeping with that tradition the elements chosen to represent the style in its revival were all heavy, rusticated, and even grotesque. Any Romanesque building, domestic or public, needed a convincing amount of rock-faced masonry, and it needed broad, rounded arches supported by multiple small columns and topped by a capital with interwoven Byzantine, Celtic, or "barbaric" designs. The overall effect was of massiveness, ruggedness, and earth-hugging, squat stability. The public responded enthusiastically.

Somehow historians manage to single out one name to describe an era or an event, although many may have been major contributors to it. H. H. Richardson was by no means the only architect to move in the direction the Romanesque concept was pointing. Nor was the style limited to one absolute form. For example, variations were exhibited in the unique works of Frank Furness, whose Pennsylvania Academy of the Fine Arts, in Philadelphia, is a masterpiece of Romanesque color, texture, form, and intent.

---

3. The Aesthetic Movement was an extension of Ruskinian influence symbolized by the peacock, the lily, and the sunflower. The movement, at its height in the late 1870's, is best remembered by the appearances of Oscar Wilde on American lecture platforms in velvet pantaloons and satin slippers. Wilde triggered such an outburst of derision and caricature that the cult came to an abrupt end on this side of the Atlantic. In England, the movement was parodied in Gilbert & Sullivan's "Patience."

Nevertheless Richardson's pre-eminence is deserved. He meant more to architecture than the architectural styles he mastered. Richardson put together a highly efficient architectural office in which he acted as corporate director supervising every step of any given project. He delegated responsibilities to well-organized departments in a smooth-flowing operation. Craftsmen in every aspect of building and design were challenged to contribute new forms that were needed to express the interdependence of the parts and the structure itself.

Richardsonian interiors were thoughtfully detailed to echo forms and textures of the exteriors. Fireplaces were massive, and outsized accessories were designed in Celtic and other robust forms to match the monumentality of the whole. Nor did Richardson neglect furniture. He drew specifications for numerous pieces that would match the muscular balusters, the exposed beams, and the golden-oak paneling that characterized his interiors. Richardson used elements of past styles for his furnishings, compacting them in a sturdy, sensible style now called "Richardsonian Eclectic." Despite his borrowings, however, Richardson's was essentially a style of its own.

Richardson also gave a new view of self to the architect. His years in Paris had a lifelong effect on his work and on his sense of mission. His Paris years (1859–65) coincided with the beginnings of the revolutionary ideals fomented by the Impressionist painters. Richardson's insistence on texture in all he produced is attributed by some to the texture of the brushwork in the paintings of Courbet, Manet, and other artists of the Impressionist movement.

Richardson adopted another concept held by the French painters of his time. The rising group of artists no longer felt that they were only interpreters of the aesthetic; they insisted also on being intellectual and cultural leaders. Given this position, the new breed felt themselves equal to any level of social or political leadership. Perhaps this spirit saw its culmination in the formation of the short-lived (1919–20) Paderewski cabinet in Poland. That cabinet was largely composed of artists and intellectuals, the pianist Ignace Paderewski serving as prime minister, and Sigismund Ivanowski, a respected painter whose years of exile were spent in America, serving as minister of labor.

Henry Hobson Richardson became the living example of the new artist as cultural, intellectual, and social leader. He was as much at home in American upper-class Newport as in the coffee houses of Boston and New York. He provided direct architectural guidance to the rich and the newly rich by directing their tastes to new spatial relationships and to the delights of simplicity.

While Richardson designed for governments and for the very rich, lesser architects and builders designed Romanesque houses for the upper-middle class. Those residences were usually planted at imposing corners of well-to-do neighborhoods. To encourage employment in the 1930's, many of the deteriorated residential areas were rezoned to allow businesses to replace houses. Imposing older houses were razed to make way for gas stations and other enterprises. Romanesques seemed particularly vulnerable to the wrecker. The cut stone was reusable, but the beautifully constructed tile roofs were smashed, and the stained-glass windows were held valueless. The painting on page 145 shows one of a gathering of fine residences on High Street (now called Martin Luther King, Jr., Blvd.) in Newark, New Jersey. It was demolished for a housing project that never happened. Much of a once-proud street is given over to rubble and weeds.

In my search for a suitable Romanesque house to paint, I was struck by the rarity of the style in New Jersey. Only the ice-house was more difficult to find. In Newark, however, the Peddie Baptist Church still stands. It is one of the finest surviving examples of the Romanesque, but its future is uncertain. In recent years fire, age, and gross denaturing have taken their toll on all the once-familiar structures. The Romanesque style was never a commonplace form. From the beginning these

A Romanesque interior in an elegant Washington, D.C. home

were costly structures rarely faring well beyond the original builders' generation. All too often Romanesque structures passed from the heirs of the builders to become rooming houses or funeral homes, only to slip into dereliction and final destruction. The success of the style was in its public application more than its use for residences. The survival rate of Romanesque public buildings is gratifying, and the efforts of preservationists have been rewarded.

Since Richardson's death in 1886, architectural historians have had the benefit of a century in which to assess his work. Richardson's building styles forked in two distinct directions: one, exemplified by his "organic" and functional building, such as his Marshall Field Warehouse in Chicago; the other, based on Picturesque antecedents. After Richardson the organic concept would be championed by Louis Sullivan and the traditionalist concept espoused by Stanford White and the New York firm he joined with Charles McKim and William Rutherford Mead. The direction that Sullivan took led to modern architecture, Frank Lloyd Wright, and the demise of Romanticism in architecture. Stanford White's route led to Chateauesque, Beaux-Art Classicism, and the Renaissance Revival styles.

Rarely does the true creator of a style, a mode, or an artistic invention receive from historians the credit due the innovator. It is the *synthesizer* or popularizer of

the style who is invariably honored. Raphael was understood to be the pivotal painter of the High Renaissance and was idolized during his lifetime. Yet the true innovators of the time were Da Vinci, Michelangelo, and Bramante, who have fared well in history but never achieved the public adulation in their own times that was lavished on Raphael. In more recent times Picasso reaped huge financial success and public acclaim as the premier synthesist of modern art, yet each of his styles is directly traceable to preceding and contemporary artists whose fame was overshadowed by Picasso.

In architecture it is sometimes the draftsmen, the designers, and even the builders who innovate rather than the architect. Credit is rarely given when the innovation is assimilated into the formal declaration of the work. As there are ghost writers, so there are ghost architects, who, without firms of their own, become freelancers to large architectural organizations. Stanford White, whose star-crossed destiny became legend, began his career as a draftsman in Richardson's Boston office. He contributed more than draftsmanship to the firm.

The synthesizer should not be denigrated. There is a special talent in those who can pull together creativity's ragtag odds and ends to achieve a style. And the acceptance of a style is often inspired by the personal dynamics of the architect/entrepreneur. A. J. Downing was never an architect, but his writings and his influence had much to do with the course architecture took in this country.

The literate public has been led to an overromantic view of the arts. Neo-Platonists held that the poet, the painter, and the architect created in a divine frenzy.[4] It is a concept cherished and promulgated by screen writers and the incurably Romantic. The fiction surrounding the

---

4. There *are* times when artists and other creators sense the presence of unusual extrasensory factors. The fifteenth-century Venetian painter Giovanni Bellini wrote that these inspirational lapses out of time denoted the attendance of God. Another, more prosaic, explanation suggests that the lapses may be episodes of self-hypnosis provoked by intense concentration. Almost always these lacunae, or time lapses, are followed by a heightened sensitivity leading to the resolution of an enigma or the achievement of a new level of aesthetic creativity or awareness. The lacunae are infrequent and cannot be consciously induced.

immortals of art have denied artists the right to be human—or even sensible. The facts are otherwise. Many of the old masters, overburdened by commissions, employed other artists or studio assistants to execute the tedious details of lace and golden filigree. There were ghost artists who specialized in the horses and dogs fashionable in paintings of the time. Vermeer was one of the first to use the camera obscura as an aid to drawing, and Canaletto overcame the shifting shadows and vagaries of sunlight with a camera obscura large enough to work inside. The Impressionists, and even Thomas Eakins, used photography as an adjunct to their work.

Composers guarded the myth of the divine frenzy all the way up to the time of Stravinsky, who cheerfully confessed that he used the piano to work out his compositions.

Richardson, among other great architects, used all the help he could get. He recognized talent, bought it, and used it. His draftsmen and his designers were the best available. His questing nature, his perceptions of the prevailing moods, his instinct for the lines that led to the future, his qualities of leadership, his gift for management, and the social graces that glued it all together—all these qualities were components of his greatness.

High Street Romanesque

The Victorian penchant for a bond between history and architecture found almost ultimate expression in the Romanesque. The form became a High Victorian symbolic ideal. The nexus between a vaguely conceived archaeology and the Victorians' insatiable desire for solidity, for bigness, and for permanency assured the Romanesque its acceptance for libraries, churches, reformatories, railroad terminals, and homes. The style combined massiveness, picturesque eclecticism, and, because of its heavy, rusticated masonry, an undefined sense of moody power. Because the High Victorian era was a time of unparalleled uncertainty and upheaval, the Victorian felt a sense of loss—and he felt vulnerable. Agrarian backgrounds were but a generation past, and many allusions, oral and otherwise, were related to the farmstead. Now the individual found himself on a stage of ever-changing scenery, and the impermanence was contrary to his ingrained ethos. He gratefully responded to the presence of the solid, psychologically protective structures that vicariously spelled security.

From the 1870's to 1890, the Romanesque was the style of choice for the upper-middle class. The style grew out of no particular Old World style, taking in elements of French Late Gothic, sixteenth-century castles of the Loire valley, and Jacobean forms of England. Unsubstantiated legend suggests that the name "Romanesque" came from the use by Dark Ages Christians of the rough-faced stones recovered from the crumbling ruins of Roman viaducts and aqueducts.

Although it is certain that the Richardsonian Romanesque style was not altogether Richardson's, nor especially Romanesque, the buildings that Henry Hobson Richardson created, and similar ones that rival firms built, are now so named. The impact that Richardson made in the world of architecture was enormous. He built an architectural corporation of twentieth-century efficiency and assumed the role of tycoon, assigning tasks to a wide-ranging and talented staff that included Stanford White. Richardson's wealth, his way of life, and his presence gave new stature to his art. In Newport, in Boston, or in New York, he was an equal, having attained the status that Beethoven predicted one day would come to artists.

High Street, Newark, New Jersey, was once remarkable for its notable families and fashionable houses. Arson

Plate 50 *High Street Romanesque*

and neglect destroyed many of them, but this handsome Romanesque and its stately Renaissance Revival companion were razed to make way for a housing project that never happened. The illustration indicates almost every element of the Romanesque style: rusticated stone, paneled chimney, grouped pillars with rude capitals, a conical-roofed tower, and a slit window or two. The house lacks only a huge arch.

Elizabeth Railroad Station

When the Central Railroad of New Jersey built a station in Elizabeth, they meant it to outshine the lackluster station provided by the Pennsylvania Railroad a hundred yards away. The C.R.R. could not compete in size or traffic with the P.R.R., but they could offer their passengers a building of eye-catching contemporary style. Since the 1890's the Romanesque station has been a source of considerable pride for Elizabeth and the C.R.R.

Today, unhappily, the C.R.R. is gone, the station clock is falling apart, and someone has stolen the bronze weather vane. The records of the Central Railroad and its handsome depots were sold or auctioned to railroading buffs and railroad magazines, and the future of the building is very much in doubt. It will be interesting to see what will replace a structure so thoughtfully built to enhance the community and reward the viewer.

The buyer of the painting of the Elizabeth C.R.R. station assured me that his purchase was not motivated by aesthetic considerations but by romantic memory. During World War II, he was aboard a troop train that was scheduled for a stop in Elizabeth. While training at a distant camp, he had written a proposal of marriage to his beloved. She was to meet him at the Pennsylvania Railroad station in Elizabeth if she chose to accept and await his return. The train arrived, and the young soldier searched for his intended—in vain. When the troop train pulled out of the Elizabeth station, it carried a very sad young man to an uncertain future on the battlefields of Europe.

Of course the proximity of the depots in Elizabeth was the villain in this piece. The young lady had waited in vain at the Central station. It took time for the mistake to be rectified, but the story has a decidedly happy ending, and the painting now hangs where children and grandchildren can enjoy the Romantic architecture and the romantic story.

The wide arches at the base of the tower are a must for the Romanesque Style. The pointed elements at the roof edge, here shown in copper oxide, are often made of rusticated stone in a form reminiscent of seashore drip-sand cones. The quoins at the corners of the tower are made of roughly hewn stone—another hallmark of the Romanesque.

In the background are the posts of the catenary lines of the electrified section of the railroad. The bridge carries the trains to the rival Pennsylvania station.

Plate 51   *Elizabeth Railroad Station*

XII. Vernacular Styles and Fashionable Alterations

THE TERMS "REGIONAL" and "vernacular" are used almost interchangeably, but there seem to be cultural connotations attached to the word "regional"—as in the Pueblo Style, a regional style of the southwest. The Pueblo Style obviously derives from the structures built by the original inhabitants of Arizona and New Mexico. Yet "regional" is also applied to the sod houses of a great area extending from Canada to northern Texas. The sod houses (1860–1900) were without cultural precedent and were born of necessity to provide shelter where neither wood nor stone was available.

A sod house in South Dakota ca. 1880

A Pueblo-style residence

Vernacular architecture arose from the expedient uses of available architectural material, forms, and details. In the late nineteenth century the local millworks gave a builder limited choices of architectural elements: window frames, doorway consoles, balusters, slate shingles, moldings, standing-seam roofing, etc. The builder might use a mixture of these items to drape a standard, practical form. There might be indiscriminate mingling of Classical and Victorian era styles, but the results could catch the fancy of the natives. Then that "style" would spread as far as the developer's scope allowed.

The little town house on page 150 is a late-nineteenth-century vernacular form in Lambertville, New Jersey, which is connected by bridge to New Hope, Pennsylvania. The style is a Pennsylvania vernacular form, and examples stretch from Philadelphia to Harrisburg. Because it is a form often repeated in this area, it is vernacular and not simply eclectic. It borrows elements from the Mansard and Queen Anne styles as well as incorporating a few Classical components.

Plate 53 exhibits a painting of a town house in Alexandria, Virginia. The building seems quite obviously of the Victorian era. But is it? A closer examination of the eaves area shows modillions—vestiges of beams that penetrate beyond the walls. Modillions are characteristic of Georgian architecture. Judging by the brick, the neighborhood, and the size of the modillions, the house could be 250 years old, despite the doorway which was installed perhaps 100 years ago to modernize the building. The entrance way is a handsome example of its kind, and while it would look at home on an Italianate or Mansard house, it was probably designed separately especially for the house's nineteenth-century owners.

The painting on page 153 is of a Gothic Revival house in New Haven, Connecticut. The house was not mentioned in the Gothic Revival pages because of a curious consideration: the structure, built in 1804, began its existence in the Adamesque–Federal style. The original, very beautiful Adamesque doorway with side lights and arcuated transom light was removed from the front entrance to an entrance at the back. In 1858 the house, named "Raynham Hall," was remodeled in the Gothic Revival style, with richly carved bargeboards, pendants, and finials and molding that suggests the pointed arch. At the time of the modernization, the Picturesque tower with its pointed windows was added. Even with its determined symmetry Raynham Hall is among the most Picturesque and Romantic houses in America.

The modillions were the telltale factors in establishing the original style of the Alexandria house. The trabeated fenestration of the New Haven house was the clue to its former character. Had it been built in the Gothic Revival style, the windows—at least some of them—would have displayed the pointed arch. It takes only a modest knowledge of the forms of architecture to be a reasonably competent architectural detective—to be able to detect Victorian era houses that have been colonialized or colonial houses that have been Victorianized.

Architectural detection—the ability to determine the age of a structure or to tell if it has been altered or modernized over the years—is a fascinating game. The classification of Victorian ceiling rosettes as a clue to the age of a brownstone, or understanding the age of moldings, or spotting elements that alter the true nature of a building, all come from knowing details of architectural history. Styles waxed and waned within specific time spans. Doors, windows, brackets, and rosettes all provide clues to that time.

Lambertville Vernacular

No specific architectural term exists for this nineteenth-century town house. "Eclectic" comes to mind for an amalgam of styles that has found favor in communities that range out from Philadelphia and Baltimore. It is an example of vernacular architecture, because it is recognizable as a type, if not a true style. The eclecticism involves a Queen Anne porch, an Italianate second story, and a Mansard third floor. Folkloristic anthropologists might classify the house as folk architecture.

Architectural dictionaries define "vernacular" architecture as a mode of building based on regional forms and materials. This meant, originally, that materials found growing, or in the ground, were used to build within the limitations imposed by the materials available. In the late nineteenth century vernacular building used elements available at the local millworks and varied with the ability of local contractors to utilize them in accepted forms.

Availability of materials was not always the motivating force in construction. In New England, where excellent building stone abounds, the colonists chose wood as the prime building resource. In Pennsylvania, where great and luxuriant forests provided every kind of wood, the material of choice was stone. This anomaly is explained by the origin of the colonists. The followers of William Penn came from that part of England where stone was the traditional and favored building substance. The New England colonists came largely from a region of England where the tradition favored wood.

By the end of the nineteenth century millworks provided regionally standardized elements of construction. Doorway consoles, preformed window frames, a variety of brackets, molding, trim, and other transportable items saved the contractor time and money. Nineteenth-century prefabrication began the trend that has had such an egre-

gious effect on modest domestic building today. Nineteenth-century millwork was standardized to a degree, but from region to region it was individual. Local mills competed with new forms and in a variety of forms. By contrast much of today's millwork is produced at the national level and distributed nationwide, resulting in the monotonous standardization that forces owners to employ a flamingo on the lawn or an eagle over the doorway to differentiate their homes from neighbors'.

The town house in the painting is on a Victorian-era street in Lambertville, New Jersey, just across the Delaware River from New Hope, Pennsylvania.

Plate 52   *Lambertville Vernacular*

Victorian Doorway

Alexandria, Virginia, is justly famed for its eighteenth- and nineteenth-century architecture. Through fashionable modernization there is some crossing over in styles. This painting of a Victorian doorway in Alexandria is an illustration of the inclination of homeowners to alter structures from original concepts to updated styles. The Alexandrian example is successful, as there is no clash with nearby elements of another style. Not all such attempts are as successful. Each month The Old House Journal *features a "Remuddling of the Month," a showcase of horrors perpetrated on fine old buildings in the name of fashion, technology, or thoughtless expedience.*

To arrive at an accurate architectural identification or approximate dating of a structure, it is important to examine every detail. The doorway here is undeniably Victorian—one of the finest I have ever encountered. But at the top right-hand corner of the painting are elements that indicate that the house it graces is of a much greater age. The modillions projecting under the eaves are a device of eighteenth-century Georgian architecture. Sometime in the 1870's an owner, feeling the fashionable tugs of the time, decided to modernize his eighteenth-century Georgian town house with a contemporary doorway and console.

The uneven coloration of the brick was caused by weathering, which washed away the white paint except where shutters protected. Sandblasting the walls to remove the paint would be ruinous to eighteenth-century brick. In time the weathering process will wash away the last vestiges of paint. Or new shutters can be hung.

The Victorian forms of the doorway are forms chosen from a vast variety of ingenious inventions in wood turnings and carvings. Some of the designs came from the drafting tools of designers in architectural offices and millworks. Many were variations on themes expressed in Renaissance and baroque modes of architecture. Other forms were the work of individual carpenters with an eye for design. When variants such as Eastlake gouging or piercing were introduced, those new decorations were promptly

Plate 53   *Victorian Doorway*

copied by craftsmen, to exhibit their skills and to keep abreast of the prevalent fashions.

In much of what has become known as Stick Style, Carpenter Gothic, or vernacular building, the role of the carpenter was significant. Of all the houses built in these modes, only a few were actually designed by architects. Carpenters in effect designed as well as built the great majority of the houses we regard as Victorian. The successful carpenter knew what could be done with materials at hand, and he knew what worked and what would be unacceptable. Plan books and trade journals gave him the broad outlines and a good deal of detailing, but in the end, the carpenter had to adapt those plans to the many limitations placed on him by terrain, budget, the whims of the buyer, and the availability of materials. He had to be a practical engineer and a creative designer. His apprenticeship was long and arduous, and a perusal of the manuals he was required to read will instill a deep respect for the carpenters of the Victorian era.

Raynham

Tudor embossing over the trabeated windows was felt to have sufficient Gothic relationship to fit comfortably with the overt Gothic modifications that in 1858 modernized "Raynham," an eighteenth-century house in New Haven, Connecticut. The house had always been a handsome place, but the restrained original Federal style must have seemed uncommonly plain as New Haven grew into a populous and worldly city. The tower at Raynham Hall does have the pointed windows to indicate it was built at the time of the extensive alterations that produced the striking results seen in the painting. The gable is less steeply pitched than the gables of originally built Gothic Revival examples, but the pendant, finial, richly carved bargeboards, and grouped Tudor chimneys almost completely disguise the Federal origin of the house.

Not all the Federal aspects are forgotten, however. The beautifully refined Adamesque doorway that once welcomed guests to Raynham has been preserved and now serves the architecturally uncertain far end of the house. The tower in the background provided a fine view, but it was also intended as a picturesque structure to punctuate the symmetry of the forms.

The view to the river is now obstructed—certainly a loss—but the real loss must have been to river travelers whose view of the picturesque landmark was ended when intervening buildings went up.

From 1790 to 1820 the Federal was the dominant American architectural style, its name deriving from its association with the beginnings of the Republic. Before its fashionable alteration, Raynham Hall was an Adamesque–Federal house with all the modest details of that style. The doorway had the typical fan-shaped transom light and delicately leaded side lights. At the eaves decoration was limited to delicate dentil molding and a reserved frieze. Porticos incorporated slender Doric columns and pilasters at the borders of the doorways. Interior elements reflected the exterior, with fireplaces and corner cupboards ornamented in the Adamesque manner.

In 1784 the Scottish architect Robert Adam (1728–1792) visited the ruins at Herculaneum and rediscovered Classical wreathes, wheat sheaves, festoons, and other forms that were to become hallmarks of the influential style he and his brothers created. Chippendale and Sheraton were direct inheritors of the Adam brothers' inspirations. In America the style embodied only Classical details, but in Europe the Adam style might include Neo-Gothic, Egyptian, and Etruscan motifs.

In New Jersey's Hackensack Valley and in New York's Hudson Valley, many of the Dutch houses of the seventeenth- and early eighteenth century were modernized in the first decades of the eighteenth century with Adamesque doorways, fanlights, and fireplaces.

"Federal," "Adamesque–Federal," and "Post-Colonial" are varying names for the same style.

Plate 54 *Raynham*

Milford Egg House

Milford, Pennsylvania, across the Delaware River from Sussex, the northwesternmost county of New Jersey, has excellent and exuberant examples of nineteenth-century-architecture in fine condition and generous supply. Two swift streams tumbling into the Delaware provided the power that encouraged the building of mills that assured an abundance of sawn wood. Surrounding forests supplied the wood, native bluestone made foundations and walls, and slate for roofs was quarried nearby. The easy availability of materials, the presence of skilled carpenters, and occasional periods of prosperity made Milford into the handsome town it is today. Milford's citizens work hard to keep it that way.

Among the Greek Revivals, Gothics, Italianates, Queen Annes, etc., is a house that first intrigued me in the late thirties, as I drove through Milford en route to college in Syracuse, New York. That house inspired my first detailed painting, which in turn encouraged me to write To Grandfather's House We Go, a primer of American domestic architecture. The Margaret and Richard Rogers house is known unofficially as the "Egg House" in celebration of the egg-shaped forms that decorate the pillars supporting the porch roof. The house itself is essentially Cube Style Italianate, but the doorway and windows are an interpretation of Greek Revival detailing. The overall effect is downright cheerful. The standing-seam roof is topped by a bracketed cupola and is low pitched in the Italianate manner. The columns are entirely original, just a little eccentric, and must have been the work of a bravura carpenter.

Milford has retained its nineteenth-century charm through quirks of history that might have discouraged a less determined population. The town was bypassed by canals, then by railroads, and never developed any large-scale industry. Without a railroad, however, Milford had no wrong side of the tracks, and without large-scale industry, there were no slums. In time the town became a fashionable summer resort. French families introduced

Plate 55 *Milford Egg House*

continental cuisine that brought gourmets flocking. The summer boardinghouse became the hub of the economy, but the Depression put an end to that delightful institution. Following the World War II years, Milford attracted commuters and a considerable retired population. Gone are the days when Sarah Bernhardt and Joseph Jefferson found Milford an ideal retreat, but it's a cheerful place very aware of its fine architectural heritage.

The painting of the Egg House is my only painting done in egg tempera. Sheer coincidence.

Gramercy Park Victorian

A careful inspection of the splendid doorway in the painting will reveal elements of Greek Revival ornamentation. The facing of the exterior jambs is slightly tapered, and the lintel board extends beyond the jambs to create an impression of massiveness. A sheltering porch roof is sup-

ported by ironwork combining Greek with other themes. The door itself is richly plastic, with glass-backed pierced elements that echo the black metalwork. Number 4 is the outstanding building on the square called Gramercy Park. If it looks familiar, it may be remembered as the base for

Plate 56   *Gramercy Park Victorian*

Helen Hayes' and Mildred Natwick's ad hoc TV detection forays.

Gramercy Park is the only private park in Manhattan. Admittance is by key. Nannies, prams, and a nice variety of dogs and birds are the principal inhabitants of the square. The Players Club and the National Arts Club occupy town houses on the little park on the east side of the city. It is an elegant enclave and a relief from the sounds of through-traffic avenues that course nearby. The bronze statue of Edwin Booth is the centerpiece of the park.

In New York's East Sixties and Seventies town houses are forbidden the luxury of stoops. Many Park Avenue residences were forced to relinquish stoops when that illustrious thoroughfare was widened. Some of the remodeling left much to be desired, as stairways were, of necessity, replaced within the buildings. Some elegant parlors were thus destroyed. From then on New York's town houses were built with principal entrances at street level, and new entrance concepts were introduced along with new styles. Chateauesque, Renaissance Revival, Beaux-Arts, and Classical Revival styles became parts of the cityscape. Sprinkled in with the residences of New York's richest families are corporate headquarters, embassies, and clubs, some of which, like the New York Yacht Club, architecturally describe the nature of the inhabitants. The Yacht Club's façade is a baroque reminder of the stern of a caravel.

Number 4 Grammercy Park, with its Greek reminders, is still predominantly Victorian. Someone passing through the doorway would hardly expect to be greeted by a hostess in a Dolly Madison gown. The visitor might better expect Belter sofas and a Victorian hostess in Mary Todd Lincoln attire.

Connected Town Houses

The American town house, especially the row house, came into its own during the Victorian era. Industrialization concentrated populations and created a demand for affordable housing. Property owners capitalized by building multiple dwellings characterized by such terms as "tenements," "railroad flats," and "cold-water flats." These places, monotonously similar, were more like warrens than homes and, at worst, were the breeding places of criminals and addicts and the cause of brutality, despair, and abbreviated lives. At their best, however, the modest, contiguous town houses looked something like the cheerful row of dwellings in the painting.

The idea of attached housing in America is as old as the Pueblos. In England connected town houses were an established form of shelter as early as the thirteenth century. The ground floors were used as storage or as shops, and the floor above as living quarters. Continental town houses grew in clusters inside protective fortifications. Again, space was at a premium, and rooms were often projected over streets and alleys, to create the picturesque look of the medieval town. In America port cities were the first to adopt the row-house concept. Boston, Philadelphia, New York, Baltimore, and major seaports to the south developed communities of connected two- and three-story houses. The houses, according to reigning fashions, embodied elements of Georgian, Federal, and Greek Revival styles. The most familiar town houses of all are the ubiquitous four-story Italianates. The dwellings are good survivors because they continue to efficiently fulfill the essential needs of privacy, shelter, and proximity to the port, marketplace, and employment.

What began as limited blocks of contiguous but varied town houses in the ideal examples shown in this painting and the painting entitled Lenoir's (plate 5) too often became monotonous, seemingly endless rows of houses, each indistinguishable from its neighbors. The conformity of the buildings seem to affect the inhabitants. If jalousies, or venetian blinds, or ersatz siding was assumed by one deni-

zen of a row-house block, soon, one by one, the entire block conformed. If the next block resisted change, it was tacitly understood that the "individuality" of that block was to be respected. I passed by a block of three-story Italianates in Baltimore once and was unhappy to note that on one house the ornate brackets and frieze so typical of the Italianate town house had been replaced by a blank plywood surface that stretched diagonally inward from the extended eave to just below the frieze band. A few years later I passed the same block to find that every one of the twelve houses had suffered the same indignity.

The pleasant stretch of town houses in New Castle, Delaware, was painted to show the progression of town houses that rise from two- and three-story houses to the more contemporary apartment building in the distance. Like Lenoir's, the Victorian storefront has been left untouched, although it has been a private dwelling for years. Painted and unpainted brick, alleyways, sturdy shutters, benches, trees, brick sidewalks, gas lamps, and potted plants all contribute to a colorful yet properly restrained neighborhood.

To most of us, the brick town house is such a familiar object that it is surprising to learn that only one brick town house existed in all of England in the thirteenth century (Little Wenham Hall, Suffolk)—at a time when there were about 1,200 castles.

Cape May September

The Republic guest house in Cape May, New Jersey, and its neighbor are choice examples of High Victorian carpenters' art. The porch of the Republic is so ornate that the simplicity of the house itself is lost in an attempt to assimilate all the dressing.

The painting of the Republic is set in September, that most poignant month at the seashore. The guests have gone, and the rocking chair is abandoned. Next summer seems a long way off! I wrote many of the descriptions of the paintings directly after I had completed the work, so that ideas generated while I was painting remained recollectible. The Republic's description was written in 1979. As it turned out there was no next summer for the Republic. A new owner changed its name, repainted, spread colorful awnings, and established what has become a fashionable gourmet restaurant. None of the architectural detailing has been changed, however.

In the early 1970's a move to modernize Cape May gathered enough momentum and attention to shake residential traditionalists into asking for outside help. Help came with alacrity from environmentalists, preservationists, and architectural historians, who were eventually able to convince the "forward-looking" groups that Cape May's greatest asset was in being itself: to bring Cape May into the twentieth century would have been disastrous. The threat wakened the community to its singular heritage, and such a sense of pride developed that preservation and restoration on a broad scale were undertaken in Cape May. The result has been a remarkable prosperity. License plates of Canada and of every state are seen in the streets.

Cape May's architecture was largely conceived and constructed by individual carpenter-builders using plan books and trade journals. As crossovers, hybrids, or eclectics were produced as a matter of course and without criticism, a recognizable vernacular developed which was once derisively referred to as "Parvenu Picturesque." Yet some distinguished architects also turned their talents to Cape May projects. Frank Furness, whose Pennsylvania Acad-

emy of the Fine Arts is a masterpiece of High Victorian Gothic architecture, and Samuel Sloan, a nationally known architect, produced buildings in the town. The name that most often appears as architect in Cape May is that of Philadelphia's Stephen Decatur Button.

Plate 58   *Cape May September*

XIII. The Stick Style

VINCENT J. SCULLY, JR., the distinguished authority on the Stick Style, places the tenure of the style from 1840 to 1876. The dates are correct in the Victorian context, but the thirty-six-year time span also can be extended forward into the world of Frank Lloyd Wright or backward to centuries-old Japanese styles, for the elements of the Stick Style are inherent in both.

Some architectural historians choose to ignore the Stick Style altogether, passing it off as an extension or decoration of the Gothic or Italianate. The red Hopewell house (plate 59), for example, is, in the main, an Italianate. Its projecting eaves and undeniable campanile say Italianate, but look more closely at all those sticks substituting for brackets, pointing up "the honesty of construction." Most modern architectural historians would defer to the brilliant architectural theories of Professor Scully, but some still feel that the sticks are but a form of decoration on an Italianate frame. Before Scully, they point out, the style had no name except, vaguely, Eastlakian.

From the viewpoint of the Classicists, the search for "Truth" in the Romantic era was a matter of some hilarity. Somehow, during the Romantic reign, the bare bones of Truth became a baroque mélange. In our own century the Bauhaus Classicists, in *their* search for Truth, provided the Romanticists who followed reasons to disdain them for the icily inhuman aspects of their work.

"Truth" has been a favorite word in every architectural age. A. J. Downing wrote a great deal about it. When not specifically calling on Truth, he wrote about "suitability," "fitness," "expression of purpose," etc. In discussing wooden cottages, Downing warned that an attempt to decorate a simple cottage in the manner applied to Gothic villas (which cost thousands more) was an offense against Truth. He suggested vines as an alternative for bargeboarding and trim embellishment. Downing also preferred vertical boards and battens for the exterior of his cottages. He felt that the vertical lines expressed the underlying construction better than the traditional horizontal clapboards.

Long before the West had contact with Japan, the Japanese regarded that same vertical effect as inherent in the aesthetics of their architectural forms. They wanted the structures of their buildings to extend from the functional to the visible. In the best examples of Japanese indigenous architecture, aesthetics and Truth were admirably joined. Just how much influence Japanese building had on the ideas set forth in Downing's writing is unknowable, but we do know that he had access to S. H. Brooks's *Designs for Cottage and Villa Architecture*, published in London. There is speculation that Brooks was directly influenced by prints and sketches of Japanese native architecture. Brooks's houses nevertheless showed only the wide overhanging eaves and immense brackets of an exaggerated Italianate style. The Stick Style aspect of his work was achieved by consciously exposing vertical members of the frame. If the house were to be of brick, then the brick was used to fill in between the vertical wooden members and to lie flush with the upright posts. If wood were the choice, then the wood was deeply recessed from the vertical members so that shadows could play their picturesque part in emphasizing verticality.

Brooks and Downing adhered to the dictum that for a cottage to be Truthful its construction must show through. That tenet was the basis of the Stick Style. Although the Stick Style itself ended in the 1870's, its spirit continued in the works of Frank Lloyd Wright and in some California construction of the 1950's. And, of course, the search for Truth always goes on.

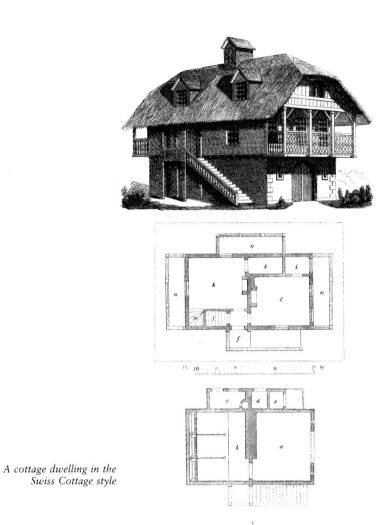

A cottage dwelling in the
Swiss Cottage style

In the beginning Stick Style houses were reasonably Truthful, but once again fashion overwhelmed Truth. The lonely little 1870's Stick Style in Ocean Grove, New Jersey, on page 167 tells us where Fashion led Truth. Behind all the curved and serrated members and the web of pierced decoration is the simplest of houses. The building at the left in the plate is an auditorium for the Methodist community once famous for its blue laws.

The Stick Style fitted nicely into Victorian philosophy. *Truly* Truthful it was not, but it did *stand for* Truth. It also expressed *character*, and character was an attribute very high in the Victorian list of virtues. Contemporary writers admired the Stick Style houses and were especially charmed by the shadows cast by the external framework. In Henry Cleaveland's 1856 plan book, devoted largely to Stick Style houses, he wrote: "The strength and character of a building depend almost

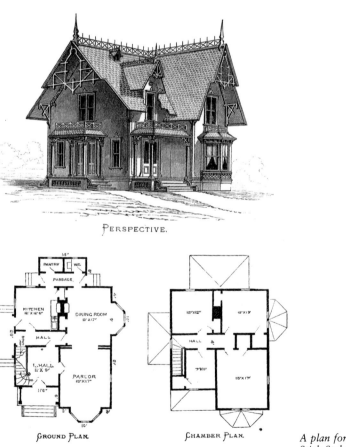

PERSPECTIVE.

GROUND PLAN. CHAMBER PLAN.

A plan for a
Stick Style house

The characteristics of the Stick Style, as it progressed over the years, include extensive verandas, an irregular silhouette, steep roofs, occasional diagonal or crossed overlays, and anything else that a builder might provide to symbolize underlying structural forces. The wood that was exposed as braces, extensions of beams, and other skeletal components were the sticks that Professor Scully seized upon for the name "Stick Style."

Another variation which falls within the Stick Style family is a sub-Gothic style known as the "Swiss Cottage" style or "Chalet Gothic." The roofs are low pitched and projecting in the manner of Alpine counterparts, and a gallery or veranda is set under the eaves. Balusters that formed the gallery were cut in "peasant" design to add texture to the already preoccupied surfaces.

wholly on the shadows which are thrown upon its surfaces by projecting members.''

Downing's *The Architecture of Country Houses* shows plans of the English-born architect Gervase Wheeler. Wheeler's plans are an important addition to *Country Houses*, as they bring elements of English thinking into Downing's sphere. Wheeler's own book (1851), *Rural Homes, or, Sketches of Houses Suited to Country Life*, refers to important English proponents of the Gothic and Picturesque styles. Ruskin and Nash are invoked, and their philosophies are thus incorporated into what Wheeler called ''Reality'' and Downing called ''Truth.'' Wheeler's houses, though basically Gothic, went another step and incorporated exposed crossbeams and free-arched members that prophesied the more decorative and less functional buildings to come.

The importance of the preservation of our architectural heritage becomes more apparent with each passing year. The need for preservation is especially pressing for the Stick Style. Of all the threats to our old houses— arson, vandalism, neglect, greed, ignorance, and indifference—probably the most inexcusable is the last. Although more people are becoming aware of the significance of architectural history through such publications as The National Trust for Historic Preservation's *Historic Preservation* and *Preservation News,* *Americana, The Old House Journal*, etc., far too many otherwise educated Americans are ignorant of the living past old houses represent.

One of the saddest acts of unconscious vandalism, abetted by indifference, is the *denaturing* of old houses. Misguided individuals, often encouraged by opportunistic home-improvement firms, mindlessly destroy the character of architecturally significant houses. Bargeboarding, brackets, decorative trim, finials, pendants, and a host of other Victorian decorations are removed, and the house is modernized by slicking over with plywood, aluminum sheets, fiberglass, and other materials totally unsuited to the original building's nature. The integrity of thousands of American houses has been ruined by synthetic siding laid over original clapboard carefully proportioned to suit the house.

The Stick Style is a frequent victim of such attentions. To paint the sticks or bones that adorn eaves or porches requires care. Owners who are unaware of the import of these members simply remove and destroy them. Because of the generous gauge of the lumber and the intricacy of the joining, the sticks are difficult to replace even if a photographic record shows the order of replacement. To duplicate the elements that make the Stick Style carriage house on page 182 unique would be costly even if able craftsmen could be found to duplicate the star-and-trefoil motif.

Plate 59 *Hopewell Transitional*

Hopewell Transitional

This Hopewell, New Jersey, house displays transition from the traditional forms of the long-lived Italianate style to a fashionable new Stick Style. Brackets were replaced by exposed braces, which are the sticks of the Stick Style.

Contractors of the 1880's shared problems similar to present-day entrepreneurs. Fortunes rose and fell through luck and an ability to produce an attractive product at competitive prices. In residential building, nineteenth-century builders rarely consulted architects (but freely adopted their ideas). Those who chose to build felt that a good contractor could provide a satisfactory house, and a recommendation from a friend was usually the only qualification demanded. Architects of the era therefore turned to public building, to planning the great houses of the rich, and to plan-book publication and its subsidiary activities.

In the east the building trade became quite sophisticated. Since costs of materials and wages were fairly standard, and experienced contractors knew every cost-cutting factor, the only quality that set one contractor above another was his feeling for style. Style was always important. Victorian conservatism is mostly myth. Victorians enjoyed change, and once an architectural style was introduced and improved, the builders were quick to employ "the latest."

The element of luck in a contractor's fortunes had to do with weather. Long periods of rain or heavy snows could ruin a time schedule—and timing was crucial to a contractor's success. Framing a house and enclosing it by summer's end was mandatory. By fall the inside work must have progressed so that the furnace, fed with scraps of waste lumber, could warm the workmen whose winter work was to finish the interior.

No form of architecture exhibited the skills of master carpenters better than the Stick Style. Every exposed beam was stop chamfered and joined with prideful precision, and the backs of exposed trusses were often chisel-dated and initialed by the artisans.

The house in the painting is an Italianate with Stick Style braces instead of brackets. It is a tentative and transitional treatment, as though the designer was not quite up to real change. The campanile of the structure is such an overwhelming statement of style that the building is classified as Italianate with Stick Style ornamentation.

Victorian Storefront

In all of Cape May only three Victorian neighborhood storefronts remain. Storefronts contribute to the character of streetscapes and were, in Victorian times, built like pieces of fine furniture, with delicate fluted columns, inlaid panels, and the ubiquitous stop-chamfered trim. Cornices were elaborate, and brackets and braces were used extensively. Windows were lettered with gold leaf or decorated with beautifully crafted raised gold lettering. Generous awnings offered window shoppers respite from the sun. Window displays were inviting and gave customers a sense of the variety, quality, and price of merchandise.

With the advent of electricity interiors were cooled by lazily rotating overhead fans, now once again in fashion. On very hot days huge cakes of ice were placed in pans beneath the fans.

Victorian shopkeepers wore aprons and looked like shopkeepers. In places like Cape May, shops had bulletin boards announcing hotel accommodations, Bible classes, houses for sale, train schedules, hayrides, swimming classes, political pow-wows, etc. There was a sense of community in Victorian shops, and their proprietors were usually well informed on any subject pertaining to their community.

Cape May's slate-and-brick sidewalks were lit by shops' gas lamps without and within. Outside the shops mounting blocks and ornate hitching posts were provided for the carriage trade, while inside, chairs were furnished for the ladies.

Storefronts disappeared when a commercial district

arose in Cape May and neighborhood services were centralized in a downtown cluster. The shop fronts were then renovated to become offices or apartments. Renovation has destroyed the Victorian nature of many streets, as the presence of modest shops added character to the neighborhood.

Gas lamps still brighten the streets of Cape May, and encouraged by prosperity and general public reaction, Cape May residents are now enthusiastic proponents of preservation. The City of Cape May, the National Endowment for the Arts, the Atlantic–Richfield Foundation, the National Park Service, and the Historic American Buildings Survey all contributed to a remarkable handbook that instructs Cape May homeowners in every aspect of preservation from profiting from new tax laws advantageous to preservationists to detailed do-it-yourself information. Architectural drawings of Cape May prototypes, including Gothic Revival, Italianate, Italian Villa, Renaissance Revival, American Bracketed Villa, Exotic Revivals (including the Octagon), Second Empire, Stick Style, Shingle Style, and Bungalow are included with brief histories of the styles to help homeowners understand what they have and to save them from the ignominy of "remuddling."

What Cape May has done with its heritage has been aesthetically and financially rewarding and should be an incentive for other communities to preserve their nineteenth-century architectural treasures.

Plate 60   *Victorian Storefront*

Plate 61   *Riverton Yacht Club*

Riverton Yacht Club

Stick Style architecture is not limited to buildings whose exposed structural members are actually supportive. Sometimes the sticks are entirely decorative, achieving no true external or internal bracing. The Riverton (New Jersey) Yacht Club is an example of a cosmetic application of a style.

Although the Riverton Yacht Club was founded in 1865, the clubhouse was not built until 1881. Catboats and naphtha launches have disappeared, but Lightnings, Comets, Stars, Dusters, and Sunfish still dart around the century-old building not far from Philadelphia on the Delaware.

The Stick Style, to many, is a catch-all category. The little houses of Ocean Grove and Cape May fit comfortably into the category, and the Riverton Yacht Club expresses no other style but the Stick Style. The Octagon

"Bonnet House" and the Hopewell Italianate-cum-Stick Style have elements of the style but are overwhelmed by more important style elements.

In his later years, the architect Richard Morris Hunt (1827–1895) is said to have hoped he'd be remembered not so much for the great mansions he planned for the Vanderbilts, but for the Stick Style houses he had designed early in his career. Hunt, who had planned the sumptuous Newport Marble House and the Italianate Renaissance palace known as "The Breakers," must have felt an utter surfeit. The integrity associated with the original intent of the Stick Style would have, in retrospect, appealed to a mind exhausted by his larger-than-life architectural accomplishments.

Very few examples of truly honest Stick Style structures exist. The style appealed to those who enjoyed its look. If the sticks played no real structural role, the owner was not concerned. Contractors understood and simply applied beams, trusses, cross braces, and bucks wherever a visual effect could be gained.

Ocean Grove Stick Style

Carpenter's lace, gingerbread, American Baroque, Stick Style, Victorian, Steamboat Gothic, General Grant— a whole clutter of styles come to mind in the presence of the little houses that form the community of Ocean Grove, New Jersey. The house in the painting is by no means the most ornamented of its neighbors, but unlike most it stands alone and can show us its full dimensions. A block or so away neighboring houses form ranks of contiguous buildings that surely tested the ingenuity of their builders, for each house had to be "different." Street after street of this seaside town exhibits variations of Victorian summer houses usually smaller than the example shown.

The late-Victorian years marked an era dominated by rich men. Wealth was obtrusive and often vulgarly displayed. People of great wealth were for the average American what the stars of Hollywood later became. The wealthy were thought to be, if not exactly exemplars, then certainly models to be imitated in matters involving taste. Building big, as the rich did, was out of the question for most, but building fancy seemed an acceptable substitution. So the jigsaws cranked and the lathes spun, and tiny gable-ended houses were dressed out in the cheeriest patterns contractors could contrive.

It worked out well for the modest builder, better than

Plate 62 *Ocean Grove Stick Style*

for the plutocrat. In time most of the enormous mansions of the very rich were given to the state or sold for a tiny fraction of their cost to nursing homes, museums, and for other uses—or were simply destroyed. In contrast the little

American baroques, if in good condition, now are valued at fifteen times their building costs.

The tabernacle in the distance was featured in one of Woody Allen's films. The awnings were his gift.

New Jersey Baroque

The nomenclature applied to architectural styles can be confusing. While architectural history is more an art than a science, and interpretation is required in it as any humanistic pursuit, the architectural novice feels misled by alternate terms of identification. Universities offering courses in architectural history will insist on a set of terms to identify styles, terms which the student will later find are ignored or disputed by the architectural vocabulary of designers, architects, publishers, and others active in the restoration field. Humanists allied to the fine arts may choose to speak of the "Greek Revival" style, while other humanists—especially anthropologists engaged in the field of folklore—refer to the style as the "Temple Form." In England the style we know best as "Queen Anne" is alluded to as "Jacobethan" or "Shavian." Only a few years ago a consensus felt that "Neo-Jacobean" was preferable

Plate 63 *New Jersey Baroque*

to "Queen Anne." "Second Empire" now finds favor over "Mansard" as a style designation, and "Adamesque" vies with, or is combined with, the older term "Federal." High Victorian Gothic is known as "Venetian Gothic" and "Ruskinian Gothic."

Admittedly there are times when some of the alternate architectural terms express the salient characteristics of particular structures better than rival terms. And rival terms at least supply us with synonyms. However, a serious confusion exists in the naming of one architectural style which went unclassified or was mislabeled for more than half a century—the Stick Style—a designation that is used to cover a multitude of forms.

The term "Stick Style" was devised by Vincent Scully to describe nineteenth-century structures in which components of actual construction *are visible members of the style*, or at least seem to be. Yet the screens of decoration that stand apart from the simple gable-ended houses of Cape May and Ocean Grove have led some to label the houses Stick Style, even though the Stick Style screens are not structural. Stripped of ornamental porches, the houses are simple gable ends with no claim to any architectural style.

In times past architectural historians linked the bargeboards and other ornaments of Carpenter Gothics to the seaside cottages and called the cottages "Gothic variants." More cautious observers named them "Ocean Grove" or "Cape May Vernaculars." The vacation houses of the New Jersey seashore are a distinctive type repeated in amazing variety, but they show strong family resemblances. Those resemblances invoke neobaroque and neorococo decoration for decoration's sake. Other than forming a screen and contributing a little triangular strengthening for the porch, the decorations perform no function as true structural members. Perhaps "New Jersey Baroque" would be a suitable name for the ebullient seaside style, or "Screen Style," but "Stick Style" is a misnomer for these houses.

The painting details a section of porch appended to an otherwise simple vacation cottage in Ocean Grove, New Jersey. It was meant to please the eye, and it succeeds exuberantly.

XIV. The Shingle Style

FROM THE 1880'S, through the Mauve Decade,[5] architectural styles were introduced that held a special appeal for the wealthy. Examples of the styles are therefore limited and appeared more often in public buildings than in private residences. The Chateauesque style has steep-hipped roofs that rise to a flat top ornamented with elaborate cresting. High, decorated, dominating wall dormers are topped by a pinnacled gable. The chimneys are decorative and paneled, and because they spring from the eave line, they are tall. Windows are deeply set, trabeated or crowned by a shallow arch. The style, of French origin, is sometimes called "Francis I." Francis I reigned for most of the first half of the sixteenth century, which saw the joining of Italian Renaissance and native Gothic forms. The American version was usually built in stone.

Chatauesque style

5. Mauve was a color favored by decorators for hotels, casinos, gaming houses, and the fashionable salons of the last decade of the nineteenth century. The 1958 edition of *The Reader's Encyclopedia* describes mauve as "pink trying to be purple." The color gave its name to the 1890's in Thomas Beer's book *The Mauve Decade* (1926), which examined the culture and society of the time.

Only the richest of the very rich could consider beaux–arts Classicism as a style for their *pieds à terre* in Newport or wherever they congregated. An exception to the rule would be the city town house in the same style, which might fit into the budget of the merely wealthy. The Classical elements of beaux–art Classicism include stone construction, symmetry, impressive paired columns, statuary, and massive flights of stairs. The beaux–arts gets its name directly from the famous school of architecture in Paris, the Ecole des Beaux-arts. One of the first Americans to attend the Ecole des Beaux-arts was Henry Hobson Richardson. By the end of the nineteenth century, architecture was dominated by Ecole des Beaux-arts graduates, who effectively formed an architectural establishment.

The growth of the profession of architecture by the 1890's was impressive. Only forty years before Richard Morris Hunt, the first American graduate of the Ecole des Beaux-arts, won a lawsuit which acknowledged architecture as a profession. In 1876 the second American architectural school, after M.I.T., was established at the University of Illinois, and the first respected architectural magazine, *American Architecture and Building News*, was founded. Despite the progress of American architecture, however, the upper classes felt compelled to commission European or European-trained architects to build their palaces. American architects, like American painters and musicians, felt the neglect of the very rich in their predilection for imported talent. Civic leaders of the time were certain that beaux-arts Classicism represented the utmost in taste and proceeded to build museums, railroad terminals, and auditoriums in that style.

The Renaissance Revival style of the 1850's was never a general style in America. The symmetrical form was introduced at a time when the public was beguiled by picturesque asymmetry; symmetrical forms seemed stodgy. The iron-front stores in the Renaissance form are the best remembered of this species. The technological novelty that New Yorker James Bogardus perfected in his cast-iron store fronts was the chief reason for the style's acceptance. In the late 1880's, when symmetry was once again an acceptable form, the style was revived. Not surprisingly it was called the "Second Renaissance Revival." Instead of iron or stucco, the façades were now stone or marble. The overall scale was enlarged, details were exaggerated, and the style's origins in the Northern Italian Renaissance were made more obvious.

White paint was reintroduced to a new generation tiring of ochre, red, and brown. White-painted wooden Georgian Revival models were "new" and pleasing to visitors at Chicago's Columbian Exposition of 1893. The Georgian Revival followed the original American Georgian and Adamesque–Federal architecture with close attention to symmetry. City and public examples were of brick with white trim. Unlike the palaces of the very rich, most domestic Georgian Revivals were scaled to suit families of more modest means.

With the neo-Classical Revival (Washington, D.C. is full of it) and the Late Gothic Revival (more perpendicular, simpler, and less ornamented than the original style), the nineteenth century ran out its string of European-inspired architectural styles. That group of Romantic styles—they all hearkened back to the past—branched away from the organic and functional directions perceived by Richardson and Sullivan. The Richardsonian–Sullivanesque direction developed alongside the neo-Classical styles in the form of the Shingle Style. At first it grew as a reaction to High Victorian Eclecticism. Because the form was malleable and areas could *flow*, the style became a basis for twentieth-century modern architecture. The earliest examples, continuations of the Aesthetic movement, were intended to show their kinship with seventeenth-century New En-

A large Shingle Style home in Spring Lake, New Jersey

gland architecture. In its time the Shingle Style was generally viewed as a modernized colonial evocation. In its simple forms it became an inexpensive and popular building style for suburban, seashore, and country living. Shingle Styles in cities look ill at ease, and most building codes forbid them as they are susceptible to fire.

To some architects the style was understood to be a revolt against style in general, while others felt the form to be a basis for an entire new discipline. Some of the earlier Shingle Style structures naturally retained strong reminders of the Romanesque—the first floor being given over to rough stones and broad arches. Others showed Queen Anne characteristics. Palladian windows, colonial details, and further nostalgic components crept into the style.

In the Shingle Style a very daring perception of form—low, flowing, serene with horizontal sweeps and an easy exchange of interior and exterior spaces—was anticipating modern architecture. Nostalgic components were gradually discarded as pioneering architects groped for means to express instincts that were, more and more, consciously guiding them.

The evolution of modern architecture from the Shingle Style never proceeded in a straight line. While pioneering architects were marching to a different drummer, contemporary critics, insensitive to the whispers of change, kept insisting that chivalry, righteousness, and probity were the sentiments architecture should evoke. And at the same time there were other anomalies: what was Truthfulness? Exposed structural members were "honest" expressions of the Stick Style builders, but in a decade or so Truthfulness found another exemplar in the Shingle Style. Covering the frame with shingles to enhance the flow of form was now truthful—or so the proponents of the style insisted. The proponents also felt the Shingle Style was democratic (as opposed to the styles adopted by the very rich.)

Color was an element of the Shingle Style that led it away from current trends. Most Shingle Style structures were stained a deep, soft brown—the softness accentuated by the texture of the cedar shingles. Some were stained a Venetian red, while others were toned in gamboges and deep greens. The most admired of the shingle tones were the silvery grays that oceanside salt air imparted to the cedar.

In the last ten years of the nineteenth century, Californians built many examples and many versions of the Shingle Style. With a certain perversity, an old rival for Truthfulness reappeared in California. *Western* Stick Style had a lowered profile and relatively slighter "sticks." Both California styles showed distinct Japanese influences.

Of all the forces directing the development of the Shingle Style into precursors of modern architecture,

the Japanese influence had the most profound effect. The golden thread of orientalism that laced so exquisitely through American decoration now found a distinct voice in American architecture. After the Philadelphia Centennial of 1876, which displayed a prototypical wooden Japanese dwelling, there was considerable fascination for the form and the delicate rectilinear details of the Japanese interior. Lattice screens and moldings suggesting the sliding partitions of Japanese households were introduced. Imitation bamboo railings and bamboo porch posts were later affectations. Owners, desiring an exotic atmosphere, decorated their homes with Japanese fans and oriental bric-a-brac.

Now, more than a hundred years after the introduction of the Shingle Style with its oriental elements, we see the duality in the style's nature. Orientalism and a fascination with the orient, are Romantic traits; but the unassuming, restrained, rectilinear forms introduced at the Japanese Pavilion were components of the Classical forms leading to twentieth-century Classicism.

As a roofing and siding material, shingles, in one form or another, reach as far into the past as history can pry. American colonists found shingling a convenient and enduring way to protect against weather and used the shingle for rough-hewn lean-tos as well as for well-finished houses and churches. The Dutch colonists in New Jersey discovered huge submerged cedars in the bogs of the Hackensack meadowlands and later in the tea-colored waters of the New Jersey Pine Barrens. Centuries of submersion in the mineral-rich waters made the cedar almost impervious to rot and remarkably weather resistant. Some early Dutch houses—sandstone to the second floor and shingled above—have original shingles that date back to the seventeenth century. Since iron nails were scarce and expensive, wooden nails were used to secure shingles to underlayment.

Colonial-era shingles were made by hand on a shingle horse or shingle buck. They were tapered with a drawknife or rived and shaped with a honed shingle

A typical 19th-century Japanese dwelling

hatchet. It was a tedious procedure, but materials and labor were both cheap. When the steam-powered epoch arrived, shingles were produced in unheard-of quantities and sawn to shape as they are today. The resulting uniformity detracts from the attractive random quality of the hand-made shingle. *Shakes* are heavy, hand-split shingles that give unusual textural qualities to roofs and walls.

In the Queen Anne era, shingling became a kind of art. Queen Annes featured fish-scale shingles rounded at the bottom and often set in decorative geometric patterns. Shingle Style houses sometimes displayed shingles set in a saw-tooth pattern to enliven unrelieved stretches of wall.

Cedar is not the only wood used in shingling. In the West, fir is favored, and the most durable and perhaps the most beautiful shingles are of the cypress from the swamplands of Georgia.

At the time that the shingle houses were at the height of their popularity shingles cost about 70 cents per square. The price at this writing is $55. Shingling was a tedious job performed by apprentice carpenters paid between 15 and 20 cents per hour. This wage was up a nickel from the 10-cent rate paid in 1878—the lowest wage since the Civil War. Master carpenters at the same time were paid 25 cents per hour, and the foreman earned 30 cents. Three thousand board feet of lumber went for $90, cement was sold for $1.50, and sand at 15 cents per cubic yard.

A good-sized, eight-room, shingled house, built from the plans of a reputable architect, cost from $7,000 to $9,000. It now costs that much to reshingle a roof, if the job is not complicated by too many valleys or curved surfaces. So enjoy those old shingle houses that grace the seashores or turn-of-the-century enclaves. Only a rare few will survive the cost of restoration.

"Valley View": A Morristown Shingle Style

Begun in 1896, this Morristown, New Jersey, Shingle Style mansion embodies many elements that foreshadow modern architecture. The chimney is an integral extension of the wall, and the deliberate lack of decoration—finials, pendants, etc.—gave the turn-of-the-century viewer a refreshing taste of things that were to come. Still there is much about the house that is Romantic. The shingles and the Octagon tower were evoked by nostalgia for "true American heritage"; the tower's design is surely inspired by early American windmills. The interior is Classical with graceful Ionic columns and Georgian elements predominating. The Georgian theme is repeated in the fenestration. The Shingle Style took many forms, but it insisted on clarity and the feeling, at least, of simplicity.

The builder of "Valley View" was Jesse Leeds Eddy, a

Plate 64
"Valley View":
A Morristown Shingle Style

New York City coal merchant and mine operator who called the house his summer residence. Where the house is not shingled, it is hand-hewn Vermont granite. It extends far beyond the limitations of the painting. Valley View has ten fireplaces, dumb waiters, a billiard room, rosewood and mahogany woodwork, and some silver doorknobs. A music room has an ornate rotunda displaying multicolored Tiffany glass lit by sunlight or at night by a hidden chandelier.

With an eye toward coming technology, the architect installed a large wooden tank at the highest point of the house to create a gravity-fed fire-fighting system. A network of air pipes provided intercommunication. By 1905 a White Steamer automobile took its place among the horses and carriages at Valley View's immense carriage house. By 1911 there were five cars and a resident mechanic. Jesse

Leeds Eddy paid $60,000 for Valley View. The Eddys used it about sixty days a year.

Valley View was not the only great house in the neighborhood. In the 1850's Morristown was a village with proud connections to the American Revolution. With the advent of the Gilded Age in the 1880's, Morristown and its surroundings were the site of a great number of the proudest estates in America. By 1896 Morristown was the home of fifty-four millionaires with a total wealth of $289 million.[8] Vanderbilts, Rockefellers, and Mellons provided the blue blood of Morristown's society, while the meritocracy was represented by Thomas Nast, A. B. Frost, and other outstanding talents.

---

8. From: "Morristown's Forgotten Past" by John W. Rae & John W. Rae, Jr.

Classical Revival

The World's Columbian Exposition in Chicago (1893) brought fame to the firm of McKim, Mead and White. Their architectural themes were thought to definitively express "Americanism." Somehow the architectural vision of Americanism had been turned around from the 1830's view of ourselves as the inheritors of the Periclean ideal of civic and political virtue to a new concept of Roman grandeur. As the nineteenth century came to a close the architecture of Imperial Rome unabashedly became the building symbol of America's self image. The architectural style that

Plate 65   *Classical Revival*

was to become McKim, Mead and White's most successful manner was named "Imperial Roman," and it was greeted with enthusiasm in government as well as private sectors.

"Manifest Destiny" was a term first used in defense of this nation's annexation of Texas in 1845. By the 1880's the term had taken on some rather glorious, imperious, and even bellicose overtones which were of concern to our neighbors. In the presence of Imperial Roman architecture, the implications of Manifest Destiny might be taken too seriously.

In the fifteen-year period 1895 to 1910, McKim, Mead and White built the capitol building in Providence, Rhode Island, the Morgan Library and the Pennsylvania Railroad Terminal in New York City; and during the presidency of Theodore Roosevelt, they remodeled The White House, all in the Roman Imperial style. There were, of course, many imitators, and the nation's capital became the site of endless grandiose evocations. The Lincoln Memorial and the National Gallery in Washington are latter-day expressions. Imperiousness, grandeur, and other qualities that would certainly have offended the founding fathers were inherent in these vast structures. Having thus written, however, I must add that the Lincoln Memorial still touches me deeply, and I mourn the mindless destruction of Penn Station.

The catch-all term for the Roman architecture of this period is "Classical Revival." It's not a satisfactory term, as Greek Revival and Jeffersonian Revival forms were also Classical revivals. A modest illustration of the form is the United Counties Trust building in Elizabeth, New Jersey. It is a well-kept and well-designed example of the style in the Ionic order. In structures of this size, columns were favored that were not freestanding but were set as pilasters on the face of the building.

For more than fifty years, the clock, an Elizabeth landmark, has told commuters to walk, run, or forget it.

Renaissance Revival Fire-Engine House

A heavy balustrade, windows topped with half-round arches, and varied Classical forms at each of its three levels give the Brooklyn Heights fire-engine house a special designation. The second floor is capped by projecting eaves supported by embellished modillions. At the outer ends of the eaves are elements usually called anthemia. An anthemion is a decorative leaf pattern of Greek origin based on the honeysuckle. The objects in the painting are actually antefixes (or antefixa). An antefix was an upright slab meant to close the open end of a row of tiles. The device shown here is only ornamentation to reinforce an association with Classicality. This architecture became a leading style at the turn of the nineteenth century—it is the Renaissance Revival style.

The original Renaissance architecture, introduced in the early fifteenth century, was characterized by free adaptation of Classical orders, round arches, and symmetrical composition. The form, succeeding the Gothic in European dominance, evolved through a Mannerist phase into the Baroque. By the seventeenth century, the form had completed its stylistic peregrinations and had returned to its Classical origins. The fire-engine house, without elaborate dimensional surface treatment, grew out of the Classical phase of the Renaissance style.

Clay Lancaster's beautifully researched book Old Brooklyn Heights: New York's First Suburb (Chas. E. Tuttle, Co.) is a model of its genre and refers to Brooklyn Heights as New York's first suburb. It became a suburb early in the nineteenth century and attracted many of the personalities who feature in Portraits of American Architecture. Mrs. Trollope visited here and wrote (with tentative approbation) of the Brooklyn Collegiate Institute for Young Ladies. Orson Squire Fowler lectured against tight corseting and held phrenological readings near where Henry Ward Beecher, Fowler's classmate at Amherst, preached at the Italianate style Plymouth Church. Minard Lafever designed Brooklyn Heights town houses in the Greek Revival style and the Church of the Holy Trinity in the Gothic mode.

Plate 66   *Renaissance Revival Fire-Engine House*

American Georgian

Three monarchs named George ruled England from 1727 to 1830. In that time, a Classical form of architecture called "Georgian" was the dominant style throughout the British Isles. Its origins are traced to the architecture of Classical Rome as interpreted by Andrea Palladio (1518–1580), introduced to England by Inigo Jones (1573–1652), and further implemented by Sir Christopher Wren (1632–1723). By 1675 the Georgian style was crystalized in its robust Classical form. The squarish, double-hung sash windows adopted after the Great Fire of London (1666) became a pre-eminent feature of the style.

The ceiling of the ground floor of the fire-engine house still exhibits the hooks from which automatic harness was dropped onto waiting horses at the sound of an alarm. The stalls which once held the horses are gone, and fire engines stand in their place. For a while the fire engines were painted yellow for higher visibility, but it became apparent that people seeing red responded more to that symbolic color than to the newer hue. Red for fire engines is once again in favor.

The paired buildings next to the fire-engine house are former carriage houses now converted into a town house and a sculptor's studio.

The early eighteenth century saw Georgian plantation houses being built in the American south and Georgian town houses, churches, and public buildings in the north. By the end of the eighteenth century variants of the Georgian form inspired by Wren and others could be found in almost every northeastern community. Unlike most other forms of colonial architecture—step-gabled Dutch, for example—the Georgian form was consciously architectural.

This painting is of a Georgian doorway in the historical quarter of New Castle, Delaware, although almost identical town-house doorways can still be found in Boston, Philadelphia, New York, Baltimore, and Charleston. The Classical pedimented doorway and the keystone decoration surmounting the window identify the doorway as late Georgian. Had the window been narrower and the Classical elements more delicate, a viewer might be tempted to accept the town house as Federal, the successor style to Georgian and the last of the Classical styles prior to the Romantic revolution.

A Georgian revival began in the mid-1860's, picked up momentum in the 1890's, and carried through to the first quarter of the present century. It was nicely timed to coincide with the life of England's George V (1865–1936).

Plate 67   *American Georgian*

XV. The End of an Era

THE TRUE BEGINNING of the modern Classical mood was nicely timed to coincide with the beginning of a new century. Classicism did not come all at once, however, nor did every vestige of Romanticism disappear on a set schedule. Moods have soft edges. In twentieth-century California the Mission Style became a Romantic revival style, to be followed by the Spanish Colonial Revival. In Arizona and New Mexico the Pueblo Style duplicated the forms of the area's original inhabitants. These styles were Romantic but were born well into the present century.

In 1899 Thorstein Veblen wrote *The Theory of the Leisure Class*, an examination of the customs of the American upper classes. With Veblen, "conspicuous consumption," and other pejorative terms describing the doings of the very rich, entered into the vocabulary of a Classical-minded audience. But twenty-three years later, Emily Post's book on etiquette was published. A great success, the book saw three editions produced in its first year of publication. The work was ostensibly directed at the affluent sectors of American society, but the vast majority of copies entered the libraries of middle-class homes. Chapters dealt with how one's cook submits the menu and how to choose the colors for the livery of footmen. To be fair, Mrs. Post also had excellent advice on how to behave like a human being, but those who bought her book were quite obviously fantasizing in the most romantic of Romantic terms.

A few years later Emily Post wrote *The Personality of a House: The Blue Book of Home Design*. The houses she favored were of colonial inspiration and expressive of history in every detail—very Romantic. The anomaly here was that Emily Post was the daughter of Bruce Price, an architect in the forefront of the modern movement. Price's Shingle Style houses in Tuxedo Park, New York, were some of the most daring designs of the time. Daughters of American revolutionists seldom exhibit revolutionary natures themselves.

Other arts entered the realm of the Classical within the first decades of the twentieth century. By 1910 modern art had begun its tenacious climb to recognition. Abstract painting had already appeared in Russia in the 1890's. The Exhibition of Modern Art, held at the 69th Regiment Armory in New York in 1913, launched a group of notable modernists with a display of 1,600 works. In 1900 Theodore Dreiser wrote *Sister Carrie*, in the naturalist tradition. The novel, a tough, unsentimental revelation of an actress in shabby decline, was not only banned, it was excoriated by "responsible" institutions. Naturalism is a Classical attribute. Twenty-five years later, Dreiser wrote his masterpiece, *An American Tragedy*, which, while fundamentally Classical, has traces of the Romantic that are murky and brooding.

Theater and dance, tiring of the constrictions of tradition, were becoming experimental. Dance, especially, became more "linear." In music an amazing American, Charles Ives, began writing modern music while still a student at Yale University. (He graduated in 1898.) Ives experimented in antiphony and curious new rhythms. In Europe Arnold Schönberg and Alban Berg dabbled in dissonances. The dramatic theme of Berg's opera *Lulu* is not unlike the story of *Sister Carrie*.

Introducing Classicism was an uncomfortable endeavor. The artists of the Armory Show were roundly castigated; Dreiser was censored and denounced; whole audiences stomped out of theaters of the experimental. The works of Schönberg and Berg, among other avant-gardists, were greeted with hisses, hoots, and cat calls. But, perhaps because he was a successful businessman as well as a composer, Ives's works were thought to be not wicked but merely eccentric.

What brought about the change in mood to contemporary Classicism? The Romantic movement began in revolution—aesthetic as well as political and social. The progenitors of Romanticism probed into dark areas of mind and society where no one had dared venture before. The institution of slavery was challenged and destroyed. Other established institutions, the church and the state not excluded, were challenged and changed. There were dangerous excursions into the uncharted realms of mysticism and drugs—Thomas DeQuincey's 1822 *Confessions of an English Opium Eater* reminds us of the underground writings of the 1960's—and of shocking departures from accepted mores. Once the shocks were assimilated and the less agitated began to sift the outrageous elements from the caldrons of change, Romantic ideals prospered. Elements of chivalry and grace now succeeded the strident cries and the raw anger of social revolution. The dust settled, and though the scars of upheaval abounded, the new generation saw itself in a vigorous, ascendant role. It was as though the forthcoming Victorian generation had fully understood William Blake when he wrote:

> If the doors of perception were cleansed, everything would appear to man as it is, infinite. For man has closed himself up, till he sees all things thro' narrow chinks of his cavern.

The ebullient spirit of the early Victorians was irrepressible. Horizons were limitless, and man was, so they earnestly believed, perfectible. With technical and industrial successes, however, there also came disasters. The Civil War destroyed an age of innocence and drastically altered our value system. Enormous disparities in wealth, conspicuous consumption, and the ostentatious, often vulgar display of power and riches spawned bitter resentment. Excesses, debauched values, political cor-

ruption, and a spirit gone stale, brought the Romantic era to an end. Like the furniture it had engendered, the era had become overstuffed, overornate, and uncomfortable. As with its voluminous dress and procrustean, corseted attempts to disguise a corrupted body, society could no longer hide the illness consuming it.

An overly ornate dining room in the Corcoran House in Washington, D.C.

The evolutionary components of any Romantic epoch are never precisely the same, but, in the order given, these are the salient characteristics: revolution—social or armed; rebellion against established orders, institutions, or mores; experimentation in untried realms; an outpouring of creativity; general stabilization and the establishment of new norms; the consolidation of norms and mores; elegance; ennui; excesses; gross excesses; and ultimate soft-edged collapse.

There is much to be compared in the Romantic revolution of the nineteenth century and Romantic onset in the twentieth. The long, unkempt hair and the affected peasant dress of the youthful French revolutionists had their counterparts in the American cultural revolution of the 1960's. The generation gap that caused such anguish in the 1970's dramatized the rift in values and mores of parents and children. In the last decade of the eighteenth century, too, families in Germany, France, and England were split by the new ideals set forth by Rousseau and his followers.

The Romantic–Classic tenets postulated by the von Schlegels are themselves part of the Romantic revolution. Classic-minded analysts will demand more concrete, more *linear* evidence to prove the existence of alternating social and aesthetic moods called Classic and Romantic. The validity of the tenet is not—nor can it ever be—scientifically established, but an understanding of the theory provided a rich enhancement to understanding architecture and the arts.

Besides the Romantic mood in its various manifestations, there were other energies that fashioned nineteenth-century American architecture. The fluctuations of the economy and the ebb and flow of populations had obvious effects. Outside immediate political decisions affecting architecture there were consequences resulting from political feelings. In New Jersey, for instance, there are surprisingly few examples of Greek Revival architecture, despite the fact that the years of its dominance, 1825 to 1855, were a period of growth and prosperity within the state. A few rather grand domestic specimens of the Greek Revival survive in Sparta and in White House, Flemington, and New Brunswick, but there are only rare Greek Revivals built by Jerseyans of modest means. The reason was political. Philadelphian Nicholas Biddle's banking philosophies were at odds with Jacksonian principles. New Jersey was largely pro-Jackson, and New Jerseymen associated Mr. Biddle's Greek Revival bank buildings[6] with anti-Jackson sentiments. While neighboring states were busy building in the Temple Style, New Jersey continued in the Adamesque–Federal style or in other forms defying easy architectural identification.

There can be no doubt that Nicholas Biddle was a believer in the form he endorsed. He is quoted as saying that there are only two truths in the world: God and Greek architecture.[7] It is pleasing to know that Biddle's direct descendant James served at the helm of the National Trust for Historic Preservation, striving valiantly to preserve not only historic buildings, but any buildings of architectural worth.

Politics, the state of the economy, and the nation's westward expansion affected building, but it was the Romantic mood, the prevailing mood of the Victorian era, that shaped the architecture of the time. The Romantic ethic insisted that architecture have historical or literary allusions, and nineteenth-century architects rose to the challenge with the fervor that gave us our Romantic monuments.

The precise temper of that time, the economic factors, the abundance of materials, and the explosive energy of the epoch can never be repeated. For this reason it is now imperative that the outstanding architectural examples—living testaments to a culture to which we owe so much—be protected, restored, and maintained. In 1981 the National Trust for Historic Preservation noted that, "since 1930, more than four thousand important landmarks have been needlessly destroyed—to say nothing of the individual homes and entire sections of our cities."

At dusk at the turn of a lonely road, to come upon an old house, remote in its years and jealous of its secrets, is to experience a sense of loss, as though we have missed something precious, very precious indeed. What elements of grace have vanished with an age that gave us these monuments to a mood? To understand the Romantic spirit, which inspired the building of the Temples, the Gothics, and the Italianates that remain brooding

---

6. One of these was modeled after the Parthenon. It was designed by William Strickland, who reminded critics that the ancient Parthenon was not only a temple, but a storehouse of public treasure.

7. Compare English architect Augustus Welby Pugin who said: "The only true joys in life are Gothic architecture and sailboating." In 1852 at the age of forty, Pugin drowned in a sailboating mishap.

over our byways, is to increase our appreciation of these treasures. The eye is sharpened, the viewer richly rewarded, by these symbols of our heritage. Each of them gives profound meaning to our past.

It has been said that the nature of the engineer is the antithesis of the nature of the artist. To achieve his ends the engineer must set a goal and move straight towards it. Linear and Classic. The artist, if he is to grow, will set a general goal and proceed serendipitously, veering off course as significant discoveries and perceptions dictate. Diverse and Romantic. As I am an artist, I proceed serendipitously in producing the portraits that follow, but my goal is always determined by a desire to share with the reader my deep admiration for these old houses and my sympathy with their moods, so eloquently expressing the character of the remarkable Americans of the Victorian era.

Star-and-Trefoil Carriage House

The decoration at the top of the gable has Gothic trefoils—symbols of the Trinity. There were probably finials surmounting the eaves, and the trefoils are pendants beneath the triangular bracing. The gables are quite steep. On this evidence we should conclude that the structure—a carriage house in Chatham, New Jersey—is Gothic Revival, but current wisdom and the 1880's origin of the building have placed the structure in the Stick Style camp. Other elements confuse any clear delineation of style. The windows are round topped, and the residence which the carriage house still serves is Queen Anne with Stick Style leanings. If the surfaces from which the star-and-trefoil motifs were sawn were eliminated, three braces would remain, and those braces are key to naming the style.

The carriage house was a status symbol. At the high end of the scale, the presence of liveried grooms, landaulets, governess carts, phaetons, and blooded horses declared the social position of a house's owners. For those of more moderate circumstances a surrey and sleigh in the carriage house sufficed. As an adjunct to the residence it served, a carriage house was usually built in a related architectural style and with consideration for style. As the structures were substantially and fashionably built, they eventually found favor as apartments, laboratories, photographers' studios, and antique shops. Because of economical maintenance and their position behind principal streets, carriage houses often survive the houses for which they were built.

Carriage houses smelled of timothy, horses, neat's-foot oil, leather, oats, salt hay, unpainted wood, lacquered carriages, kerosene, and tallow. That fragrant paella was matched by the sounds of stomping hoofs, creaking harness, sleigh bells, itinerant blacksmith's tools, squeaking hickory, and choleric coachmen.

The carriage house in the plate stands behind a residence on the main street of Chatham, which, once known as Fishwack, is an immediate neighbor of Madison, once known as Bottle Hill, New Jersey.

Plate 68   *Star-and-Trefoil Carriage House*

The House at Flemington: "Roselawn"

"Roselawn" grew from the viewer's left to right. The original house under the tall, leaning chimney at left was a farmhouse built in the earliest years of the nineteenth century. Sometime in the 1870's the Italianate porch was added, and in the eighties the Stick Style elements were attached. The Second Empire tower was possibly part of another house moved to the site. In time a porte-cochere, extended porches, and a twentieth-century addition were added at the right. In the center of the building a cube with a slight Mansard roof was built on the porch. Legend insists that it was a fresh-air infirmary for the ailing wife of the owner.

The chimney leans back a little. Old chimneys facing south gradually bend away from the sun to the north side, which is always in shadow.

Roselawn, in Flemington, New Jersey, is only one in a living repository of nineteenth-century Romantic architecture. The main street of Flemington is a delight to preser-

Plate 69   *The House at Flemington: "Roselawn"*

vationists and architectural historians. Greek Revivals, Italianates, Mansards, and Queen Annes grace the streets in numbers. Flemington lacks only an Octagon to be a complete model of nineteenth-century residential architecture. The Greek Revival Hunterdon County Courthouse, Flemington's nineteenth-century hotel, and a handful of Victorian storefronts give scale and harmony to the principal thoroughfare. The dazzling whites of the Temple Style houses, law offices, and public buildings are in visual counterpoint to the ochres and reds of the Italianates and Queen Annes.

Roselawn, this Victorian eclectic, fell into disrepair and neglect shortly after its portrait was painted. In 1981 the property was bought by a group of businessmen to be converted into individual apartments. The interiors were so changed as to honor the architectural elements of the house yet provide attractive apartments. The exterior has been handsomely restored, and the reds, blues, and creams make the splendid old house at the end of the town a source of community pride. In 1987 developers razed half of the structure to accommodate an out-of-scale office building entirely alien to the community. Residents of Flemington were outraged.

The builder of Roselawn began as a clerk in a grocery store near Flemington. At the end of the Civil War he went west to Kansas City and parlayed a $5,000 investment into a $6,000,000 fortune. William Edgar Emery became a director of a large insurance company and of the Lehigh Valley Railroad. Roselawn, at first a summer house, became Emery's permanent home. He died returning to it on the Lehigh Valley.

Flemington Detail

The preceding painting, titled The House at Flemington, *does not show a significant detail in Roselawn's eclectic assemblage of styles. Since it is obvious that Roselawn was built in stages and that no single overall plan was ever developed, it is reasonably certain that, with the addition of the elevated, octagonal, and red-roofed raised gazebo at the left of the painting, the builder meant his collection of styles to be Picturesque.*

The Picturesque, with a capital "P," was a concept articulated by architectural historians in the England of the 1790's. It looked back to the kind of architecture produced at the onset of the eighteenth century, which ran countercurrent to revival styles of Classicism. The Picturesque expressed fervid Romanticism with an emphasis on broken skylines. Perhaps the ultimate example of the Picturesque movement is the aforementioned Gothick fantasy Fonthill Abbey built in Wiltshire, England, in 1796. John Nash lived in this period and was the most prolific of the Picturesque architects. He incorporated themes from the Romanesque, Tudor, Gothic, Italianate, and Castellated

Plate 70   *Flemington Detail*

styles to achieve his Picturesque ends. Most Romantic and Picturesque of Nash's creations were his rustic cottages, which gave rise to a new architectural form called, in England, not surprisingly, the "Rustic Cottage" style. Rustic cottages began as follies (Englishmen call them "fabricks") and came into acceptance as suburban retreats decked out with thatched roofs, undulating roof lines, and other pastoral allusions. The Rustic Cottage style gained enough prominence that its form was adopted for use as gate houses, hunting lodges, dairies, and church adjuncts.

    Many of the raised gazebos, pinnacles, and turrets that were part of Picturesque structures showed the influ-

ence of orientalism. The eclectic vacation house at Cape May (plate 40), with its pierced-wood decorations, indicates a modest enthusiasm for orientalism. Fascination for things oriental was nothing new in America, but John Nash's Royal Pavilion at Brighton gave impetus to the whimsically minded on both sides of the Atlantic. That assemblage of onion domes, Moorish minarets, and crenelated keeps has always been referred to as a "confection." It was built for the Prince Regent, who was soon to become George IV. The confectionery was too sticky for the Regent, however, and he promptly forgot it and turned his attentions to the remodeling of Windsor Castle.

End of An Era

There are two Newports. The one I find most to my liking is the old Newport, with its eighteenth- and nineteenth-century houses clustered in the seaport area. Restoration and rebuilding has changed the original character of the area, but a new character has grown that is alive and spirited. The scale of the old town is human, and traces of the original enterprises link a scene of good restaurants and shops with the distant past. The other Newport, the Newport of the great and resplendent mansions, is fascinating and at the same time eerily disturbing.

Newport's Gilded Age of the 1890's projected images of such unbridled opulence that a reaction from society was inevitable. The reaction was mixed. Some regarded the scene with amused tolerance, others with alarm and indignation. Edith Wharton mourned the old Newport of restrained and cultured elegance and Gothic cottages that were cottage sized. Of the immense palaces of the newcomers, Henry James wrote that, in time, they would be useless, that there would be no other course than to "let them stand there always, vast and blank, for a reminder to those concerned of the prohibited degrees of witlessness, and the peculiarly awkward vengeances of affronted proportion and discretion." James's rebuke was mild compared to Thorstein Veblen's published feelings. Veblen, an economist and social philosopher, was scornful not only of the new Newporters' "horrific waste" and "conspicuous consumption" (it took a staff of forty to operate some of the Newport "cottages"), he also felt that inflated and irrelevant tastes were being formed by the examples set by "vulgar wealth." Veblen called these examples "pecuniary canons of taste."

There is little doubt that the opulence exhibited in Newport's palaces projected such exclusionary airs of hauteur that something had to give. Lopsided wealth arrogantly displayed has always brought change. Change was on its way. The Romantic era had progressed from elegance to excess to gross excess and now to soft-edged collapse. A new Classicism was to have its say.

Years have passed, and values have changed. Many of the great houses of Newport are splendid museums and as such are richly rewarding to the half million visitors who come to this ocean-girt, sparkling community.

The painting is of a lawn sculpture on the grounds of "The Elms." That sculpture speaks too well of a pose that ended the Gilded Age. The Elms was bought in 1961 by the Newport County Preservation Society for $75,000. In 1901 it cost more than $1,000,000 to build.

Plate 71 *End of an Era*

Gothic Finials

From the introduction to these portraits, I repeat a single purposeful sentence: "At dusk at the turn of a lonely road, to come upon an old house, remote in its years and jealous of its secrets, is to experience a sense of loss, as though we have missed something precious, very precious, indeed." This painting is an evocation of such an experience. Wende and I were pleasantly lost somewhere between Ithaca and Elmira, New York, at an hour when the last rays of sunlight picked out gold in the tallest treetops.

Plate 72   *Gothic Finials*

We came to a rise and a bend in the road, and suddenly it was there—an unexpected Gothic set away from any neighbor in an area that could once have been farmland. And what a Gothic! The painting shows only two of the three gables that graced all sides of the house—twelve inspired statements of the carpenter's art expressing ingenuous and unashamed aspiration.

The sense of loss that the house conveyed was real. We no longer live in an age where sentiments can be articulated in something as monumental as a house. More than any structure in the book this house is a monument to a mood—a mood that held Americans in an enthrallment hardly comprehensible today. The gables seem to reach back directly to the spirit that built the cathedrals of the fourteenth century, bypassing all the novel-inspired sentimentality and agreeably exciting enjoyments of dolor. Even the finial, with its mysterious, somehow Viking epi, seems more aspirational than any I had ever seen. Perhaps it was that lingering glint of sunlight that brushed the finial—and profoundly touched me.

Something like Gothic dolor overcomes me when I think of the future of such places. When I came upon the house in 1974, it was in good enough condition, but I am aware that the owners of such architectural jewels are faced with unusual maintenance costs and obligations to our heritage. Old houses may not attract the heirs of their owners, or future buyers. Somehow such houses must be preserved. Other nations less prosperous than our own preserve their architectural treasures and profit spiritually and materially. To allow our monuments to perish is to forfeit our heritage.

INDEX

PORTRAITS OF AMERICAN ARCHITECTURE

has been composed by
PennSet, Inc., Bloomsburg, PA
in Linotron Sabon, a face designed
by Jan Tschichold. The roman is based on
a font engraved by Garamond and the italic on a
font by Granjon, but Tschichold introduced many refinements
to make these models suitable for contemporary
typographic needs. Designed by Lisa Clark,
the book was printed by South China
Printing Company, Hong Kong.